Earl Hart Miller

DECORATING FOR CELEBRITIES

Other books by the author

Architectural Digest Celebrity Homes
Architectural Digest American Interiors
Architectural Digest International Interiors
The Worlds of Architectural Digest, 4 Volumes
   Traditional Interiors
   Historic Interiors
   New York Interiors
   California Interiors

Val Arnold / Mario Buatta
François Catroux / Stephen Chase / Harrison Cultra
Leo Dennis / Angelo Donghia / Ted Graber / Bruce Gregga
Albert Hadley / Anthony Hail / Sally Sirkin Lewis
Loyd-Paxton / Billy McCarty / Lorenzo Mongiardino
Mrs. Henry Parish II / Lee Radziwill / Valerian Rybar
Jay Spectre / Michael Taylor

DECORATING FOR CELEBRITIES

*Interviews
with Twenty of the World's Best
Interior Designers*

CELEBRITIES

*By Paige Rense
Editor-in-Chief of <u>Architectural Digest</u>*

Doubleday & Company, Inc., Garden City, New York 1980

ISBN: 0-385-14810-0
Library of Congress Catalog Card Number 78–22644

Copyright © 1980 by Paige Rense

Dedication

For Bud Knapp

Acknowledgments

You can't do it alone! My thanks to:

Charles Ross, graphics director of *Architectural Digest,* for designing this book in cooperation with Alex Gotfryd at Doubleday.

Photographers Robert Emmett Bright, Arthur Coleman, Billy Cunningham, Robert Hemmi, Pascal Hinous, Russell MacMasters, Derry Moore and Tony Soluri, who photographed the interior decorators' portraits. (Photographers' credits for the interiors are listed on page 219.)

Margaret Redfield, for copy editing as well as for creative assistance.

Gayle Moss Rosenberg, for writing all the captions with accuracy and style.

Susan Heller Anderson, for interviewing François Catroux in French. Jany Gade, for translating the Catroux interview.

My assistant, Bill Casper, for somehow coordinating both the book and me.

My friend Earl Blackwell, for writing the Foreword.

And, of course, all twenty of my friends the celebrity decorators.

Contents

Foreword

The star figure in the drama of interior design today is not a designer at all. She's Paige Rense. As editor-in-chief of the prestigious international interior design magazine, *Architectural Digest,* she has brought the once fuzzy outlines of decoration into sharp and splendid focus. She has made the names of the most gifted interior decorators of our time familiar in almost every part of the world. And in *Decorating for Celebrities* she has gathered twenty of the top designers to explain their theories of design, tell of their successes—and even a few failures—and offer some advice and words of caution to the do-it-without-a-decorator types.

Designers are basically idea people. They are innovators, rule breakers, but with a sure knowledge of what rules can be broken without creating disaster. In short, they have the gift of perspective, that discipline of the artistic sense that makes the difference between excess and success.

Perspective is one of those trick words that people find hard to define—even decorators will get around it by using other terms: balance, scale, a sense of proportion. Poet David McCord had perspective pegged about as well as anyone when he wrote:

> It keeps the windows back of sills
> And puts the sky behind the hills.

Of course, today's designers being a creative, innovative group, it's possible that even as this is being written, one of them is busily engaged in designing a room with the windows in *front* of the sills—but generally speaking, perspective is the common denominator in good interior design.

There was a time when the "decorated" home too often meant one that was so precise and sterile that it evoked a feeling of invisible velvet ropes and Do Not Touch signs. "Perfection is a very dangerous thing," Angelo Donghia comments. "Pillows puffed perfectly, tables devoid of anything. A home devoid of life."

There's not much of that around today. Home can be whatever we want it to be: a retreat, a showcase, a show place; even, in the words of designer Albert Hadley, "a sentimental scrapbook." The important thing is that it must be livable, no matter how elegant, no matter how filled with a collector's treasures. People today want to use what they have, to bring the antiques down from the pedestal, out of the cabinet and into everyday life. Part of the peculiar genius of the interior decorator is a talent for integrating the treasures with the more mundane possessions. An eye for color and form. A sense of which chair is right, which rug is wrong, for a specific room.

"Every room speaks," observes designer Albert Hadley. "But you've got to listen to what it's saying." Undoubtedly, these are twenty of the best listeners in the world of interior design today.

Earl Blackwell
New York City
1980

Introduction

Once upon a time, only a few decades ago, there were no decorators. Today they are a major influence on the way we live. Their interiors are shown in magazines year after year. They design furnishings that eventually impact the marketplace. They are copied. Admired. Often excoriated. Sometimes rightly so. Most often not. But this is the era of the decorator.

Interest in our personal surroundings has increased in direct proportion to the complexity of contemporary life. As individuals, we cannot seem to control the "outside" world. So we turn inward to our homes. We can control furniture. Objects don't hurt us. We want our homes to be supportive, comforting. And we turn to decorators as never before, because furnishing a home today is costly, as are the structural changes that are often an integral part of the design.

For this book, each decorator interviewed was asked the current approximate cost for a room of quality, *not* including fine art and antiques. The average was forty-five thousand dollars. Mistakes at that level would make the most confident do-it-yourselfer think 45,000 times and then turn to a professional for help.

The decorator today does not sweep in leading a pair of Afghan hounds and announce censoriously, "This won't do. Throw it all out!" Decorators work *with* their clients. Each interior they create, whether refuge or showcase—and often for today's celebrity it is a combination of the two—must reflect a special sensitivity and practical knowledge.

As editor-in-chief of *Architectural Digest,* I see, either personally or in photographic "record shots," almost two thousand homes each year, in all parts of the world. I have space to show less than 10 percent in the magazine. The majority of that percentage are interiors by professionals. The reason is simple: Rarely does a non-professional have the talent, visual sense, knowledge of quality, choices, eye for scale and authoritative style to create the interiors with the magic I seek for *Architectural Digest*. I regret that only twenty decorators could be interviewed in this book. The criterion was *not* the twenty best decorators. It was, instead, twenty *of* the best.

DECORATING FOR CELEBRITIES

VAL ARNOLD

When I first saw Val's work, "comfortable" seemed to be the one-word summary. More than eight years later, "comfortable" still seems synonymous with Val Arnold, whose photograph here was shot in his new house in the Outpost section of the Hollywood Hills. The same sofa has been in at least three of Val's residences because it is comfortable. Clients who agree are: Dinah Shore, John Austin du Pont, Mel Brooks, and Anne Bancroft.

I was the homemaker . . .

My mother and father worked long hours during the Depression years, and I was left to take care of the house and my younger brother. I constantly rearranged the furniture, although we didn't have that much. When we got a little money together, my mother decided we were finally going to have some new furniture, so I went with her to Detroit, which was about twenty-five miles away. She wanted fancy Victorian furniture, but I made her buy a very simple rolled-arm sofa in pale green mohair, and a Chinese rug.

Then we moved to California, where, after high school, I was part of the J. C. Penney management training program. But I found myself getting involved with display. My department always looked the best. I had thought about decorating for a long time, but didn't quite know how to get into it. I didn't know any decorators and I didn't know anything about decorating.

I decided the best thing to do was to get into merchandising, so I worked in the best men's shop in town. One man did all their window displays, and I started setting up props, clothes, and accessories for him. In a short time he wasn't doing the windows anymore. I was. Then I was hired to manage a store that sold lounge chairs. I re-covered all their ugly chairs in attractive fabric and put them in the windows. Business doubled the first month. In San Francisco I ran into a friend who told me about a job opening with a furniture store. Their design department was doing model homes at the time, about 1956; and business was booming.

I was told I didn't have enough experience, so I asked the head of the department to see my own apartment before making a decision. He did and liked it. I told him, "I decorated this apartment for five hundred dollars. Think what I could do with five thousand dollars." They gave me a model house to do; the worst house. My decorating budget was thirty-five hundred, but I spent about forty-eight hundred and was told I was in big trouble. Then the house sold. In two years I did 150 model homes. I had the chance to experiment and get every bad idea out of my system.

Not long after that I opened my own decorating business. The first year I went into debt for eighty-five thousand dollars. I didn't know anything about business. I learned how to type, keep books. I did everything myself until I got out of debt. Now I do two or three major jobs each year and ten or fifteen minor jobs, working with a staff of five. The major jobs take at least six months, and sometimes two or three years. Some take a lifetime; they never stop. Today I live in Los Angeles and new clients come to me usually because they've seen my work at a friend's house.

Being social helps, even though the people you meet may not use you themselves. Socializing leads to publicity, and people like to hire a designer whose name is established. Many of my clients are wealthy, but for every one who is, there are ten who aren't.

When I begin with new clients . . .

I like to see their home and how they live. We discuss what they want to do. I used to tell people too much at the first meeting. Now I try to remember to talk about money first. Most people don't tell you what they really can spend. They lie. You have to drag it out of them, because that tells you what price range you can be in when selecting fabrics and floor coverings. Today a lot of people say, "Look, I don't want to spend a hundred dollars a yard for fabrics. I'd rather have an antique or a painting."

If we agree to proceed, there is a retainer fee that applies to the projected budget. The retainer fee is because the preliminary layout is the creative concept and I will not present that until there is some kind of financial agreement. My fee is generally 50 percent above the net, or wholesale, price of the merchandise. Sometimes people expect the fee to be less, if the job is small. But a small project takes as much time as a big project. Sometimes more. The less money you have, the more you have to stretch it and the more ingenuity it takes.

I try to avoid hourly consultations, because the client does not realize how much time it takes to get things

For the master suite at his country house north of San Francisco, Mr. Arnold designed a restful contemporary setting of classic, functional simplicity. Since the suite is located in a restructured garden house, separate from the main residence, he concealed a heating unit in a painted antique stove; above it is a Michael Dailey painting. Color and pattern are replaced by the subtle, practical textures of raked paint, cotton fabric, and sisal matting. Says the designer: "The most lasting rooms I've seen have been white and beige."

done. Making a pillow, for example. We have to find the right fabric. That may take one hour or ten hours.

Then we have to write an order for that fabric, send it in, receive an acknowledgment. We do the same paper work for pillow stuffing, the zipper, and perhaps fringe, which may have to be custom-dyed. Then the whole pillow has to be fabricated, and that's another purchase order. On an hourly basis, one pillow could cost three hundred dollars or four hundred dollars at my hourly rate, which is one hundred dollars.

The words "interior designer" are misused . . .
We're really interior decorators. An interior designer is supposed to be able to design a piece of furniture as well as an entire home. Does designing a cabinet make you a designer? But whatever we're called, people need us. I've seen very few rooms by nonprofessionals that come off. They just don't have an eye for scale, color coordination, quality. In the eighteenth century, if you had money, you went to the best furniture maker. The styles were limited and you couldn't put together a bad house. If they were building, the architect was also the decorator. And fabrics were limited. Today there are so many choices. Years ago, I used to show my clients lots of fabrics. Now I know they don't really want that. They want to be told. Almost 6o percent of my clients tried to decorate for themselves before they came to me.

The mistake most people make
when trying to do their own decorating is . . .
trying to duplicate rooms they see in magazines. They like that, but they also like this. They don't know how to get it all together. And most people have no sense of scale. Of course, most decorators don't either. Easily 95 percent of the decorators in America should not be decorating. They have no sense of style, and they don't have that important thing called *click*. You can't explain it, but it is there. Some people have it, some people don't.

If you are decorating your own home, take everything out of the room and ask yourself, "What would I do if I didn't have all of this?" Then put things back one at a time and try to eliminate as much as possible.

Don't listen to your friends. Taste can be improved, even acquired, by reading and exposure. Go to the best galleries, the best furniture stores, the best showrooms; read the best magazines and books. A tasteless room might be defined as "opulence without any awareness of architectural standards or design." Ostentatious. Over-embellished. My mother thinks any furniture that is carved is automatically an antique.

Your home may reveal a lot about you. However . . .
some homes look serene and wonderful, but the people living in them certainly aren't. Bedrooms reveal a lot about people. They are one of the biggest problems I have with my clients. If a husband and wife can't agree on how to decorate the bedroom, you know they're in trouble. Also, complicated bedrooms usually indicate a lack of sex life. If you have to fight pillows, covers, and spreads to climb into bed, there won't be much lovemaking. Not even napping. You know the sex life is good when the bedroom is pretty, attractive, warm, voluptuous, soft and easy. Cozy, yet with a sense of humor. Colors should be warm, perhaps toasty and beige and into chocolate brown and pink or any derivative of red. I like bedrooms with pictures on tables on both sides of the bed, because it is the personal chamber.

Today most of the important designers are men . . .
Maybe it's because of the rigors of this business. Everyone who is tops in the field flies all over the world, working very long hours. Maybe women just don't want to do that. Most of the women I know in decorating are married; that seems to be the important thing to them.

A designer can become intimate
with a client to the point . . .
where it's disastrous. When you're dealing with people in their homes, you really get to know them. Sometimes very unhappy people will try to seduce the decorator.

I don't think most of the top decorators really give a damn about their clients or the way they like to live. We're talking about an incredible bunch of survivors. And I am certainly a survivor. I am also unabashedly selfish, selective, snobbish, and self-centered. I see it in my decorator friends as well.

Clients are funny people—sometimes . . .
When I did my first house in Palm Springs, I visualized a wonderful old Spanish look with tile roof, tile floors, wonderful arches and beams. My client said, "Stop! David Janssen is already building a house down the street that is so Spanish you can't drink the water."

And I had one client who kept the whole top floor of his house for sex. Just beds. Businessmen, most of them married, brought in girls for overnight parties.

Another client had an elevator hidden by a bookcase. It went down to a tunnel that led to a secret hillside exit. I've had requests for false doors, hidden compartments and, of course, mirrored ceilings over beds. One client installed closed-circuit television focused on his bed.

Wealthy clients are less difficult but . . .
more demanding. People with less money to spend are terrified of making a mistake. Wealthy clients want their money's worth, but it's not a matter of life or death.

All clients expect you to be on call at any hour of the day or night. I train their servants, set their tables, tell them how to create interesting menus. I've even bought their children's clothes and layettes for their babies.

The most expensive home I've done was . . .
for a client who spent a million dollars on antiques and rugs. In the first year we spent about half a million dollars on paintings. That was seven years ago. The collection is now worth at least seven million dollars.

My least expensive interior was done about five years ago. It was a funny little Victorian house for a young bachelor who had only ten thousand dollars to spend. He said, "I don't care how you do it, just get it done." We made it very attractive, using a lot of imagination and not much else.

Today's cost for a quality room is astronomical . . .
I'm doing a job currently for an intelligent client who has money and wants the best quality. We're working on an atrium, a library, and a breakfast room. My budget is between thirty-five thousand and forty thousand dollars. It should be closer to seventy-five thousand dollars.

*Today for someone who wants
a big look on a small budget . . .*
I would suggest simple classic pieces. Proven things. Nothing gimmicky. Canvas director's chairs. The sling chair is still a classic. Go to big import stores for white Indian rugs. Straw rugs are fabulous. Buy inexpensive fabrics and slipcover everything. Keep it simple. When in doubt, make everything one color: ceilings, walls, window coverings, woodwork and carpeting.

Sometimes you can make a mistake work . . .
Once I presented a fantastic fabric to a very wealthy client. It was hand-woven silk, only twenty-seven inches wide and so incredible that you could see four or five layers of delicately woven threads. At that time it was $365 a yard, wholesale! The client loved it. There was one thing I hated in that room; the ugly red velvet draperies. I couldn't get rid of those damn draperies. One day, kiddingly, I said, "Wouldn't the fabric we used for the chair be fantastic for the windows?" I held it up. The client said, "Fabulous." Then he added, "How much would it cost?" I said, "Forget it. It would be outlandish." The client insisted. The price was fifty thousand dollars for four pairs of draperies. I left in a state of shock and with a check in my hand.

One of the best things to collect for investment is . . .
the Oriental rug. The market is going up, up, up. And I would probably collect Roman antiquities if I could find

In a colorful vignette from his home in Los Angeles, an Oriental tablescape indicates designer Arnold's attention to quality and fine detailing. A bouillotte lamp illuminates the similar hues of a fearsome nineteenth-century cinnabar-lacquered frog, studded with turquoise, and an elegantly restrained Lang Yao vase, which share the sleek reflective surface of an antique chinoiserie black-lacquered desk.

Local artisans executed the latticework cabinetry designed by Val Arnold for the master bath of a home in Puerto Vallarta. Tiles, handpainted on the diagonal, form an arresting, shiny, hard-surface pattern that is also easy to maintain, while recessed lighting above the counter functions with unobtrusive effectiveness. A wicker hamper and ferns in clay pots complete the luxuriously simple look.

them. The modern-art market is sort of iffy. My instincts tell me to stay away from it.

A person who is secure about decorating is . . .
one who has dealt with many decorators. Someone who has never used a decorator is unsure of the role of the decorator and of his own role. There are many reasons for decorating houses, and they are not always the obvious ones. You have to find out what the real reason is. It may be that the marriage is shaky. Or that the children are all gone and the clients' life style changes. In actuality, loneliness sets in and decorating is a time-consuming project that keeps them busy. Once you find out, it makes your job much easier.

Wealthy clients are very concerned about . . .
budget. They want to know where the money is going and why. Every decorator has a problem collecting fees. And it's always the very last bill you have a hard time collecting. They'll argue about the last bill forever.

If I could choose any client . . .
from the past or the present, it would be Coco Chanel. Or Pauline de Rothschild. It would be wonderful to be around someone that clever and tasteful. I wouldn't mind working for Mrs. Onassis, although I hear she's very difficult.

Decorating likes and dislikes . . .
I like beautiful curtains. Very few people do them anymore. Not elaborate, just beautifully made. Interlined properly with real quality and handwork. I don't like a telephone directory lying on a beautiful English table, *without* a leather cover. Or a note pad without a beautiful leather case. An overabundance of candles. Beautiful objects made into lamps. Too many pillows on sofas bore the hell out of me. You have to push them around just to sit down. Lacquer is getting to be a pain. It scratches, it's impractical, it doesn't make much sense. Wallpaper is out, except in powder rooms, and even there it should be limited. Powder rooms should be simple and plain.

I'll dislike bedspreads for the rest of my life. And I'm awfully tired of seeing beds piled high with pillows. White sheets are still the most luxurious. White towels are luxurious. Or off-white, eggshell, or champagne. Black and white looks good today, especially with gray. Beige always has been and always will be good. Tan and camel are good. Canvas is a wonderful fabric. Bright colors are over. Dark rooms are too trendy. The most lasting rooms I've seen have been white and beige. Plain white damask tablecloths and napkins are classic. Big napkins are wonderful. Cute little napkins on luncheon tables are not. Place mats in pretty colors, no.

Val Arnold

Word Association

Color	Variation of lacquer red.
Furniture arrangement	Close.
Living rooms	Spacious.
Entrance halls	Important.
Bedrooms	Complete.
Bathrooms	Luxurious.
Dining rooms	Versatile.
Studies	Private.
Floor coverings	Practical.
Window treatments	Quixotic.
Fabrics	Practical.
Wallpaper	Ugh!
Lighting	Restrained.
Television sets	Ignore them. Put them on a stand and leave them.

Individual chairs for people to sit in look very good to me as opposed to big sofas. I'm beginning to tire of votive candles, except in churches, where they belong. And candles in colors. They should always be white or ivory. Mirrors have always been great. But mirrors for a reason. Mirrors that do something, that seem to enlarge a room or to reflect a beautiful view. I love tinted mirrors like that wonderful *pêche* mirror made in the thirties. Contemporary glass and steel tables are boring now. If you can't have real suede, don't have a synthetic. Suede when it's worn is very good. Leather when it's worn is very good. Velvet when it's worn and crushed is good. No on plush carpets, unless they're outrageously plush. Crystal chandeliers, unless they're real, are horrors. Chandeliers made of paper fans are almost as bad. Trying too hard is bad. Not trying hard enough is worse.

In the future, wealthy people will . . .
buy fewer but better things. Quality. Homes will be very stripped-down, but there will be more upholstered furniture, more comfort. Rooms will have to serve a multitude of purposes, because the days of twenty-room houses are over. We never really needed that number of rooms. It was pure luxury and status.

If I had millions to spend on a home for myself . . .
I would have four or five architecturally perfect large rooms; a master bedroom and sitting room combined with adjacent bathroom and dressing room, an incredible living room that would serve as a dining room as well, with a multipurpose table that could be used at any time. I don't mind a dining room, but it is not mandatory. I would like a kitchen where I could have people sit around and talk to me while I cook and where we could also dine. It would be on a small lot in Los Angeles, on a hill with a view. Almost Japanese in principle of design. Contemporary, with beautiful floor surfaces. Perhaps marble. It would be an open house, very light and breezy. Most of the furniture would be classic, upholstered; several beautiful rugs, fabulous objects and space to store objects so I could bring them out and change them from time to time. Incredible art, both modern and traditional; antiquities; a marvelous Roman torso, a fantastic Greek head; a beautiful Japanese screen; an incredible piece of sculpture, which might be outside. A game table, a wonderful secretary or a beautiful cabinet, one or two great mirrors. That's my dream house.

Some wealthy people know
how to entertain; most don't . . .
When people come to my home, they say, "Why doesn't my house look like this?" Well, it's because I care so much that I spend a lot of time getting ready for that evening. I try to anticipate every person's needs. Most people don't get the right combination of guests, the right food. And most either have too much help or not enough. There's nothing worse than having too much of everything, unless it's having too little.

The rich are spoiled, certainly . . .
Most of the wealthy people I meet are really not in touch with reality. That's the biggest problem. Another problem is that it's costly to be a decorator. Unless you live like the rich, you cannot decorate for them. But there's one thing a decorator can never forget when working with the rich. You're an employee.

"I try to see the architectural content of a room, first," says Mr. Arnold. Lacking such content in the master bedroom of a converted San Francisco firehouse, he installed a Franklin stove, which at once brought design interest and cozy warmth to the cheerful setting. Traditional furnishings include a nineteenth-century French red-lacquered desk flanked by Louis XV–style painted fauteuils. For bedrooms, the designer says, "Colors should be warm, perhaps toasty and beige and into chocolate brown and pink or any derivative of red."

MARIO BUATTA

Mario Buatta's interiors are usually upbeat and cheerful. So is Mario. Greatly influenced by the late John Fowler, England's grand master decorator for many years, Mario has brought a touch of English country house interiors to the New York homes of many clients throughout his career, including Geraldine Stutz, Mr. and Mrs. S. I. Newhouse, Alexander Cushing, and Henry Ford II.

*I*t all began for me when I was five . . .
My uncle, who was an architect, died, and my grandfather thought, "Ah-ha, here's my little architect." I wasn't really precocious, but I decided to be an architect.

During my school years I spent most of my time drawing houses in my textbooks. Then, after high school, I studied architecture at Cooper Union, and hated it. There was so much math involved. I thought you just drew pictures of pretty houses. I didn't want to be bothered about where the pipe goes or what holds up the wall. I was only interested in the way it all looked.

It was really the decoration I liked most, so I studied in Europe, with the Parsons School, under Stanley Barrows. That opened my eyes. But it wasn't until I was twenty-six that I really found my own style. I realized that what I really liked was the feeling of an English country house. The English travel a great deal, so their houses are filled with furniture and collections from all over Europe. A lot from Italy. Their architecture is basically Italian. I like a mixture of things, and I love the way the English really *live* in their homes. It's not studied, the way most decorating is today.

I had no background that led me toward decorating. My father was a society bandleader in New York. He was with Rudy Vallee for about twelve years and traveled all over the country. I spent part of my childhood in Hollywood. In 1940 my father started his own orchestra, for the Savoy Plaza in New York. He always said, "Oh, you don't want to be a decorator." But I did. I think much of my life has been spent proving to my father that I wasn't just a crazy kid who liked furniture.

Actually, I don't feel formal education is necessary for a decorator. You either have it or you don't. You can take all the cooking courses in the world, but if you can't improvise, nothing's going to make it right for you.

I've been in decorating professionally for twenty years. Two years at B. Altman & Co. in New York, and then with decorator Elizabeth Draper. Later, with Keith Irvine, who had worked for Mrs. Henry Parish, and for John Fowler in England.

I've been on my own for about fifteen years. There are forty or fifty clients on my books. But one client might be just a pair of curtains during the year. I have a secretary and an assistant. I design everything myself. I'm actively working on ten residences, in different phases.

Most of my clients were well off
when I started decorating . . .
I was lucky because a few important clients came with me. Today clients come to me mainly through word of mouth. You can have all the magazine pictures in the world, but people are afraid to come to you on the strength of an article. It's basically what they've seen of your work in person, what they've heard about you, whom they've heard it from, whose life style they want to emulate.

Socializing helps in making contacts. But a lot of decorators spend too much time socializing and not enough time at the drawing board. However, it does help, because you may meet people who need a sofa re-covered, and end up doing their whole house. Once you're established, you don't have time for extensive socializing.

When potential clients contact me . . .
I like to see them first in their environment, although the word *environment* sounds like the kind of decoration I'm so against. But by visiting clients in their homes, you get to know them better—the way they live, what they're like, exactly what their needs are. When I first started my business, I had a theory that I'd like to spend a weekend with clients. I don't have the time anymore. I wish I did. Now you spend weekends with them and eventually wish you hadn't.

I need a decorator.
Every decorator needs a decorator . . .
I'm trying to complete my own house. We all need somebody to throw ideas back and forth with. I can tell everyone else what to do, but I need to be disciplined, because I see so many things I want.

For the living room of a Manhattan apartment he once
enjoyed, Mario Buatta created a cozy, English–country house
atmosphere with a Regency flavor. "I loved that room—it
was my favorite," he recalls, "so I re-created it in my present
house—but with green walls." Warm colors and floral motifs,
velvet and chintz fabrics, provide a harmonious decorative
basis for a mélange of treasures, including a diverse and
interestingly arranged porcelain collection. "I am a collector,"
he explains. "I love a house full of things that have been
collected for years. Each one tells a story."

Another view of the same living room reveals the seating
arrangement that faces the fireplace. A contrastingly somber
eighteenth-century still life with animals, above the sofa, is
flanked by giltwood-framed oval chinoiserie paintings on
mirror suspended from blue faille sashes—a homage to
English designers Colefax and Fowler. The Adam bracket
supports an antique Chinese porcelain double-gourd vase.
"It's all in the balance," designer Buatta maintains.

My financial arrangement with clients is . . .
basically, retail. It's the most honest, because people know what things cost. Unfortunately, they think I make a lot more money than I do. I rarely work on a consultation basis, but when I do, it's a hundred dollars an hour or a daily fee.

The difference between an interior designer and a decorator can be very confusing . . .
when the sign on a painter's truck says DECORATOR. A decorator can be someone who makes slipcovers or paints your walls. An interior designer, on the other hand, designs a given space the way an architect would. But I prefer to be thought of as a decorator.

Everyone needs a decorator. Somebody who gets to know you and facets of your personality that you know nothing about. A decorator can introduce you to yourself. Today, every books tells you how to, why to, where to. They don't tell you why *not* to. A lot of people are decorating on their own, but they don't have a clue about what they're doing. Even decorators need decorators. If I were starting my life all over again, I would not be a decorator. I'd be a client.

When starting with a new client, it's important to . . .
see how they live, what their needs are, find out what they want. The first thing to think about is what's appropriate for them. If it's a major job, I like to make the architectural changes. Once you have a good background, anything can happen in the room. You're bound to have success, because a room will always work if the doors are in the right place, the entrance is in the right place, the fireplace is right and the windows are set properly. If you're faced with poor architecture, you have to decorate in a way that makes the eye "see" things that aren't there. You work around the architectural faults and try to make them look right.

I have very few clients who come to me and say, "Here's an empty house. We need everything." Most of my clients have inherited or collected things. It's harder, because you've got to make everything they have work.

Sometimes I work with a floor plan. If clients have a lot of furniture, it's more fun just to push it around and let them see it all working in various ways. I always like to show them two or three different arrangements, then perhaps let them live with it one way, over a weekend.

If you're working with a client who is starting out with very little furniture, you have to do floor plans. A draftsman does the plans from my sketches. Then I like to show clients several ways the plan could be done, doing sketches and floor plans in front of them. That way, they see what it's all about. Showing them the completed plans doesn't offer any other possibilities. It's like meeting people in a restaurant when they've already ordered

dinner for you. But you don't really feel like having duck. You want to have what you want. Also, choices make people feel more involved. They feel it's *their* house rather than your house.

The biggest mistake amateur decorators make is . . .
architectural. They never think of the possibilities a room could have by just heightening the door frame five or ten inches. That alone lifts the ceiling two feet. They never think about scale, they never think about color. They're very timid about color. They have too many so-called accent colors going on at one time, or too many objects in the room that don't relate to anything, but they're all the latest "in" things. They're self-conscious about what they're doing, and consequently the rooms look self-conscious. People tend to overdecorate. I like to think of my work as *undecorated*. It doesn't look as though it all arrived fresh from the shops yesterday. It looks as though it's been assembled over a lifetime. There's an art to making something look as though it was always there. Elsie de Wolfe said it in three words: *suitability, simplicity,* and *proportion.* That's good for would-be decorators and decorators to think about.

Don't think about what's in fashion. Don't think about fads in decorating. Don't think about whether blue is in or red is out. Do call a professional decorator. I like to think of decorating the way an artist paints a picture, and then the composition will come together. There's no such thing as "Yes, it should be red, yellow, blue or green." Answers may come in the middle of the night. You suddenly think, "This client should have yellow."

Recently I redecorated a dark apartment. I thought, "How am I going to make this apartment bright and cheerful?" It had a red library, which was a pleasant surprise, but everything else was sort of beige. I painted the hall a wonderful sky blue and glazed the walls. You could see lots of trees from the hall window, so you felt that you were in a walled sky garden. Then I did the living room walls in a deep, shining green.

Taste. Everybody thinks their taste is good . . .
We live in a world in which everybody has been told to be themselves, be individualistic, don't follow the next guy. So how can we really define good taste? But if you accept that there is a standard, a level, I do think you can acquire good taste. It has nothing to do with money, and exposure isn't always the answer. You could have been brought up in the richest world, surrounded with marvelous paintings, marvelous food, brilliant people; you could travel all of your life and still not *absorb* any of those things. You have to leave yourself open. Relax. Eventually you'll absorb a little, then more and more. Good taste is timeless.

If a room looks trendy, it's tasteless. If the house looks as though an enormous amount of money was spent, it's tasteless. A room is tasteless if the money shows; if it has become a showcase of status symbols. All the most expensive fabrics, the newest tables, lamps, chairs, but not put together in a stylish way. Of course, maybe it does reflect you. Maybe you are gaudy. Maybe you want to show that you've got the money. You can tell a lot about people by their interiors. You can tell whether their personalities are warm or cold. You can tell if they're afraid of color, or if they're adventurous.

My personal dream house would be . . .
a penthouse in New York. And I'd have a fantasy cottage in the English countryside for weekends. I'd like to have an apartment in a London square. And I would like living in Italy. My favorite house is *Malcontenta*, outside Venice. It's a classic Palladian house. In France I would love to live in *La Fiorentina*.

Entertaining . . .
Guests should be made to feel as comfortable as they would be in their own home. The whole point of entertaining is making your guests happy, giving them the best of what you can offer. Guests want to feel they are being taken care of. Don't overdo with flowers. Don't plump up the pillows so perfectly that people are afraid to lean back. Allow things to happen. Spontaneity is the most important thing. Throw all kinds of people together and let them have a good time.

To get started today as a decorator . . .
apprenticeship is more important than schooling. Work for a decorator whose work you really admire. It's difficult, because most of us don't need more help. I receive many telephone calls from people who want to work for me, even for nothing. But past experience has taught me that this is a great mistake. They take more from you than they give.

My favorite room to decorate is . . .
the bedroom, because it is so totally personal. You don't have to consider whether or not there are enough groupings, enough chairs, and so forth. It can be a mélange of everything you own in one room. It's your personal little cave. Your retreat. You should have everything that makes you feel, and be, at your best.

If you don't have it within you, the bedroom isn't going to make you sexy. But in decorating terms, it's color, fabric, lighting. When I think in romantic terms, I think of the rainbow, of sunshine, of light. It's the play of light that's so important. Actually the most important. If the lighting isn't right, the room doesn't come off. You create the mood with light. I don't like bedspreads. Never have. I like a bed to be inviting, to look as though you can sleep on it any time of day. I hate anything that looks overdressed. Beds always look overdressed when they're made up with a big bedspread. I like just a blanket cover and a lot of pillows, so that it looks terribly inviting. It's a great luxury to be able to use your bed twenty-four hours a day, not just at night for sleeping. I like curtained beds. If they're relevant to the space, it's the most wonderful feeling. It's like living in your own special little world.

My own home is a series of fantasies . . .
There are so many things going on, because it's the home of a collector. It's the home of somebody who has traveled a great deal; somebody who fantasizes a great deal about whether he is in England, Italy, France, or New York. It's filled with color.

It's a part of a house in Manhattan, a house that was built in 1920 for George Whitney. There were four private houses originally, the last big houses that were built in New York. They are landmarks. I have the parlor floor and half of the floor below, so I have the drawing room, the library, the reception hall and the big flying staircase. It's the feeling of an English country house, and I've filled it with everything I love.

The colors are all like the inside of a melon. The walls in the hall are very pale watermelon pink. My library/office is the color of a honeydew melon.

The living room is 34' x 23'. It's the old drawing room. I've made it into a one-room apartment. It is a plum color. And it's all cooled off with blue and white porcelain. The walls of the library/office are covered with Victorian paintings of dogs. Pets were very popular in those days. People often had their dogs' portraits painted. Almost everything pertains to nature. A collection of vegetable and fruit forms in porcelain, in paintings. Lots of flowered chintzes. It's what I love.

My apartment is revealing, but I'm not afraid of that. I'm not afraid of having a pink hall because I'm a man. None of those things have to do with whether you are a man or a woman. It has to do with what you like to see.

The design excitement in the world today is . . .
in New York. It's the center of everything. It's American decoration at its best, the strongest. It's the best of all possible worlds. We have a life style for every kind of person. The amount of California-style decoration that's happening in New York now surprises me. It works so well in the right place. And I'm amazed to see an English country interior in San Francisco. It's wonderful. And why shouldn't it be that way? That is what makes American decoration so good. There are so many different people with so many different ideas, people who have traveled, who have come from different parts of the world. The big thing today in Europe is to have

Mario Buatta

Word Association

Color	I love it. Color is my strongest weapon. Stanley Barrows, at the Paris Museum of Art, told us as students that if we did not understand the color usage of Matisse, Bonnard, and Vuillard, we would miss as decorators.
Furniture arrangement	I hate rooms that look so well thought out you are afraid to move an ashtray.
Living rooms	Not trendy.
Entrance halls	Inviting and impersonal. It's quite often nice to have a dark entrance hall leading into a bright, light room.
Bedrooms	Very personal. The place where you are yourself. The bedroom should reflect you in every way, cater to your every whim and fancy.
Bathrooms	Functional. Everything you need within reach. White. Decorated with personal things.
Dining rooms	Useless today. We don't have the help people once had. The space functions better as a combination library-dining room or sitting room/dining room. Or no dining room at all. Lots of people like to have dinner in the bedroom.
Studies	Books.
Floor coverings	Suitable.
Window treatments	I love curtains. They add to the architecture. Curtains are architecture.
Fabrics	Durable. Real. Real silk, real cotton, real wool.
Kitchens	Clean, functional, undecorated.
Children's rooms	Organized.
Wallpaper	Not much. In the right places they are terrific: kitchens, bathrooms, halls.
Lighting	The most important, and the cheapest, decorating ploy. With lighting you can create any kind of space you want. Any mood.
Lamps	Good lamps are the most difficult thing to find.
Television sets	It's such a luxury to have a television set that is concealed. If you can put it in a wall and hide it with a picture, terrific. Otherwise, put it out where you need it.

Fresh coordinating linens appoint Mario Buatta's canopy bed; other accoutrements—flowers, photographs, reading material—are comfortably close at hand. "I like a bed to look as though you can sleep on it any time of day," the designer says. "Beds always look overdressed when they're made up with a big bedspread. I just like a blanket cover and a lot of pillows, so that it looks terribly inviting."

an American interior. Especially in England. They want American, American, American.

In this country, we've had so much contemporary, I think people are weary of it now. They were more supportive of contemporary five years ago. Young people don't want the glass-and-chrome look. There is nothing worse than those stilted rooms filled with the furniture designed in Milan today. That hard-edged look has no feeling, no personality. It's like walking into a hotel lobby. What could be more boring?

Most people fear decorators, and rightly so . . .
when I see the things some decorators do. The only way to overcome that fear is by working with one you feel can be trusted. You will probably meet that decorator through a friend whose home you like.

Some of the most affluent people
have the most ghastly taste . . .
They haven't a clue about how to live. They don't know a table from a chair. And they are not interested. They're only interested in what's going to benefit them.

However, there is a breed of "old money" people who have a feeling of ease and elegance instilled, which seems to show through in their houses. It's a certain elegance and grace that new money can only try to copy, but never quite achieves.

"My favorite room to decorate is the bedroom," says
Mr. Buatta, "because it is so totally personal. Your retreat.
You should have everything that makes you feel and be at
your best. In decorating terms, it's color, fabric, lighting."
The focus of his own bedroom in Manhattan is a canopy bed
draped in a toile-de-Vence print and lined in a sun-bright
solid. "The use of blue and white with yellow happens to be a
great love of mine," he admits, adding, "I like curtained beds
if they're relevant to the space. It's the most wonderful
feeling—like living in your own special little world."

FRANÇOIS CATROUX

We met for the first time at a garden party in Paris, after several years of just-misses in various countries. Catroux's wife, Betty, is well known to those who read the picture captions in WWD. *François is one of the few decorators in Europe highly regarded for contemporary interiors, by decorators in the United States. His work takes him to the United States so frequently he has now opened an office on Manhattan's East Side. His client roster lists Mr. and Mrs. Gardner Cowles, Mme Michele Morgan, Mr. and Mrs. Antenor Patino, Mme Hélène Rochas, Baron de Rede, Baron and Baroness Guy de Rothschild, Mr. Stavros Niarchos.*

*O ne day a lady who was visiting
asked me to do her palace in Rome . . .*
because she found my apartment very attractive. She
was the fashion designer Mila Schön. But I have always
been interested in interior design, although I only
started working in this field ten or twelve years ago.

I believe it is important to have some training, but not
indispensable. It is more a question of taste, of the "feeling" you have for design. It is not because you attend a
school for four or five years that you have talent when
you graduate.

Today I average about fifteen jobs a year, with a staff of
five, based in Paris on the rue du Faubourg Saint-
Honoré, and I also have an office in New York.

Now clients come to me because they have seen apartments I have done for their friends or through my work
shown in magazines.

With new clients, I test people . . .
to know more about what they like, to know more about
their taste—if they have taste, or if they do not. Whether
or not they are ready to give me *carte blanche*.

Then I go into more intimate matters. I want to know if
they have children or not, if they have live-in help or
not. Also, I want to know a little more about what kind
of style they want, if they want something formal or
something a little more relaxed.

I explain about my fee, which is 20 percent of the cost
of the interior.

A decorator chooses . . .
material and furniture in existing shops, and puts everything together.

A designer is more someone who takes into consideration
the internal structures of an apartment; someone who
can redo a whole apartment, starting from the basis;
who puts walls where they should be and bathrooms
next to bedrooms where there are none.

A designer is someone who can redo the whole *architecture* of an apartment—from the inside.

Interior design is a job for . . .
professional people. You should use a designer, in order
to avoid mistakes.

Unless you are gifted in this field, you will make mistakes, because you do not always know what really has
to be done, and you do not always do what is important.
Then you have to do it all over again. And it will be
twice as expensive.

You might not know the structure of the apartment,
where things such as electrical and plumbing fixtures
can be put. Most people do not know, when they see an
apartment, how to give it a completely new shape.

The best kind of clients are strangers with charm . . .
The worst kind, the most boring, are the very rich.

*In America there are more
decorators than designers . . .*
There are many more people who go around collecting
samples in various shops than people who completely
redo the apartments. The reason, in New York, for example, is that apartments are not very old. There is not
that much to do. One is not going to demolish everything, mostly because it is already pretty well built.

In America, when you take on a new job, already, in
general, the plan of the apartment has been well
thought out.

In France, we have to demolish everything because all
the older buildings have one room followed by another.
Also, there is no bathroom.

I do believe the design excitement today . . .
is in Italy, although the contemporary things are accepted less today than ten years ago.

American decorating is a little standardized, a bit repeti-

The multicolor evening splendor of a vista across Lake Geneva, including the monumental thirteenth-century silhouette of St. Peter's Cathedral, is framed by sliding panels of latticed wood. Conceived by François Catroux for the living room of a Geneva penthouse apartment, the contemporary architectural grid—which the designer specified before the space was structured—conceals a temperature system and provides privacy and light control, without obliterating the view. Says M. Catroux: "I love architecture in the decoration world. It appeals to me before anything else—before material, carpet, furniture." Ancient objets d'art include an Egyptian mask, Etruscan head and Wei horse.

Sycamore bookcases trimmed in brass frame a view of the
master bedroom in the same Geneva apartment. A large
fabric-covered paneled screen stretches across the headboard
wall, becoming an architectural diversion, while a
Chippendale giltwood mirror above a draped table accents
the otherwise tailored and simplified setting.

Closely coordinated fabrics in varying intensities of the same
warm hue give the master bedroom a restful unity.
M. Catroux used the brass-trimmed sycamore bookcases he
designed to create a cozy sitting alcove, which is graced by a
Georges d'Espagnat painting. Louis XVI chairs counterpoint
the modern European flavor of the design.

A gleaming master bath illustrates the consistent use of luxurious materials in the Geneva apartment. Mirrors that conceal cabinets above twin oval brass sinks extend the strong linear quality of a lighted ceiling overlaid with a sycamore grid faced in brass. A painting by Christopher Wood is seen in reflection beyond the travertine tub. "I like bathrooms the best, because there's no furniture," says François Catroux.

tious. But I do not think it is the decorator's fault. It is more the fault of the living space they have to play with. The "volumes" of space are always the same. All the rooms have the same shape, all the windows are alike. Then, inevitably, it is always the same size sofa that goes in the room. And then also, one must say it, there is not a background, a past behind the Americans for them to have a taste that goes with the objects, the furniture, the antique paintings, a taste that exists more in Europe.

Opulence is in very bad taste . . .
A room decorated with bad taste is one hundred things. It is the choice of the furniture, it is the choice of colors, it is the choice of what covers the walls, it is the choice of the carpet. It is all of that. And if all of that is ugly, then inevitably the whole room is in bad taste.

Men are better interior designers than women . . .
They have more feeling for it than women. But I think women decorators are better for the charm they give to a home.

Recently a client asked me to . . .
make it possible to cook three sheep in their dining room. I am doing a château for some people from the Middle East, and they want to be able to cook three sheep in their dining room, not in their kitchen.

I do inexpensive as well as expensive interiors . . .
The most expensive home was about three million dollars. The least expensive was around twenty thousand or twenty-five thousand, in 1968.

The average cost for a room today is over two thousand dollars per square yard. That includes all the decoration, but what is missing is art and the very personal objects. The Picasso, for example, is not included.

If the budget is low . . .
I would suggest no luxury at all. Try to do the most with charm and simplicity. Because, really, there is no mystery. Sometimes you get the feeling that decorators are expensive, but it is not really so. It is mainly all the labor of the different specialists.

Anyone can have a home with style without much cost.

It is exactly like fashion. There are a great many women who are very elegant, naturally chic, who cannot afford high-fashion designers. If someone who has inherited objects, furniture, and already has a certain feeling about apartments, is given the choice between two apartments, one in a modern building and another in an eighteenth-century building, for the same price, inevitably, the most elegant apartment will be the one that is eighteenth century, and not the one in the modern building.

Do not follow fashion . . .
to extremes. It will not last. In the era of Italian design, everyone was ready to throw away their antiques, to have a low table for the living room, two white sofas and paint all the walls white. One should not go along with a fashion. Each time you should learn how to interpret. Never go all the way with something that will not last.

You can tell when someone is not very secure . . .
during the first interview, when you ask them what they want. I start asking about their special likes or dislikes of colors. You have people who tell you, "I like all colors." Then you have other people who say, "I do not know," or, "I am not sure." There are some people who have no idea of anything. They do not know about their likes or dislikes for colors; they don't even know what style of apartment they would like to have.

I do not like colors . . .
I do not like a combination of rich fabrics.

I love architecture in the decoration world. That means I like well-proportioned spaces. That appeals to me before anything else, before material, carpet, furniture.

In decorating for the next few years . . .
there will be a kind of going back to classicism. For the moment, it is the nineteenth century. After the infatuation over the nineteenth century, people will come back to the eighteenth century.

The wealthy know how to give parties . . .
but after all, it is the function of the very rich. Often they do nothing but entertain, so they do have the training, the know-how. They make no mistakes.

The rich are different because they have more . . .
time than others. The very rich are inevitably more capricious, because they can have everything with their money. They use their time to annoy the designer.

François Catroux

Word Association

Color	Beige.
Living rooms	Big and spacious.
Entrance halls	My favorite room to decorate because there is no furniture.
Bedrooms	Big.
Bathrooms	Average.
Dining rooms	I hate them. I enjoy eating in my kitchen.
Studies	I adore the study.
Floor coverings	In certain houses, hardwood floors are much better than carpeting. In other homes, it is the contrary. If you have a very small space, it is somewhat better to have carpet than hardwood floors.
Fabrics	Very simple.
Wallpaper	I do not like.
Lighting	That you cannot see.
Television sets	They do not bother me.

STEPHEN CHASE

*Steve Chase, a partner in Arthur Elrod Associates, favors a certain
amount of formality with his clients, which usually helps him
control the situation. But—not always. I was once present, although
I tried to pretend I wasn't—when a difficult client upbraided Steve
for something for which he was clearly not responsible. His
handling of Mrs. Monster was masterful. I've been an unabashed
fan ever since. Most of his clients—such as Johnny Mathis, Sonny Bono,
Farrah Fawcett, Suzanne Somers, and William Lear—are too.*

*My first present, when I was a child
in New Hampshire, was a dollhouse . . .*

That was of no interest to me. But the furniture was. I painted it all black. I really wanted to be an architect. I'd buy magazines with the fifty best floor plans and draw the houses in detail. But when I was older and realized all the math and engineering I would have to take, it seemed to me I'd be happier in decorating. So it's been my whole life since I was seventeen.

I got into decorating professionally when I came home to California after being in Switzerland. I was traveling in Europe with another family and I stopped in Geneva to show pictures of some model buildings I had constructed, to Mr. Lear of Lear Jets. I had gone to school with his son and daughter. One model was huge—eighteen feet long, seven feet wide and about eight feet high, in quarter-inch scale, with hotels, banks, office buildings. It was filled with forty thousand pieces of furniture.

But everyone saw the models instead of the rooms. They looked at it as a curiosity, more than anything else. Instead of seeing the rooms from a design standpoint, they were dumbfounded that anyone would take the time and trouble to build such a complicated project. It was an oddity, whereas I intended it as a portfolio.

The architectural firm Welton Becket offered me a job immediately in the model apartment. That was the last thing in the world I wanted. It all left me with such a negative feeling that today I can't put two pieces of paper together straight. I went to Art Center school in Los Angeles and took all the courses except interior design. I don't even know what they do in those courses. I've seen people with little pieces of paper putting furniture around, but it doesn't seem to mean too much.

I don't think formal education is actually necessary. Unfortunately for people starting today, it's the first step. I was fortunate to avoid that step. But when I started, twenty years ago, only the swells had decorators. I was essentially selling furniture, wallpaper, drapery fabric. There's nothing as good as an apprenticeship. Today I would insist on the formality of education, if for no

other reason than if someone wants to be a decorator enough to go through four years of the training, that gives me a clue that he or she is at least serious.

After I left Art Center, I started working in a furniture store for fifty dollars a week, selling and doing the display windows. My first morning I moved five hundred pieces of furniture to redo the display floors and the windows. That day they sold six pieces of furniture out of the window, the dogs they had never been able to sell.

Sunday of that same weekend, the parents of another kid I went to school with came in to see their decorator. She had not shown up that day. The owner suggested, "You work with them, since you know them." The girl lost that account right off the bat. I made my first sale and I never had to "do the floor" again.

Then my work received some local newspaper publicity and the late Arthur Elrod of Palm Springs saw it. He was famous and I had admired his decorating for a number of years. Everyone told me, "He won't give you any publicity. You'll dissolve into his corporation and disappear in Palm Springs." But he was very helpful all the way along.

Today I handle about twenty-five jobs per year, more than I intend to do in the future. Not because I want to do less, but because I want to do better. We have a staff of fourteen.

So much of our work is with houses under construction or reconstruction that we are inevitably ready before the house is ready. We have done jobs in three months; I would prefer six. We have jobs that go on for several years, only because they're so far away. A recent job in Singapore took a couple of years, but we finished the house right on the date we promised. We've done jobs in Germany and Mexico, and I have a new job in Switzerland. Palm Springs accounts for no more than 40 percent of our work. We're based there because we like it.

When I started in this business, any budget over ten thousand dollars was a major job. Today, a hundred thousand just fits in the door.

"It's the way a ranch house might look in the twenty-first century," says Stephen Chase, of an elegantly scaled hillside residence at Rancho Santa Fe, California, where he designed a sunken conversation area for the living room. "You need a lot of courage when you pick the fabric for forty feet of sofa," he adds, "and you have to have a lot of courage when you decide to *have* forty feet of sofa." A tapestry by Roméo Reyna unifies the subtle neutral color scheme.

I don't want any part of the social game . . .
It doesn't help. It hurts. I learned that from Arthur Elrod. My expense account for the year is so small, it's almost embarrassing.

I have fallen into the great luxury of having clients come to me. I will not go to a cocktail party in order to meet people. I will not do business that way. Not that I'm a prima donna about it, I just prefer people to come to me and say, "We want you to do this. Will you?" My answer is almost automatically "Yes." Usually they're not people who have seen work we've done for their friends. Friends are often not that anxious to have the same designer, and I can hardly blame them. The old saw, "Do a house for me, and all my friends will hire you," doesn't necessarily prove true. Publicity in *Architectural Digest* is the strongest source of new clients.

I don't like shopping with a client, because it hurts the job. They want to buy things they shouldn't have. It only costs them money. I get along famously with all my clients, but it would be impossible for me to maintain a social relationship with so many people. It would hurt the current jobs if I were going out three or four times a week. I studiously avoid the cocktail-party circuit.

By my own choice, I'm not on a first name basis with my clients. They call me Steve—I wouldn't have it any other way—but I address them as Mr. and Mrs. It is very hard to work with "Betty and George," eat with them, stay at their house, and then say, "By the way, you owe us thirty-five thousand dollars." It's amazing what trouble you stay out of by maintaining a little formality.

The decorating begins when . . .
we talk for the first time, perhaps even on the phone. I tell new clients how we work and what we charge. Then I see the house that's to be done. Probably 50 percent of my clients have never set foot in my office. I ask if they have an idea of what they want to spend on decorating. They inevitably say "No." Of course they have a figure in mind, but they want to hear *me* say it. You have to get the money out of the way so you can begin with the aesthetic. The aesthetic cannot come first. So, initially, I work with the man. Very few husbands say, "Honey, you do it. Anything you want." The woman has maga-zines and friends to sway her. The man knows what he wants, what he likes. It's my duty to expand on that.

You have to explore the look they want, right off the bat, after you've settled approximate costs. Sometimes we put the job together on the third meeting. I'm not one for surprises. Clients see the basic style. They always see a floor plan. I cannot work without that and I frequently do the scale drawings of the room myself. We rely pretty heavily on *design* as opposed to *things*. It's a little more architectural. Clients see fabrics, they see the basics. I don't show them the little geometric wallpaper we're going to put in the closet. I show them a floor plan and samples. "This is the fabric, this is the carpet. We'll do this chair in this fabric, and this is a wool sample."

Color often comes up on the first phone call. I ask about it immediately and it is one of the very first things people think of. It tells me a lot about the person right away. I'm very anxious to broaden people's color taste. If someone says, "I love orange," I suggest shrimp or melon—something other than just orange. I think of color in conjunction with the people. Color, when it relates to a space, isn't really that critical.

Rules are strictly to be broken, as far as I'm concerned. I wouldn't want to live in a canary yellow room, but there are people who would. And I would love to do it for them. I like enough colors, enough things, so that I can do their way *my* way. And everybody thinks they've got exactly what they want.

It's important to talk about money right away . . .
We have a brief contract for our services that outlines what we are going to do and how much we are going to charge. Once we're all in agreement on that, we present another contract, with a complete list of each item and its approximate cost. Things like: "Wallpaper, $300, not including hanging." A few extra words of explanation help make sure everything is absolutely clear.

Design fees vary according to distance, size, complexity, length of time. Most are in the fifteen-thousand- to twenty-thousand-dollar range. And the client also pays net for the furniture, plus 35 percent. The net is whole-

For the living room of a totally remodeled Beverly Hills residence, "the real excitement is in the palette—colors the owner specified," Mr. Chase explains. "I ask about color immediately, and it is one of the first things people think of. It tells me a lot about the person right away." A tapestry by Roméo Reyna weaves together the unusual hues, while organically shaped table lamps provide a parenthetical essence of contemporary Italian design.

"If any place ought to be dramatic and special, it's the dining room," maintains designer Chase. The mirrored wall of a large dining room in Rancho Santa Fe, California, reflects the interesting glass roof at the other end of the room, where another glass-topped table and a set of chairs are used for breakfast or more intimate dining. "Mirrors on the walls do fabulous things," he says. "A sheet of mirror can do more for a room than any other single thing that I know."

sale. If the client spends one hundred thousand dollars and you charge a fifteen-thousand-dollar fee, and 35 percent above wholesale on your furniture, the client is probably getting about sixty thousand dollars' worth of furniture at net. Nobody can balk at that. You can go into a furniture store, spend maybe one hundred thousand dollars at the retail price but you only get fifty thousand dollars' worth of furniture. Also, you are not getting the design and architectural help a top designer would provide.

Designer or decorator? The difference is . . .
an interior designer thinks of the structure, the whole plan of the interior: function, lighting, architectural details, windows, even the air conditioning. The decorator finds a nice paper, a print, and a pretty rug. But I have no qualms about referring to myself as a decorator, because some people find "interior designer" a little pretentious. We definitely fall into the interior designer category, and I prefer that. I don't care about decorating at the expense of the architecture. If the house is great, if the structure is right, decorating follows. The worst jobs have been decorating jobs on bad houses.

Today everything costs a fortune . . .
A decorator saves money and time. From a business standpoint, someone who has one hundred fifty or two hundred thousand dollars to spend would be wise to turn it over to a professional who will distribute it responsibly through the whole project and finish it. If you do it yourself, you must know exactly what you want. I've seen some lively things that people did themselves. Many of my clients have the aesthetic instincts. But they don't know how to control the whole picture.

Men are not better designers than women. However . . .
in addition to the creativity, which the woman certainly possesses, the man traditionally has been more organized. For whatever reason, he is more able to handle the business at hand.

In most instances, design is a full-time career for the man, foremost in his mind. The woman may have a family or interests that keep her from a total devotion.

Most women prefer a male decorator because there is no ego conflict. That's part of the problem. When women are together, it gets to be a social thing. They have so many things in common. I have nothing in common with many of my female clients other than our mutual affinity. We don't compete.

Intimacy between designer and client is . . .
total. You become a member of the family. And a lot of name designers are often seen socially with their clients. It's not for me. I'm thirty-seven years old. When I'm forty-seven maybe I will want to do that. But I'm not

that comfortable socially, anyway. I could go to a client's house for dinner, but a big to-do doesn't thrill me.

Seduction? Perhaps if . . .
you give the impression that you are seducible. I suppose it could happen. When I'm working I'm so asexual that it doesn't occur to me. It would seem funny, because it's not where I'm at. Socially is where it happens. If you've worked all day with a client, fine. But if you go out that night, have four or five drinks and dance, then at the door you may get into a whole new scene. I've avoided it all for that reason.

Wealthy clients are easier . . .
to work with. They expect to spend money. They want to spend money. That's the first thing I tell my assistants. Don't bring me a selection of ten-dollar-a-yard fabrics when there are gorgeous forty-dollar-a-yard fabrics the client will really love. They'll bitch about the price, but they'll be happy with it. The ten-dollar fabric will be replaced next year—by another designer. Because you didn't give them enough. People *want* to spend. They don't want to be cheap. That's no fun. Wealthier clients are easier, more secure, because they have money. I'm a great believer in money. "Money doesn't buy everything" is a swell idea. But it buys *almost* everything.

My clients know better than to . . .
expect me to be on call like a doctor. I have a gut feeling about whether an appointment is necessary. If one client had his way, I would come in at nine in the morning and sit there until something comes into his mind. Los Angeles clients are very demanding, very difficult, and those jobs cost you money.

The most expensive interior I've done was . . .
about seven hundred and fifty thousand dollars. The least expensive was an apartment for about ten thousand, a few years ago. Today I couldn't do a four-room apartment for less than thirty or forty thousand dollars. About twenty-five thousand dollars will do a basic fifteen-by-twenty-five-foot living room.

The most important thing
when doing an interior on a small budget is . . .
mood. You can't always buy mood, and mood doesn't always cost money. It's easier to do that for single people, because they're looking for style. To give a family style for very little money is very difficult, because so many basic requirements just can't be fulfilled.

But you can't go wrong with shape. Shape and proportion and forget the fine points of decorating. Forget the details and the finishes. Abandon quality. A cardboard box with a sheet over it may work better as an end table than a boring factory-made table. I'd rather go for the charm of something that doesn't cost anything. Slipcover the whole room. Buy used furniture and cover it all in the same paisley fabric and you've got a look. Chairs with sheets tied over them as slipcovers have a lot of style. It's temporary, but it works.

I live more like my clients . . .
than I used to, but not as well. I don't have any concept of opulence for my life. I choose not to have a Rolls-Royce. But I feel no qualms about living in a very expensive house. It assures my clients that I know how to handle their houses.

However, I don't know how to entertain well. My clients do it much better. They have big dinner parties. I would like to come to that point some day. But for now, my maid makes a big salad and I throw some chicken on the broiler and that's comfortable for me. But a black-tie dinner is totally out of my realm.

I would tell anyone to collect . . .
what they understand or have some knowledge of. Everything is not going up. Art has proven that. You hear at parties about a painting someone bought for a thousand dollars and sold for ten thousand. But there are an awful lot of people who have paid fifteen thousand dollars for a painting they couldn't sell for two thousand.

Signed antique furniture is going up only because handmade things are disappearing.

I like to see collections approached in an informal way, where things are used in daily life, if possible. I am not in favor of twenty-two different collections all over the house and twenty-five pieces on every end table. That's just cluttering.

Insecure clients always say . . .
"Money is no object." There's absolutely no reason for anyone to say that, because it *is* an object. And if they say that, you *know* it's an object. Even worse, because I hear it more often, is "We're easy to work with." What they're really telling you is, "You are not going to have to work hard, so you shouldn't charge us as much."

*If I could choose
any client in the world, it would be . . .*
the late Margaret Rutherford. I would do a wonderful faded, dusty English chintz room because I assume that's what she would want. And I'd like to do a house in collaboration with a great architect like I. M. Pei and have him say, "I love what you did with my architecture."

If a sheikh asked me to build a great desert palace, I could do a beautiful structure. A mile of marble. Not a *Beau Geste* set.

*For the next ten years
the important thing in decorating will be . . .*
mood. I'm doing some things now because they're uncopyable. Other things—Lucite, skins, bone—all of those things can be copied if you have enough money. Mood cannot be copied; it requires an assembling of things that are so exotic the untrained person can't copy it.

Decorating for the rich will be more exotic. An odd amalgamation of things past, present and future. It's the 1980s version of that tired word *eclectic,* and it seems to me not far off. For myself, I'm hoping that ten years from today I will be designing houses or working with fine architects, and a lot of the decorating will have gone away.

I really would like to see "less is more" happen. I have a conflict today. I love fine architecture with no furniture. But I know I can't sell it to my clients. Philosophically, I want to go to the land of nothingness—that's my goal. I will do it for myself.

Decorating likes and dislikes . . .
I like wood, marble, steel. I like today's materials; Formica, aluminum. I like things that are handcrafted, although they have to be well designed, too.

I hate shag carpeting, but I really don't dig carpeting, period. Draperies have no merit. The philosophy of hanging a lot of fabric and pulling it across windows doesn't suit me—it's so antiarchitectural.

I still use lamps, but I try to avoid them. In a well-designed room, the lighting is there and you don't need a lamp. Chandeliers are out of the question. Lampshades bother me. The concept of a wad of silk stretched around a metal frame with a light bulb inside is really pretty ugly. Little metal reading lamps of floor or table height are functional and attractive. I like torchères. And lights around plants, corny though it is. I like underlighting because it's a wonderful mood. Tubes of light under sofas, under tables, under consoles, in cabinets. It's flattering. And it's one way to get a lot of mood into a room when the architecture doesn't provide it. I can't deny the use of the coffee table, except that I would prefer tea tables, so people could really use them. I like tables behind seating areas.

We haven't done actual bedspreads for a long time. My preference is a quilt. You just throw it over the bed in the morning and that's that. An architecturally boring room requires upholstered walls. It's not design, but it certainly is decorating. A nice look, though. Very European, very pretty. I don't like plain, painted walls. That's very unfinished to me.

I love big, beautiful quality plants. Plants that mean something and say something. When I have a problem room, I stick a big plant in the corner and it looks a lot better. It's camouflage, but I like it and I don't foresee plants becoming dated.

Television sets are a problem. I like to hide them. I put them in boxes and they pop up from out of nowhere. But that's very expensive. I prefer them on a bookshelf.

I like mirrored ceilings, to conceal architectural faults. If you've got an eight-foot ceiling in a room that's twenty by thirty feet, you've got a problem. And if it's an acoustical ceiling, you've got a big problem.

Ceilings have been underemphasized for years. Recently I saw a room with pretty apricot walls and a white ceiling. What would be wrong with an apricot ceiling? The rule of the white ceiling is just about over.

Mirrors on the walls also do fabulous things. A sheet of mirror can do more for a room than any other single thing that I know.

I prefer big paintings, although lighting is a problem. I have no objection to small paintings with picture lights, but it's boring to go through a house and see five hundred lights everywhere. I'm not convinced that pinpoint lights from the ceiling are the solution, either. They say, "Look at the paintings. They're precious."

If any place ought to be dramatic and special, it's the dining room. You're not in it very much. It's a room for entertaining. You want to get away from the everyday, the ordinary. So start with a room that's a little exotic. The long rectangular dining room table with pull-up chairs? No way!

I love multiple tables, banquettes, odd arrangements pulled off to one side, something with a little character. The concept of glass on glass on Lucite on glass for dining, while it might make a very pretty picture, seems a little cold to me. A glass table needs something to make it look warmer. And glass tables make me nervous. I don't like looking at a lot of knees.

People get carried away trying to make children's rooms little fantasy lands. Children should have a place where they can really play and create. Formica is a great material for a child's room. In my generation, the children who were brought up in rooms done like little princes' and princesses' often grew up to reject material things because they were always so surrounded with them. It also takes the creativity away from the child. A child would probably prefer to live in a tent than in a fifteen-thousand-dollar room.

I love to do kitchens. Nothing is more wonderful than a flawlessly perfect modern kitchen that just gleams and glistens. Although the old English kitchens with heavy tiles, wood floors and wood paneling are pretty too.

My favorite room to design is a bathroom, because it's fun to add a little fantasy touch. In the house I live in at

Stephen Chase

Word Association

Color	I love it!
Furniture arrangement	None. Less.
Living rooms	Unstructured.
Entrance halls	First impression.
Bedrooms	Sexy.
Bathrooms	More sexy.
Dining rooms	At ease.
Studies	Intelligent.
Floor coverings	Practical.
Window treatments	Simple.
Fabrics	Luxurious.
Wallpaper	Carefully chosen.
Lighting	Important.
Television sets	Unimportant.

present, my shower is five by six feet, without a door. There is a wall of glass and a little garden area.

If I had unlimited wealth, my house would be . . .
near the ocean. Sardinia, Greece, Bali, the Galapagos. Somewhere off the beaten track, all by itself. It would be a strong architectural statement and it would be simple. But it might also be very big and grand. Lavish use of beautiful materials. One material in one room. Hammered copper walls. Opulent things. Lacquers and gold, but in a modern way and in great quantity. Mother-of-pearl would make a fabulous room.

One day I will live in one great big room about the size of a tennis court, with a roof and trees and a running stream. Lots of glass. Glass walls that disappear. It would be almost like being in a temple. A wonderful temple of the dawn. It could be twelfth century B.C. No furniture. Lots of pillows. No art. The house would be art.

My own house is . . .
a fifty-five-year-old Spanish hacienda that was in need of attention when I bought it, but had a great deal of charm and character. It does not have noble architecture. It's a beautiful piece of land, an acre and a half in the old section of Palm Springs. It has a beautiful view of the mountains. Big trees. A lot of rooms. It has a comfortable ranch quality. Corners to curl up and read in. Lots of different colors. The main entry is elephant gray. The living room is pink and the bar is terra-cotta. My bedroom is off-white; the bathroom is white. Lots of wood floors and tiles, brick floors, stone. Most of the walls are adobe. It's not a normal house by any standards. I have rooms to go into in the winter, rooms to go into in the fall. And rooms not to go into at all.

*The home builders of today
underestimate the taste of the average person . . .*
They are doing them a disservice by continually erecting fifteen-hundred-square-foot Colonial, Early American, and high-Spanish reproductions. A good, simple, con-temporary house would be a much better solution. Within the house, people may want to go in another direction.

The best interior decorating is . . .
in the United States. The Orient suffers terribly. South America and Mexico, once in a while something. When it's good, it's out of this world. And when it's good in Italy, it's better than anything in this world.

In the United States, if you asked ten New York designers for their best house and ten California designers for their best house, the East would win. It's more sophisticated. A little more advanced. They're competitive and they see so much of one another's work. It's intense and closed in. In California there is very little social or professional contact among designers. The work is not as similar on the West Coast.

Acceptance of contemporary in America has been slow because examples are so few. But I think it's coming. In architecture, definitely. Not in the single-family house. The single-family house is the last bastion of true nonsense. Condominiums are getting modern, getting good. But great modern houses are rare.

People fear decorators, so . . .
I try to put clients at rest in one meeting by telling them everything. Take out all the mystery immediately. Initially they say, "I was afraid to call you, because I thought you'd be too expensive." Once they understand that you are not going to race around the room and scream at them, everything is fine.

The rich are not better but . . .
they are different. They're exposed to so many exciting things. They have had a lot of experiences the non-rich have never had. Therefore, their attitudes toward things are much more credible. It's very easy to say, "I have money and I don't care about it." That's credible. To say, "I don't have any money and I don't want it," is not credible. The rich are different and they have good reason to be.

Mr. Chase created a sensuous Moroccan mood for a guest
room of a large residence he designed on an estate near
Honolulu. A twenty-four-panel screen depicting Old
Marrakech, executed for the space by Richard Kishady,
provides an atmospheric backdrop for the interplay of five
fabrics inspired by Persian designs, and for the lightly scaled
Islamic furnishings. "Mood cannot be copied," explains the
designer, "because it requires an assembling of things that are
so exotic to one another the untrained person can't copy it."

HARRISON CULTRA

Although he is younger than many of the decorators who have established themselves as masters of traditional interiors, Harrison Cultra's feeling for antiques and his knowledge of history have set him apart in the few years he has practiced his profession in New York. His country house claims most of his affection, and is, he feels, a suitable ambience for working on traditional interiors for his clients, including Jacqueline Onassis, and Richard Jenrette, who collects Greek Revival houses.

I *always cared about the way things look . . .*
My whole family did. As a child, when people asked me what I wanted to be when I grew up I always said "a remodeling architect." Building was actually sort of an important pastime for us. And we did move a lot. We lived in Arizona, Mexico, and Canada. My father felt that you should see everything.

We settled in Arizona because my parents finally decided we should all be in schools at the same time. My father was a serious farmer with many other interests; some were intellectual and scientific. My mother was interested in antiques and decoration.

When we lived in Arizona, I visited every Frank Lloyd Wright house possible. I remember thinking one of his great houses, the Price House, looked exactly like a luxury yacht. He did have a little problem with livability, but he was an absolutely incredible architect.

I once went to one of his lectures at Arizona State University and asked several pointed questions. He said, "Harrison, that's a very red shirt you're wearing." That was about as much of a reply as you got from Mr. Wright in answer to pointed questions.

Architecture fascinated me. I always drew houses. Before I was sixteen, I built a house with my aunt. Later, in Paris, I took courses at the Louvre because I was very much interested in early Chinese pottery. At the same time I visited every house I could.

When I came back to the United States from France, where I had been working in an import/export business, I had to find a job. I had all the background. An old friend of mine, the duchess of Argyll, had been a great friend of Rose Cumming, who was also a friend of mine. She knew that since Rose's death, Eileen Cecil, Rose's sister, was looking for someone to run the interior design business and the shop on Park Avenue. They hired me to assist her to continue the business and make it work. So I just dove in.

I started decorating professionally then, although I had already decorated for myself and a few friends. Actually

I did jobs that were bigger than my average job today, and that's eventually the way I'd like to work again. Six or seven jobs a year, of a certain scale. Today I do about twenty jobs a year, with a staff of three. My New York City office is in my apartment, which works very well for me because I also work from my country house several days a week. That's my real home.

To become a decorator, it's very important . . .
to first work with someone who knows what he's doing. One of the problems of decorating is going into every workroom and hearing people say, "It can't be done that way." You have to be able to tell them how it *can* be done that way. Working for a good firm with a large volume of business is wonderful training.

My jobs take longer than most decorators'. I usually take the clients around to shops and museums and find out what is going on in their heads. I take them to fabric houses and let them choose. But I never give a client anything I don't like myself. After all, clients come to you because they like what you do.

Most of my clients are not wealthy, in fact . . .
a lot of them are on the rise. Many are young people who are professionals in their own field, so they understand the importance of advice.

My first major clients came to me because . . .
they liked my own apartment in Paris. When I found it, the place was dreary and unattractive. Nobody had seen its possibilities. I painted it white and put in a yellow broadloom carpet. Bright lemon yellow on parquet floors. I found some good architectural elements in the Flea Market along with late-seventeenth- and early-eighteenth-century overdoors. I used natural materials and the least expensive curtain material I could find. That was it. White walls, lemon yellow carpet, and curtains.

At that time I learned that the French couldn't scale lampshades, which absolutely amazed me. And the idea of slipcovers seemed beyond their comprehension. That

"I try for colors that have seasonal personalities," says
Harrison Cultra. "The drawing room of my Hudson River
country house is a color I matched to that moment of spring
when everything turns green. That very special perfect green;
in summer it appears very yellow." He describes the room as
"slightly formal and cool . . . spare with a sort of modern
feeling. The furniture appears to float." Appointments
include an Art Déco leather-upholstered chaise longue by
Jules Bouy and a parchment-finished waterfall table by
Jean-Michel Frank; an églomisé mirror that once belonged
to Syrie Maugham, and a Louis XV chinoiserie commode.

Mr. Cultra considers the library in his 1773 country house "the coziest room because it's all down-filled and overstuffed and comfortable, with some period furniture. The sofas are upholstered in a familiar old seashell chintz, and they have fringes on them to anchor them." He adds: "Over the fireplace is a large nineteenth-century landscape, possibly painted by Thomas Cole. It looks almost as if you had cut a large hole out above the fireplace—it's what you'd see: a vista of mountains and a valley in strong blue and green colors. The rest of the pictures are memorabilia to do with the house, which was once owned by Robert Fulton."

was what somebody's aunt made for them. In the Flea Market I found a low table—and I still have it—which you could eat at comfortably from low armchairs. So with my low table and low chairs I gave "children's parties." The people who visited my apartment loved the comfort, the color, the elegance. My first clients were young friends who wanted a comfortable home that was different from their staid family houses.

I don't like clients to come to my office . . .
I like to see them in their homes and try to find out how they live. How many people do they like to have for dinner? How many children? How many people do they like seated in their living room? If they don't have pictures of things they like, I always ask them to find some. That helps enormously and you generally find that they like a lot of different things. I try to help them develop their own style, which is very often much different from what they thought it was when they started. The best result is when clients say, "It's exactly what I wanted, only I didn't know it." And sometimes things just evolve.

When I first spoke with Mrs. Onassis, she asked me if I could find a hanging backdrop for a piece of Egyptian sculpture. I told her I really didn't feel the problem was the backdrop. She said, "What do you think the problem is?" I said it was really in the room across the hall. She asked what I would do. I had to say, "I really don't know, because I don't know enough about you." Eventually I got the job and started with the basic premise of what she liked and what made her comfortable.

I start at five hundred dollars a day . . .
Sometimes on a consultation fee basis, but it varies. I don't even know what it is now and I'd prefer not to. "Discuss it with the office" is what I tell people. But straight retail is the way we almost always work.

*I don't know the difference
between an interior designer and a decorator . . .*
An interior designer is presumed to be capable of design-ing and drawing. But it has become a term meaning that interior designers are one step above all those others. When anybody asks me, I say I'm an interior decorator.

People use decorators because . . .
they don't want to be too involved. If they have the taste, of course, they can do it themselves. Often people have very good taste, but they are involved in other things. A year ago, I gave a talk to a museum group and said that if women spent as much time making their husbands happy as they do taking decorating courses, they'd be much better off.

When beginning a new job . . .
you have to first make sure the architecture is correct. I like to begin with plans. We place everything on paper, but I don't find it's really necessary. Most clients don't read plans well, either. You ask what colors they like, what colors they wear. I try to find out everything. Many decorators charge for the time expended in finding out about the client, and I do think one should be paid for that. I've spent weeks with basically indecisive people who lead you merrily hither and yon. I like working with businesswomen. They make decisions.

*The mistake most often made
by people doing their own homes is . . .*
choosing every perfect detail. The greatest chair, the greatest rug, the greatest fabric. But they don't work together. Overblown. Just too many things. Nothing becomes important. Decorating is not finding the most beautiful chintz. You have to ask yourself, what does it have to do with everything else? How are you going to look sitting on that chintz? Does it mean you're going to wear only plain dresses in your living room for the rest of your life? There are women who are perfectly dressed, who love luxury and comfort, who have no luxury or comfort in their own homes. You have to decide where each piece will go.

People buy on impulse in the supermarket. That's the

key. It's the whole American way of buying. Generally, their major mistake is asking other people's advice. You have to believe in your own taste. Do keep it simple. And, because decorating costs a lot, don't indulge in fads. You have to think of the future. Good taste is really timeless, but it becomes commercialized, and then you have to think of something else.

Decorating likes and dislikes . . .
Basically, I don't like skirted tables, but if you end up with lots of good period furniture dancing around like a corps de ballet, you've got to anchor it somewhere. Very often you can't get enough upholstery in the room, and a skirted table is the only way to pin it down.

I don't like synthetic fabrics, but there are exceptions. I like parachute nylon. It can be used attractively for window treatment and creates a light and airy effect.

Curtained beds have been overdone, but I still like them. Often there isn't enough attention to detail on curtained beds, and people just slap something up on the ceiling and let it hang. However, curtained beds give people a very cozy feeling. They're luxurious, warm, and attractive. And if you like to sleep with your windows open, it cuts the draft.

I'm basically opposed to lamps. To have a well-lighted room you have to think of a room without lamps, then add the lamps for specific purposes such as reading. One can't really get by without lamps, I'm afraid, although I try. I do like large, colorful, transparent lamps.

You can't get along without coffee tables, but it's one of the last things I put in a room. Although I don't dislike them, I do dislike "arranged" coffee tables. They should be minimally arranged so you can put a tray down and use the table for what it is intended. It also takes the stiffness out of period rooms.

I like area rugs. I don't like Oriental rugs per se, but I do like certain kinds. I like Samarkands. They are the only pale rugs you can get, other than resorting to a durrie or a kilim. I basically dislike animal skins and disapprove of using them, but I don't mind cowhides and sheepskins on the floor. I like sheepskins next to the bed to put your feet on.

I do like mirrors and I subscribe to the French theory of having one in every room. It's good for people if they get used to them. A lot of people are shy of mirrors because they don't like to catch their reflections and they don't want to see their bad posture.

Mirrored walls can create a chilling effect, unless rather carefully used. I like mirror-paneled dining rooms because they reflect candlelight and sparkle and create a very elegant dining atmosphere.

I would prefer everything to be real and I would also use good furniture reproductions, if they created a good effect and were pure in style. I don't tend to use them, because you can usually find something real that works.

I do like good wicker. It is a very good way to achieve a feeling of informal charm. I am basically opposed to period dining chairs. They are a very expensive proposition. People eventually lean back in their chairs, and if one Louis XVI chair gets broken, it turns out to be the most expensive dinner party you've ever given.

I don't like cloths on dining room tables, as a rule. I like bare wood tables with a highly polished surface that reflects. And I like the reflection of silver and crystal and candles. I like, when the situation allows, a square dining room table. Eight is a good number, because the conversation works better across the corners and in groups than it does at a round table.

I like candlelit rooms, fires, and shiny hearths that reflect the fire. I like tactile fabrics. I like silk pillows to be soft and underfilled, so that one can create a sort of comfortable spot to nest in. I like fabrics that feel good. I don't like velvet. But I like silk velvet.

Children's rooms should be functional and with ample open space where the children can play. Bulletin boards, blackboards—all are important to allow changing décor. The rooms should not be overdecorated.

I don't like curtains as such, but they do create an atmosphere, an ambience, that becomes an architectural feature of the room. Where woodwork is lacking, a good curtain treatment can provide the missing architecture for a room. It can set the entire tone, if you want an Edwardian study or a very elegant modern living room. There is a certain time when nothing else but fabric will do the trick.

I like hanging things on mirrors over a fireplace. I like a mirrored chimney breast with a picture hung on it, so it gives you an additional dimension. It maximizes the picture's importance, and at the same time, diminishes the focal point of the fireplace itself. When a fireplace is not used, it's just a black hole. So it needs to be sparked up in some other way.

My New York apartment
is where I hang my hat and spend the night . . .
but it also has to function for cocktails and dinner parties. I use it for business, so it has to be "townish" and have a certain elegance. At the same time, it's my own living room, so it has to be comfortable. I must be able to spread books and papers around.

My country house is my real home . . .
The approach is down a long driveway and it's just the way you'd like your house to look. It's foursquare, solid, massive, and rather simple from the outside. The driveway leads directly to the front door. There is no question as to which door you're entering through.

The entrance hall is a twenty-two-foot cube and it has the things that entrance halls should have. I keep trying to take the lamps out, but the room is basically lighted from above, so I have never really succeeded. It has a bench where you can take off your galoshes or your muddy shoes. The painted floor was dictated because this is a period house, built in 1773. But I have insisted that it not be a period restoration as far as decoration goes, because I want to be totally comfortable. My halls are a very good warm apricot color, a dry-brush paint treatment that appears to be three colors. The floor is done in a painted false marble, a large design that makes the hall appear larger. It has a very imposing

Harrison Cultra

Word Association

Color	Friendly.
Furniture arrangement	Comfortable.
Living rooms	Livable.
Entrance halls	Dramatic.
Bedrooms	Luxurious.
Bathrooms	A retreat.
Dining rooms	Cool.
Studies	Cozy.
Floor coverings	A unifying feature.
Window treatments	Simple. They make or break a room.
Fabrics	Natural.
Wallpaper	Good.
Lighting	The most important thing of all.
Television sets	In or out.

Chippendale staircase and a large painted green lantern in the Georgian-Chinese style that fills the great space. A big Louis XVI mirror hangs over a demilouvre console table with a Chippendale fret and a marble top, which creates a kind of solid feeling in the hall, as if it had always been there.

I basically don't like blue, but the library is blue. It's a cool feeling for a warm room. I came on blue because the seashell chintz I wanted to use is a familiar old chintz to me. The sofas are upholstered in the chintz and they have fringes on the bottom to anchor them. It is a very lively room. There are lots of books, of course, but they are all behind doors. It's the coziest room because it's all down-filled and overstuffed and comfortable, with some period furniture. Over the fireplace is a large landscape possibly by Thomas Cole. It looks almost as if you had cut a large hole out above the fireplace. It's what you'd see. A vista of mountains and a valley in strong blue and green colors. The rest of the pictures on the walls are almost all memorabilia to do with the house.

From the library you go back into the hall, then into the drawing room. It has five French windows and no curtains. There is an Italian carved marble fireplace, a later addition to the house about 1800. The room is spare with a sort of modern feeling. I try for colors that have seasonal personalities. The drawing room is a color I matched to that moment of spring when everything turns green. That very special perfect green. In summer it appears very yellow. The room appears to be slightly formal and cool. A big Chesterfield sofa is covered in a natural woven fabric, rather Edwardian looking. Over that sofa is a very modern contemporary picture in strong purple, orange, and yellow, very bright. There is a beautiful and architectural American chaise longue of the Art Déco period, upholstered in leather, with a fur throw on it. The room also has white painted Louis XVI furniture, which lends itself to the Neo-Classic fireplace and the elegance of the French windows. The furniture appears to float.

The dining room is "serious." It is connected to the drawing room by two very large, overscaled doors. When they are open, you have a big expanse of dining room, and the two rooms join. The dining room has four French windows, which are treated with curtains in a rather strong orange. The table is a small oval folding campaign table by Jansen. It will seat eight. I like space in the room, and it's cozier to sit at a smaller table. Surrounding that is a set of painted, off-white armchairs. Over the fireplace is a Georgian two-part mirror.

One of the largest rooms in the house is my bedroom, which is upstairs. There were no closets, but each bedroom had what was then called a "powdering room," so I adapted those to bathrooms and closets. I have a big, comfortable Louis XVI bed, a chaise longue, and a couple of the original pieces of furniture from the house.

There is a yellow guest room with all my furniture from my room as a child, including the bed in which I was conceived. You can't very well throw that out. Fortunately, it was a nice American canopy bed.

I would really like to have a modern house . . .
built with natural materials, with classical lines and proportions. It would be oriented to the views and the sun. I like stone, slate, natural materials. I also like a lot of glass and a lot of view. It would be a combination of French country manor house and American farmhouse, yet it would somehow still be modern. Inside would be a greenhouse and fireplaces. Plenty of large, squishy sofas. That requires a large room, so you can have three or four people lying down and talking to each other, which I think is very often good. There would be a movie screen and television set. The house should have a very comfortable bathroom and dressing room with access to the outside. A workable kitchen with a slightly open plan that can be closed. I would furnish the house with a mixture of antiques. I might buy a very good Oriental rug. I would have things of all periods and styles.

My fantasy client would certainly
be someone who is interested in collecting . . .
someone interested in decoration who also knows about

The pink-painted living room of Mr. Cultra's Manhattan pied-à-terre is airily appointed with natural linen slipcovered seating and lightly scaled tables, split-bamboo blinds and sisal matting, and plants. A fragile painting by Kenzo Okada hangs above a Louis XVI caned daybed. Says the designer: "The room was originally designed all in pink—upholstery, too—to flatter everybody, and to look cool and fresh in contrast to the uncompromising New York out-of-doors."

gardens. It would be Lord Merlin, from Nancy Mitford's novels. His character was, I believe, drawn from life. Sir Philip Sassoon was, I think, the prototype. He was a gentleman of great means, interested in the arts, very worldly and a great personality himself. He would work with me in the decoration and design, taking advantage of all the great contemporary artists.

Homes are revealing . . .
I very often look into people's bedrooms to see how they live in that room. It tells me what they like at hand, how they like things to work, about their comforts. A home has to reveal.

I love a spare, Spartan house. Monastic places. Perfect simplicity. I like people who don't want anything around them. Yet I also like people who want clutter around them—I just wonder how they live that way.

In the bedroom, you have to know more intimate details. Where do they keep their tissue boxes, their cigarettes, if they smoke? Are they extremely tidy? Is reading in bed important to them? And I have clients whose sex lives are extremely important. I've designed some extraordinary mirrored bedrooms.

The trouble with women designers is . . .
either that they're not serious enough or they're married and take a secondary position. I don't think men are better designers than women. There are women with extraordinary taste, but they seem content to keep the home fires burning brightly. They are very good wives.

People criticize me for being too close to my clients . . .
but most designers do become very intimate with clients. I shop with them for clothes and jewelry. I don't want to, but that's how you find out about them. I don't want to go around holding their hands. I don't want to be everybody's buddy. I definitely don't want to go to everybody's house for dinner. And I don't want to be everybody's best friend. But almost invariably, the people I work for become friends. You get to know each other over the period of time you're working together. You know when they're not happy. They can talk to you. You can be a friend at those times. It's like being someone's doctor. And you must be just as discreet.

I once had a client who told a friend, "Whoever walks through this door as the recommended decorator, I'm going to seduce." I got the job anyway, but not on that basis. I don't think sex necessarily gets in the way, but you have to be clear whom you get involved with.

Wealthy clients are easier to work with . . .
because they're busier. But lots of wealthy people have nothing else to do but decorate. And they're the ones who are difficult.

The focus of a bedroom in suburban New Jersey is a fanciful Chinese Chippendale pagoda-top bed. "It's a splendid, unique bed—it was mine," says Harrison Cultra. "I used natural handwoven cotton for the canopy hangings as a kind of contrast to the stateliness of the bed, and they are filled with down to give them a puffy look." Chinese paintings, a Queen Anne japanned tea table, Regency chair, and durrie rug reinforce the tradition, while contemporary fabrics update the look. "The fabrics encourage a contemporary feeling in what could have been a very stuffy room."

LEO DENNIS

Leo Dennis and his partner, Jerry Leen, have been quietly influencing interior design for many years, since they opened their extraordinary shop, Dennis & Leen, in Los Angeles. They have shared their taste and style with the top decorators, who, in turn, have purchased for clients those things deemed acceptable by their discerning eyes. You are considered fortunate if Leo Dennis and Jerry Leen will do your interiors, because they do only what they want to do—and that is very little.

*My background, before I went
into interior design, was checkered . . .*
to say the least. I was with the Lester Horton dancers, a modern troupe in Los Angeles. Then I was hired by Earl Carroll, but the draft board was after me, so I joined the Merchant Marine. I was in the service for five years and read every book and magazine about interior design I could put my hands on. Afterward, I bought some property with money I saved. At the age of twenty-seven I retired. I didn't do anything for three years. One day I talked to some people who were driving to Alaska, and the next thing I knew I was up there. I was going to stay two weeks and I stayed eight years.

I got into decorating professionally when . . .
I returned from Alaska. My partner, Jerry Leen, was working for a decorator, and we decided to go into business together. We opened our antique shop twenty years ago and started doing a little decorating on the side. I don't think formal education is necessary for an interior designer. If I wanted to get into decorating today, I'd go to the best person in the business and offer to work free. That's an offer no one can refuse.

We only have time for about three jobs per year. We do all the decorating ourselves, without any staff at all. Our clients, in the beginning, were moderately wealthy, and we met them all through our antique shop. Most of our clients now come to us through referrals from other jobs. We're not very social. I'm sure socializing helps, but we don't have the time or the inclination.

Our first conversations with new clients . . .
take place in our shop. There they can point out things they like and we can tell if there is a continuity of taste. We have a wide variety of antiques, paintings, ancient Greek statues, crystal chandeliers, and a big collection of Egyptian pieces. We also design furniture in the style of the eighteenth century. Before we go much further, we take a look at the client's house. Then we just go ahead and start making suggestions and placing things.

Our fee is one-third above wholesale. The client pays the retail price and we pay the wholesale price. For example, the client would pay fifteen hundred dollars retail. We pay a thousand dollars wholesale, or net. Our commission would be five hundred dollars. We don't work on a consultation basis anymore.

The most expensive interior we've ever done was under half a million dollars.

*An interior decorator furnishes
the existing architecture. A designer . . .*
does built-in furniture, changes wall structures, floor plans, that kind of thing.

*The average person is just not capable
of decorating. It takes . . .*
ten or fifteen years of experience to know how to make a house look good. Only professionals have devoted that much time to it. Everybody wants to be a decorator, just as everybody wants to be a movie star. They think it's easy, but it's a lot of hard work. There are only three professions that you can follow without experience: art, interior decorating, and prostitution.

I decorate to the architecture. If it's an apartment with no architecture, then you have to get a feeling of the way the client wants to go. Most people play down what they want. They may say they want their home to look very humble or very "country," but it always ends up closer to *grand.*

When we begin we look at everything, and sometimes when a room is about half visualized, we just deliver the furniture we think will work and place it around the room. It's faster. We don't draw little chairs on floor plans. I don't care how it works out with a pencil. That's theory. It has to look right in reality. That's why we don't have rules about too many chair legs in one room or a smooth surface next to a rough surface.

Amateur decorators make the mistake of . . .
trying to be careful, and it all ends up bland. They do

"My apartment in Los Angeles hasn't changed in twenty years," Leo Dennis states. "I've never moved a piece of furniture; I don't know how it could look any better." Two eighteenth-century Pierre Puget wood figures survey his distinctively stone-colored living room, with its cosmopolitan assemblage of furnishings that exude a rich patina of age. Exotic accessories include a maharaja's snakeskin walking stick, encrusted with diamonds, resting on an Egyptian stool. "The living room is the whole thing for me," he says.

In his living room, Mr. Dennis placed a framed Venetian floral fresco above a William Kent console, and a nineteenth-century Mexican woven-leather trunk beneath it. The table itself supports an eclectic array: Chinese lotus blossoms, a Han vase, eleventh-century Persian bowls, a Wei dragon. "I have things from every part of the world," he explains. "I don't play any favorites. I don't care if it's old or new or where it came from. I like things first for their form, second for their color, and third for their quality."

everything else wrong too. Wrong scale, wrong character, wrong color.

The total design concept should come first. Backgrounds are the first thing you do. Color and fabric are part of that. We use a lot of beiges with a little blue violet and lime green for accents. But backgrounds are the most important. Nothing is more important in a room than the walls.

The first thing is to decide on the walls and the floor. That's the background. If that isn't right, nothing is right. You should not do anything without a complete plan. If it's a matter of money, buy things one at a time. Don't buy anything half good as a make-do or a fill-in. If you can't afford a marquetry commode, then have a draped table.

Good taste is timeless . . .
if you're thinking about the good taste I'm thinking about. Taste can be acquired to a certain extent. You can imitate it and fake it and get by, but you have to be born with the kind of spontaneity that makes great taste.

A "no taste" room is just that. Everything is wrong with it. Fabrics, furniture, colors. No redeeming social value. I've gone into houses where there isn't one thing I would want to steal.

An interior reveals people as much as their clothes do. Bedrooms especially. If the bedroom is pink and frilly, with a lot of cherubs, there's no sex.

Men are better designers than women . . .
I can't explain why, but they are.

Regardless of sex, some designer-client relationships are completely business. But with some it's all the way. Clients may not try to seduce their designers physically, but they certainly try in every other way.

Some clients are crazy . . .
One lady told us she was looking for a cabinet eight feet tall with space for books. I happened to have one, so when she came in, I said, "Would you like it to be oak?" "Yes." "About eleven inches deep?" She said, "Oh, that would be just fine." So I took her around a corner and there it was. She looked at it, and I asked, "Isn't that exactly what you've been looking for?" She replied, "Yes, I've been looking for exactly this cabinet for ten years." Then she added, "Oh, and another thing I want. . . ." I was furious. "I know how disappointed you must be to finally find it. Now you won't have anything to talk about for the next ten years." Then she looked at it again and wanted to know, "Would this pull out and make a bar?" I said, "No. And being eleven inches deep, it doesn't hide a television set. It doesn't have an ice-maker, it doesn't open cans, and it doesn't

get in bed with you. What you're looking for is a man, not a piece of furniture."

The best client is one who doesn't have to ask her husband everything.

Wealthy clients are often difficult to work with, because they are spoiled. Designers have told me they are expected to be available to their clients at all hours, but that's something we've never experienced. Mostly they just expect attention. Some people think decorating will be their salvation. One client had a way of making me think I was always wrong until finally I realized she was insane. Sometimes a client can lead the decorator along until you realize you're not decorating at all. You're taking care of them.

You have to talk about money and . . .
it's no use asking what people want to spend, because they always give a lower figure and always end up spending more than they say. You just tell them about how much it's going to cost. We don't give a total figure. Instead, we say, "An antique console and mirror will be so much, and this will cost that much, and that's your entry hall." We take it one room at a time. Then we can stop at any point if we want to or if they want to, because we don't have contracts.

My advice for people on a budget would be . . .
to start with the right color. That's the most important thing that can happen in a room. Usually I do pure white ceilings and a stone-colored wall. If the floors are hardwood, I make them medium walnut. If it's a carpet, it should be compatible with the wall color.

If people are on their way up economically, they should not buy inexpensive things. Buy one good thing at a time. Buy basics. The best box spring and mattress. A good sofa. Keep it simple. Use seashells as ashtrays. Use white canvas at the windows. Then gradually start acquiring better things. But if you find a small accessory that's wonderful and you love it, buy it right away because you'll never find it again.

If I had to, I could do a wonderful room with five hundred dollars. The only trouble is, I couldn't afford to put my time into it.

Anyone can have a home with a lot of style without spending a lot of money. Of course, if you have style, you'll soon have a lot of money.

Our biggest decorating mistake was . . .
with a client who wanted a magnificent room. We did a beautiful layout. He couldn't have been more thrilled. Then he started thinking about it. He liked everything, but couldn't it be a little bit more subdued and couldn't it be a little bit more this and a little less that? Finally he

made it ordinary. But we did the room. Although we received compliments on it, we never liked it. We decided then we would never again allow a client to water down a design.

But we rarely have problems with clients, because before they come to us they've thought about it for eight years, discussed it with everybody they know, and have even made attempts at doing it themselves. So they're usually in a good frame of mind to go right ahead.

The secret of our success in buying antiques is . . .
knowing about many things and covering an enormous territory. It's just incredible what turns up. Recently we bought a yellow Creil pitcher worth four hundred dollars, for eight dollars. The next time it turns up somewhere, the price will be eight hundred.

We stay with the old standbys: the coromandel screens, French chairs, rock crystal accessories. I never think of what something is going to be worth. I buy it if I like it. And I very often pay more than I can afford and more than I should. I even pay more than it's worth. But I have it. And ten years later, I'm glad.

If I were asked to choose any client, it would be . . .
Alexander the Great. He built some magnificent buildings. From what I've read, he was a very cultured and tasteful person. He had enormous power and wealth. A client like that is really beyond comprehension, but you could certainly get a lot of things done.

My likes and dislikes in decorating are very definite . . .
I like bare wood floors. Parquet, if possible. I do not like hard red and blue Oriental carpets, and that's about 80 percent of them. The most marvelous carpets in the world are Polonaise and they're still available for about a hundred thousand dollars.

Wood ceilings are wonderful. I like painted walls. In some instances, I like fabric walls. I'm not fond of wallpaper unless it's antique. And certainly not wallpaper in living rooms and dining rooms. Maybe in bathrooms and kitchens.

I prefer windows to be as bare as possible. Shutter treatments are fine. I don't like venetian blinds.

Lamps have to be either very good or terribly simple. One of the two. That applies to lots of things. If it isn't good, it has to be simple. There are an awful lot of bad lamps, especially modern lamps. That's one of the biggest problems for decorators.

I like more accessories than you really should have. If they're good, there is no such thing as too many. If they're bad, one is too many.

I hate all the art that clients have. I hate everything they own. They bring in their ghastly paintings after we've done the house.

I'm mad about mirrors. One beautiful mirror or mirrored walls. That's one of the major considerations in laying out a room. Where would a mirror look best?

Higher coffee tables work best. They should be eighteen to twenty-four inches high.

I'm crazy about chairs. I think of chairs as accessories. I own chairs you can't sit in, just because I like the looks of them. As a look, it's awfully hard to beat a sofa with a coromandel screen behind it, a chair at each end, a coffee table and a couple of lamps. It's awfully trite; it's been worked to death, but there are certain things you just can't beat.

I like elaborate beds: four-posters and canopied beds.

Dining room tables should conform to the size of the room *only*. It doesn't matter how many people or how few people. It's architectural. A dining room table should fit the room. If you need to seat more people than the dining room accommodates, you have to seat some guests in another room or buy another house. It's the same with chandeliers. When we design chandeliers for a dining room, everyone tells us what size the dining table is. We're not interested in that. Just because the table is the wrong size for the room, that's no reason to make the chandelier wrong, too. The chandelier is architecture. It should conform to the room.

I've never been interested in trends. However, some of my ideas that were not popular at a certain time became the rage fifteen years later. For example, doing English dining chairs in very precious materials. I had some beautiful wheel-back English dining chairs executed in solid mother-of-pearl. That kind of thing is the trend today—classic forms executed in unusual materials.

An unknown benefactor gives you millions on condition you spend it on a home . . .
I would build a house in southern California on level land with a view through the mountains. The exterior would be clean, simplified eighteenth-century French. But strong French. Louis XIV.

I would furnish it with a mixture of things: French, English, Oriental and modern. Not just one period.

The core of the house would be a period room I would buy from a dealer like Jansen in Paris. A simple Louis XV boiserie, stripped down to that bare oak that has a wonderful gray color. A fifteen- or sixteen-foot ceiling, about twenty-five feet long by forty feet wide. That would be the main room. Then I would just build the rest of the house around it.

I'm not very interested in any other part of the house.

When I go to a client's house and they start showing me the guest rooms and the broom closet, I just walk away. If a house doesn't have an interesting living room, I'm bored. The living room is the whole thing for me.

Entertaining . . .
I like a party with vast differences in people, occupations, ages, and cultural backgrounds. When people are too similar, it's monotonous. And there should always be some kind of surprise. A point of departure for everyone to talk about. Something other than the butler being completely nude. That's been overdone.

Things that make a bedroom sensuous are . . .
wall-to-wall carpeting continuing right into the bath. An elaborate bed, preferably a four-poster with drapery. The psychology of color would be important. Red is supposed to be exciting and stimulating. Certainly, if you want a sensuous bedroom, it has to be done with warm colors. White is too sterile. I would do a very elaborate bedspread. Something easy to throw on, in a very unusual and luxurious fabric. An antique silk or a wonderful fur.

In my own house . . .
I've never moved a piece of furniture. I don't know how it could look any better. The color is like a stone. Actually, there is a lot of color but it's played down. Every morning when I awake I look at a Chinese painting of a little pheasant hen, and it's perfection. You never tire of something like that. I have a fountain on the balcony off my bedroom, which I hear day and night.

The apartment is in my own building. It was California Monterey but I turned it into a "Portuguese palace." There are antiques from almost every period. All the fabrics are luxurious. And I have some new tie-backs. A big vine has grown through a window and wrapped itself around my white canvas draperies about eight times. That's a new look.

My bed is covered with a black mink spread. The headboard is upholstered in leather and studded with nails.

My apartment hasn't changed in twenty years.

The interior design excitement in the world today is . . .
everywhere. In London, they do nothing but talk about it. In Paris, they're doing more and more. But we have the best interior designers in the world in America.

When you look at magazine photographs of French châteaux, the wonderful thing you see is the sunlight streaming through the twelve-foot-high windows, which look out onto the orchard where baby lambs are gamboling. But the chair isn't good, the fireplace isn't good, the mirror isn't good. There's nothing really good. It's

"A dining room table should fit the room," says antiquarian/designer Dennis. "If you need to seat more people than the dining room accommodates, you have to seat some guests in another room or buy another house." In the dining room created for the Los Angeles apartment of Mr. Dennis's partner, Jerry Leen, Henri II and Louis XIII chairs pull up to a glass-topped eighteenth-century stone pedestal for dining; a mirrored wall visually enlarges the small room and reflects a Queen Anne mirror on the opposite wall. "I'm mad about mirrors," Mr. Dennis admits. "One beautiful mirror or mirrored walls. That's a major consideration in laying out a room. Where would a mirror look best?"

just an incredible photograph. If an American designer worked with that kind of architecture, you would have the most stunning interior in the world.

West Coast decorators are tops. East Coast decorators have to work with small rooms, and it all gets too refined, too perfect. I like the flamboyance and the throwaway quality of California decorators working with unlimited space.

European designers cannot touch an American designer, but maybe that's because I've grown up with American taste. But I've been in many private homes in Europe over the years and, typically, I'll see a desk put crosswise in a corner and those horrible red and blue Oriental rugs going crosswise. With that they'll put a beautiful black lacquer and ormolu desk. These objects do not go together. They only cost a lot of money.

In America there's a big acceptance of contemporary interiors. I'm not against them, I'm just not for them.

Most people fear decorators, and . . .
the good ones do instill a certain amount of fear in their clients. It's the only way they can control the design.

Some of the rich are only poor people with money.

Leo Dennis

Word Association

Color	Walls.
Furniture arrangement	Sofa. Where the sofa goes, everything else follows. Although you don't necessarily have to use a sofa. You can use six big chairs.
Living rooms	Ceiling height. It's my favorite room to decorate because it's the biggest and most dramatic room.
Entrance halls	Depth. You don't want to open a door and walk into a wall.
Kitchens	Light.
Children's rooms	As far away as possible. I think of distance. I think of foreign countries.
Lamps	Nothing.
Bedrooms	A canopy bed.
Bathrooms	Space.
Dining rooms	Chandelier.
Studies	Comfort.
Floors	Parquet.
Window treatments	Let in as much sunlight as possible.
Fabrics	Rich.
Wallpaper	Chinese and other antique papers.
Television	Another room.

"A few of the things that make a bedroom sensuous are wall-to-wall carpeting continuing right into the bath . . . an elaborate bed, preferably a draped four-poster . . . warm colors. White would be too sterile," says Leo Dennis. He describes his own bedroom: "My bed is covered with a black mink spread. The headboard is upholstered in leather and studded with nails. And I have a fountain on the balcony off my bedroom, which I hear day and night."

ANGELO DONGHIA

Everyone likes Angelo Donghia. He is warm, outgoing, bright, and thoroughly professional. When I was trying to establish Architectural Digest *as the preeminent international publication reporting interior design, Angelo allowed me to photograph his own townhouse first, although every magazine in the world wanted it for their pages. It was a turning point. It meant a great deal to me that Angelo believed I would do with* Architectural Digest *exactly what I said I would do. His integrity, loyalty, and talent have attracted some rather illustrious clients, including Diana Ross, Barbara Walters, Ralph Lauren and Marvin Hamlisch.*

Because of my father's tailoring business,
I learned to sew . . .

making pillow slips, and reupholstering, as a hobby. I can still remember doing my first display window for my father's tailor shop. He loved it, and it was then I realized I had a talent for putting things together.

When I decided to go to Parsons School of Design in New York, I planned to return to Pittsburgh because I had always wanted to work as a designer at Kaufman's Department Store. But I never went back. New York was it. I finished my schooling at Parsons, took a trip to Europe, then went to New York University to complete my degree. But just before my finals, I decided to make three phone calls. There were three names on my list: Yale Burge, Billy Baldwin, and Michael Greer. I said, "Well, I'll just call them all." It was the day after New Year's, and Yale Burge said, "Come in and see me," so I didn't make the other two calls. It was my first job interview. He said, "I do need somebody and I like your portfolio. How much do you want?" I said, "Well, I'd like a hundred dollars a week." He said, "You'll take seventy-five dollars." I said, "I sure will." So I began assisting Yale Burge, who was running an antique business and a decorating business, and had just started doing reproduction furniture. My first big opportunity came in 1960 or 1961, when Yale asked me to do a room window display at the Design Center. I used a daisy chintz on a black background, straw rugs, and some French antiques. That led to more windows. A national magazine photographed one. It was my first publicity. Three years after joining the firm, I became a vice-president.

At that time Billy Baldwin was designing the Opera Guild Room at the just-finished Metropolitan Opera House and he suggested that I do the Opera Club. I did, and it was a success.

All of these steps were very important because they were feeding devices. Success needs the food of reassurance, acceptance, acknowledgment.

In 1966 I became a partner in the decorating business, which we then called Burge, Donghia, Inc., and Yale started putting more emphasis on his furniture-reproduction business. At the same time, our decorating business grew because we were commissioned to design the world headquarters of Pepsi-Cola, Warner Bros/ Seven Arts. The commercial jobs came to us because we had done homes for major corporate executives. In 1967 I told Yale I wanted to design fabrics and open my own business. He supported me completely and I set up "& Vice Versa." In 1970 I began designing sheets for J. P. Stevens. A year later I opened White Walls Gallery to promote young artists. In 1973 I began Donghia Furniture, which was all made-to-order. In 1976 I opened Donghia, Inc., my showroom "to the trade" in Los Angeles. I designed a line of retail furniture for Kroehler in 1977. In 1978 Donghia, Inc., opened showrooms in Chicago, and Troy, Michigan. I feel my mass-market designs have as much integrity as the designs for my most exclusive clients.

Formal design education is necessary because . . .
it gives security to people who want to get into this business. It doesn't give them the design background, because only experience gives that. Design is not a science. It's not factual. It's a point of view.

Yale allowed me the experience of working with his important wealthy clients almost from the beginning. My first big residential budget was two hundred thousand dollars. Today the same interior would cost four hundred and fifty thousand dollars.

Clients were coming to Yale Burge, but they were getting Angelo Donghia, and they'd never heard of him. I quickly learned that two things were very, very important. Integrity and a strong point of view. When you make your statement, you *don't* say, "Well, we could do it this way or that way." When people are spending a lot of money they want to know they are spending it the right way, that you have thought it through. So I say, *"This* would be perfect for this room. I've thought about it very carefully, done many trials, and I've found that *this* is perfect."

All a client wants from the designer is to be able to feel, "I've gone to the right person, and thank God he's

"I've spent many years redecorating my own home," says
Angelo Donghia of his 1925 Manhattan townhouse, "but for
the past six it has been exactly as it is now." The living
room's ten-foot-high ceiling, covered in reflective silver foil,
harmonizes with pale, bleached parquet flooring and
deep-toned walls accented by crisp white Georgian moldings.
"Walls, ceiling, and floor all must be designed together to
relate to one another," the designer counsels, adding; "the
furniture is a series of large, fluffy, upholstered pieces covered
in cotton. There is a large painting by Mark Strong, a table
sculpture by Bob Bruno, and my most important possession,
the coromandel screen purchased from the estate of Chanel."

Slipcovered chairs cluster flexibly near a diagonally placed
sofa in the living room of Mr. Donghia's Florida residence,
a late-Victorian house he restored. A white-lacquered fan
turns lazily overhead. "When I'm in a tropical environment,
I want to feel it," says the designer. White paint has been
rubbed into the raw wood walls. "Having stripped
everything down to this most basic form, I would have
been content to live in the rooms as they were—quite bare,"
he recalls, referring to the structure's fine proportions and
sensitively placed windows. "Of course, I took some license
here and there. I couldn't resist adding moldings and
painting them high-gloss white."

handling it." When a client feels the designer is not secure in his or her beliefs, they start questioning everything. And the designer's strength has to go from Day One to Day End.

One of the biggest things I've learned is that the most beautiful moment with the clients is when they sign the contract. They are your greatest friends at that moment. But if you are not consistently strong, that feeling of friendship dissipates to the point of their not wanting to pay the bill. To get the job, you've done everything to make them feel comfortable, wanted, loved, and secure. But then designers have a tendency to say, "I've got the job now, let's go on to the next thing." You can't let yourself think like that, because the client still needs what you projected originally.

Clients must feel they are Number One. They don't want to know that you have other jobs. You can never be too busy for them. I call every client daily. Too many people treat decorating like an art form. It's not. Decorating is a business. It's buying and selling. Along with selling your taste, you're selling furniture and the works.

There are many decorators, but only a few designers. A decorator says . . .
"I think we should re-cover all the furniture," or, "I think we should take this furniture out and use a different style."

A *designer* can take the space and totally conceptualize it. Certain people are great designers and some are great decorators. The design concept cannot be abstract. It must resolve the client's needs.

I just finished a two-room apartment for bachelor Joel Schumacher, the screenwriter. He entertains very little— one or two people at a time. He does not cook. He dresses fantastically, so he needs well-thought-out space for his clothes. He needs a place to mix drinks and perhaps heat up some food he's had sent in. He needs a comfortable place to sit and good lighting. And he needs a place to work. Now you take those needs and design everything around them, utilizing scale, shape, color and texture. That is the process of designing space.

The solution for Joel Schumacher was to take the bedroom and think of it as a space connected by a long hall to a living room. Let's make both rooms look like they're one. So there's one common ceiling, one common floor. All the walls are white, all the doors go to the ceiling. The living room furniture is low and loungy. Joel is tall and likes to slouch, so there's a big banquette with two leather chairs facing it, and a big rough-granite coffee table. The fabric is plain canvas, channel quilted. Windows are covered with bleached-wood slats that roll up. The fireplace is mirrored so that it all seems bigger than it is. Very low lighting. The kitchen is used as a bar, so

it has a brown marble floor, walls of brown tinted mirror with nut-brown lacquered cabinets, stainless-steel counter tops and a brown lacquered ceiling. That's the way Joel's needs were resolved with design.

Interior designers have enormous expenses because . . .
the more jobs you do, the more services you offer, the more space you need, and the more people you need. Working on a fee basis and buying the client's merchandise at cost is a much easier way to operate. Clients are willing to pay if they believe you're worth it.

If I charge retail, the markup is 50 percent. But I always say, "I would like to give you a choice. Whatever suits you best. I will break it down into two stages: the design stage and the production stage. Two stages, two fees. The design stage is the floor plan, colors, specifications, and a list that explains where everything comes from, how much it costs, how much you need. If you want to buy it wholesale, fine—pay my design fee and that's it. But the production stage takes a lot of time. That is getting it done. I will do that for a percentage of the contractor's cost and a percentage of the purchases."

People love financial alternatives. And they want to know exactly what they're getting into. Secrecy causes doubt and distrust. There are no secrets about wholesale and retail. Everybody knows what that is. So you just lay it all out in front and be very honest. Of course, clients can lie, too—usually about how they're going to pay, or that they can't afford as much as they say they can. Also, that the husband has agreed to whatever the wife wants to do. But he hasn't.

With a staff of sixteen, six are designers. We do at least seventy-five jobs per year, major and minor. Major jobs take ten to twelve months; five hundred thousand dollars is a major job. There are a lot of those, but not as many as people might think.

Clients usually come to us through . . .
clients. Usually their friends, relatives, or business associates. Generally, publications don't bring in jobs, but they are the endorsement of your work. And the strongest endorsement is *Architectural Digest*.

If I played social games . . .
I could be doing four times as much work. But I don't want to. I don't believe in it. I refuse to do it. There are a lot of people in our profession who love socializing and make it their lives.

I go out to see what's going on. It's very important to feed the eye. You can't sit in an enclosed box and create beauty. You run dry, become stagnant. To keep the great freshness and aliveness, you have to find out what has to do with today. See what's being done in window displays, theater, museums, discotheques, movies. Travel is very important. You've got to smell the air.

Clients. More than 80 percent are millionaires. The others are about to be . . .
After the initial meeting with a new client, I like to see the space to be done tomorrow, then see where the client lives today. I want to find out if there's anything that's going from one space to another. And it's very important to find out how the client *really* lives. "What is the first thing your husband does when he comes home from the office? How do you entertain? Do you have a drink in the evening? Do you play cards?" You want to know all about their everyday lives.

The worst thing is to have a perfect home, but as soon as one extra person comes you have to rearrange everything. If that happens once a year, fine. But it shouldn't happen once a week. I find out how people live and what makes them feel terrific and comfortable. Sometimes they don't tell the truth, because they're saying what they think *other* people feel, rather than what *they* feel. Sometimes they don't know the first thing about themselves. So I ask lots of questions.

Rich or not, people who use a decorator avoid the costly mistakes amateur decorators make, such as . . .
scale. People buy pieces of furniture that really don't fit in a room. Then they say, "I didn't realize it was so big." Or so small. Some people have a much better visual facility than others. Scale is easy for me. Yet there are designers of great talent who have to work at it by taking things down to half-inch scale on paper. Lighting is another thing that is not understood by amateurs. They either underlight or overlight.

The other mistake nonprofessionals make, and even professionals, is excluding the ceiling. Ceilings are the most neglected part of the decorating process. Track lighting and down lights have been commercialized. You have to really look at that complete effect. Walls, ceilings, and floors all must be designed together to relate to one another. My important rule is: Make the background work. I finish the background totally before I put in one piece of furniture.

Some people want to light paintings. I don't really care for that look. Art is part of the ambience. You don't spotlight furniture, even if it's great, so why spotlight a painting? I like to light a room so that the source is not recognized. The more indirect, the better. Lighting was done much better in the thirties and forties than it is today—indirect lighting, cover lighting, uplighting, wall lights that shot light up to the ceiling so that it reflected down, creating a soft, easy light.

Mirrors are wonderful, but they should be used very carefully. People should not be aware that they're watching themselves. They become self-conscious. Mirrors in a dining room are horrible. There's nothing worse than watching yourself eat.

Other mistakes amateur decorators make are overcoloring and overpatterning. Patterned rooms sometimes overwhelm people. And if there are too many outrageous colors, the people don't show up. Thought has to be given to the way people dress. There's no reason why a sofa should be more important than the person sitting on it. I've seen rooms so blatant in pattern and color that the people disappear.

People often put enormous emphasis on hiding their television and stereo. Why hide them behind closed doors? Why put them away? They are what they are.

I don't care how "married" people may be, they prefer to function privately in the morning. It's very nice to have two separate bathroom areas. No matter how much in love you are, it's important to have private space.

People overdo kitchens—overequip them. They buy anything that's new, and then don't use it.

Children's rooms are overdecorated. Most people, especially young people today, want something for the children that they didn't have. It's not important. You don't have to design children's rooms. They should be whatever makes a child enjoy the room, not what makes *you* enjoy it.

If you are decorating your own home, always . . .
paint first. Don't buy the cabinets first, or the table. Buy two chairs, or a sofa, and a good reading light. Make one little space so that two people can sit together and be comfortable. The decoration process for most people is very long, sometimes five, eight or nine years. Not everyone does it all at once. So it's wise to have something for your comfort, rather than paintings or a console or an armoire. And personal relationships are better. When you're decorating, the decisions, disagreements, the waiting, all those things can harm relationships. The guy gets home, he's put in a hard day. He says, "Where can I put my feet up and my drink down?" And many women say, "I can do my home myself. I don't need a decorator." Often they feel they have to prove something to their husbands. They're the ones who are in the greatest trouble. There's nothing wrong with getting a little professional advice. Many women end up in really bad situations, with unfinished rooms and expensive mistakes. A professional decorator is a good investment.

Taste is like religion because . . .
it will be discussed forever and there will be very little agreement. Beautiful to me is not always beautiful to someone else. Today, a lady who weighs ninety pounds is considered beautiful, while in the nineteenth century,

Bamboo, wicker, and cool Indian cotton casually appoint
Angelo Donghia's Florida sitting room. "This house is part of
a new way of looking at myself—of paring down," he says,
emphasizing the intangibles: "The way a curtain moves in
the breeze, the way a rug is arranged, the distinctive scent of
a special person. These are all terribly elusive things, and I
wanted them all to resonate at Key West."

women who weighed two hundred were considered beautiful. There are changing standards in taste. No one thing is right. Taste overlaps style, and style is what we do with taste. A person can have enormous taste, but a very low range of style. I have developed my taste by seeing, feeling, doing, and making mistakes. So I really do feel that taste can be acquired if you are open to it.

Rooms are often tasteless because . . .
most people don't know when to stop. Often when I'm near the end of a job, I omit the last few things. It's those last-minute add-ons that are usually dangerous. People also tend to forget the original concept and change in midstream. I can always spot a room that started out one way and ended up another. It begins with, "I want to do an all-white room." Then, midway, "Oh, it's too white. Maybe we should add a color." Almost always your original concept was better. Stay with all-white and overcome those midway fears. The original thrust of feeling and thought about a situation is usually correct.

Anyone can have a home with style.
It has nothing to do with money . . .
Style, to me, indicates that which might be somewhat unexpected, a pleasant surprise. Something out of the ordinary. Style might be injected into a room by making it less full. Or it could be an overstatement. Personal style is something that people understand more readily, the way we dress is easier to figure out. But when it comes to having style within a room, people are definitely intimidated. But it should be approached the same way, because it's what you really feel comfortable with, the image you're trying to project, and *then* going just a step further to let it be more special.

I've learned from my mistakes
and I'm still making them . . .
I have always loved the use of mirror. It adds a lot of sparkle, glamour, dimension, and a long, focal point. But when mirror is not applied to a space architecturally, it can be very dangerous. Recently, even though I have been using mirrors for years, I tried something that didn't work. It was a major mistake and had to be changed. Only one surface of a corner was mirrored, rather than both. It reduced the volume of the architecture. The safest way to mirror, architecturally, is between two points. Between two columns or two windows, for example. And the one thing you must always ask yourself is: What will the mirror reflect?

Some decorating has to be secret . . .
Businessmen who have an apartment no one knows about. This is always a difficult confidence to keep, because we have to put a fictitious name on our records. I pass no judgment on it, but it has always been a tricky thing to handle. Recently a woman asked me to decorate her secret apartment. Maybe that will be a new trend.

I like to see clients live as I do because . . .
I live very comfortably. Not ostentatiously. Anyone who comes to my home is overwhelmed with comfort, not luxury. They feel attractive. I've always been shocked to find people who have never really understood what it means to live attractively.

I don't believe in collecting . . .
If a client asks me what to collect, I always say, "Whatever you love."

Secure or insecure. They both show . . .
You can always tell someone who has had experience decorating, and someone who has never had any. I'm very cautious about people who say they're going to give me a lot of freedom, because they're usually the ones who don't. I love it when people come in and tell me very frankly what they want. Some clients are totally intimidated and afraid to express their own opinions. They're the ones I have the greatest problems with. Decorating is like personal relationships. You should express your feelings honestly.

The smartest, most astute clients all have . . .
budgets, no matter how affluent they are. Those who are insecure are the ones who say, "The sky's the limit! Just do it! I want it to be really great." But I like definitions. What is "great"? I prefer it when clients tell me, "This is what I have to spend." That's the way it works best.

Decorating likes and dislikes . . .
I don't like decoration for decoration's sake—unnecessary decoration.

The lamp has been overdone. It has become decoration, and it should not be. Trees are overdone. You can overplant a room. Billy Baldwin always said, and I've always found it to be true, "A room should stand on its own before you put a plant in it." Plants should enhance a room, not dominate it.

Don't collect paintings unless you like them. A room doesn't have to have paintings. It doesn't have to have anything. A room can have just shadows on the wall from an up light. It can work well with just a few simple accessories—books, a basket of fruit, little plants, single flowers in vases. That's reducing it to zero. But if you work your way up from there, you will realize that a room doesn't need that much. Most people today want to simplify their lives. They want their homes to be open, easy to manage, easy to live in.

I like industrial carpeting, but I do not like a lot of industrial materials used inappropriately.

I have an antipathy to light fixtures. I simply do not like track lighting.

There's always too much of everything. Too many of one thing or too many gimmicks. I really like everything that is appropriate. The most common problem in decoration today is inappropriateness.

Decorating is going through a transition . . .
In the sixties and the very early seventies there was an overabundance of everything filling the space. In the sixties it was most often because people wanted to prove they had made it. The young executive who has been climbing, the past ten years, is now saying, "Let's get rid of all that and have something much simpler." There seems to be a trend to want less, need less.

There will be more compact, preplanned living space. A feeling keeps coming to me that within twenty or thirty years there will be quite a big change, and that we're going to witness just the beginning. It's something like when the radio first came out and then television changed our lives. Something is going to happen and electronics will again change the world we live in. It's a very exciting time.

A home usually reveals a personality . . .
at least, warmth or coolness. Honesty or pretension. Some people like to live very tidy lives and others like to live very casually. You can always sense that when you walk into a house.

Perfection is a very dangerous thing. In their quest for being perfect, some people make their backgrounds perfect. That is very intimidating. Pillows puffed perfectly. Tables devoid of anything. A home devoid of life. There is a way of making things look as though they just happened.

Few people know how to entertain . . .
to make their guests feel special. Entertaining groups is a very special talent. For example, any table of over eight people is too much. There is always someone who talks too much at a large table. With eight, there is much more sharing. And people are much more comfortable when they're dressed casually. Black-tie dinner parties are a bore.

Serving too much food is a mistake. Almost everyone is dieting in one way or another. Sometimes entertaining becomes showing off. "How can I impress them?" People don't come for that. They come to be with you or to meet other people. A production can be overwhelming. Too many drinks is not nice. Guests should not be invited for dinner at eight and served dinner at ten.

Angelo Donghia

Word Association

Furniture arrangement	Overscaled.
Living rooms	Comfort.
Color	Personal.
Entrance halls	Coat closets.
Bedrooms	Your own.
Bathrooms	Warm bath.
Dining rooms	Intimate.
Studies	Private.
Floor coverings	Good and bad.
Window treatments	Let the light in.
Fabrics	Necessary.
Wallpaper	Practical backgrounds.
Lighting	Discreet.
Television sets	Unhidden.
Kitchens	Home base.
Children's rooms	Too small.

There are so many rules about entertaining. Mine are simple: I like people to feel comfortable and at ease.

If decorating is what you want to do . . .
don't keep your intention a secret. Associate with people who might be able to provide that opportunity. Why waste time being with people who can never give you a path to the first client? Let everybody know you are out to become a decorator.

How does someone get to know people in the decorating business? Anyone can call me up and tell me they just saw and loved something I did and they wanted me to know. Flattery gets you everywhere. All you have to do is tell people what you want from them.

My favorite room to decorate is the bedroom . . .
because the most important moment of life is waking up. And it is the most difficult time. Your defense mechanisms are at their lowest. You need the most support possible when you open your eyes.

Sensuousness also has to be considered in bedrooms. Soft shapes, comfort and the very best lighting.

I've spent many years redecorating my own home . . .
but for the past six it has been exactly as it is now. It is a three-level townhouse designed in 1925. The floors are all hard surfaces from wood to marble, except in the master bedroom, which is carpeted wall-to-wall. All the rooms have ten-foot ceilings. In my bedroom, the ceiling is gold Chinese teapaper. The ceiling is silver in the living room. The windows are not covered in any way. All the moldings are painted chalk white. The floors are pale, bleached parquet.

The furniture is a series of large, fluffy upholstered pieces covered in cotton. There are some white tables in plaster, two large paintings by Richard Giglio, and my most important possession, the coromandel screen purchased from the estate of Chanel.

My bedroom is also very, very comfortable. It's soft, sensuous and changeable. One of the keys to my house is that I can switch the furniture around from wall to wall, area to area, without destroying the effect.

My favorite kind of client . . .
is honest about what she wants, and what she wants to spend, then leaves me alone and lets me create for her. The worst kind says, "Just do what you want," then later says, "Oh, that's not quite what I had in mind."

There are some people who hire designers because they know they can't do it themselves, yet when asked who's doing their decorating, will say, "Well, so-and-so is helping me, but I'm really doing it myself."

The interior design excitement today is in . . .
New York City. The greatest decorating talent in the world is within a few square miles in New York City. Equally talented people are scattered around in various cities, but nothing as concentrated as in New York. It seemed for a while that Europe might take over, that Italy might become the new center, but it's not so. New York now has designers with an excellence of professionalism and style unlike anywhere else in the world.

I deal in the mass market and in the class market. The uptown or the downtown. In the mass area, Europe is ahead of us. In the class area, Europe is behind us. Something has happened.

The rich are not different . . .
Everybody is totally, totally the same. We all have the same basic needs.

"I love to live by the sea," says Mr. Donghia, whose Fire
Island, New York, weekend retreat comes as close to the
Atlantic as you can get. "What I wanted to do was to bring
the outside in and let the ocean become a part of the
interior," he explains. He left bare the sliding glass doors that
open onto the pool, and to the ocean beyond, and decorated
the living room with the simplified contemporary furnishings
of his own design that fill all his residences.

TED GRABER

*I first met Ted Graber when interviewing the late William Haines,
over seven years ago, in the firm's contemporary building in Beverly
Hills. Haines, a former actor, was charismatic, and a fine
decorator as well. Graber was just as knowledgeable and involved
in the Haines look, but behind the scenes instead of center stage.
This marks the public debut of Ted's talents, already appreciated
by such clients as Ambassador and Mrs. Walter Annenberg, Betsy
and Alfred Bloomingdale, the late Joan Crawford.*

I *always knew what I wanted to do, so . . .*
instead of college, I studied at the Chouinard Art Institute, in Los Angeles. My grandfather and my father opened the first antique shop in the city of Los Angeles. On Saturdays, when I was seven years old, I had to work in the shop to start learning the business.

I was given my first job when I was seventeen and still in school. There was a wonderful old woman, Miss Cora Le Seur, who was Joan Crawford's aunt and a great friend and client of my father's antique shop. Miss Cora told my father, "It's time Ted got a little experience; I want him to decorate the house we're remodeling."

After Chouinard, I went into the Army during World War II. All those long marches, dreaming up color schemes. Anything, it was so dull! My father died while I was in the Army, and we had to sell the shop. After I came home, in 1945, I did some design jobs on my own. I had always known the great decorator William Haines, but I hadn't seen him since returning from the service. He was a client of my father's and grandfather's.

When I went in to say hello, Billy asked what I was doing. I told him I was playing Fox against MGM. At that time I was thinking of going into designing motion picture sets. He said, "That's no place for you. Why don't you work with me?" That, of course, was what I'd always wanted. If you're going to do it, start at the top. Working with Bill Haines was the best possible way to start out. Although I do think some formal training or education is necessary. Only a few people have the innate taste to become interior designers without training.

Bill Haines died in 1973. Today we design anywhere from three to six houses every year. The jobs come in waves. And for our regular clients who have been with us for years, we just keep refreshing, redoing. The staff is very small, because we like to keep our work very personal. My assistant, Jean Hayden, has been with me for twenty-five years, as a bookkeeper and a driver.

Socializing helps, so I'm told . . .
and there are a lot of decorators who do lots of it. I've never really been too social, because I didn't have to be. Bill Haines was. I think your reputation is more important. Basically, clients come to us because they've seen houses we've done for their friends.

The first conversation with a client is important . . .
If it's new work, a total design job, I like to meet with them in my office. If they already have a house, it's best to meet there. But the first thing is talk. Do you relate or don't you relate? Is it going to be good music? And if it's not good music, say so right away and that's it. Because you want no surprises.

We charge a flat fee only for . . .
architectural design and supervision. All the decorating is on a straight retail basis. Once we show the scheme, and everything's agreed upon, we estimate the entire job. One lump sum. If there are antiques to be found, that is noted in the original estimate. The client signs the estimate, pays one-third, and we start the work.

A decorator is a fetch-and-carrier . . .
A designer is capable of designing backgrounds and furniture. A decorator picks up a piece here and puts it there. A decorator selects fabrics. We design fabrics. People come here because they want something individual.

To begin an interior design . . .
you have to start with floor plans. If it's right on the plan, it's right. And in my opinion there's really only one way to do any room to put it in balance. If you try to force it, it's going to look forced.

You're thinking color all the time. You ask clients what color they *don't* like. Not what they *do* like. Invariably, a woman will say, "I don't like blue," and she's wearing a blue dress. And a man who says, "I don't like brown," is wearing a brown suit. You do it all in toto and then you refine it. *Most* important is that you keep editing. Have your flights of fancy in the initial design stage, then go back and edit all the way through a job.

"When I go home after a day's work of coloring, I want to
wash my eyes, so to speak," explains Ted Graber, referring
to the neutral palette of his own West Los Angeles apartment.
"Not to say that each area isn't dotted with color, but in the
main, it's off-white, beige and brown." A view from the
living room toward the library reveals a Regency table
attended by mahogany wheelback chairs, and accents of
primitive sculpture and plants. "It's furnished with antiques
I've collected over the years, and masses of accessories—really
too many," he adds, "but it all happens to be what I like."

Amateur decorators are not . . .
in a position to edit. It's like sitting down to a banquet. They want everything they see. They can't make up their minds, so they just have it all. They push it together. And that's the way it looks.

If you're doing your own home, *do* be simple. *Don't* try to use every color in the rainbow. We've all seen a woman walk into a room and what she couldn't wear, she carried. Rooms can look that way, too. Tasteless. Good taste is timeless if it's simple, although I suppose I've done some things nobody would consider simple. If clichés are included in an interior, then it's not going to be in good taste, although today it may be very acceptable. Redundancy doesn't wear well. The moment something is declared in, it's out.

*An interior reveals a great deal
about the people who live there . . .*
A designer can only do so much. You can create perfectly beautiful interiors, but once you walk out the door, *they* have to take over. People have to breathe life into it.

Bedrooms are especially revealing. There are very few women who play to the husband in the bedroom. You don't put a man into a pink master bedroom.

Although there are many men who don't care if the bedroom is pink. Their masculinity is not in jeopardy. But usually, the lady has the largest bath, the largest dressing room and the largest closets. And sometimes the man is just shoved off into a hall bath. Some women are selfish and some men don't care. "Give her what she wants."

Years ago, Billy Haines was doing a house for a famous comedian. He had been away and his wife had ordered a lot more work done than he knew about. Billy said to her, "When he comes home, put on your best negligee and be in bed, so that he'll pay for all of this."

There have been some sensational women designers . . .
but Robert Adam was the first to do the total look. Ar-

chitecture and interiors. There's a virility to the work, so it would be natural that there would be more men. You have to think architecture to be a designer.

*You have to know more
about your clients than a doctor does . . .*
If you're doing somebody's drawing room, it's one thing. If you're doing an entire house, it's quite a different matter. You must know the details of how they live. If something doesn't work, you'll hear about it, because you have been retained to make the house work for them. You are the problem solver.

The difficulty is when the client is insecure. You can smell it. But it's an attitude, rather than anything they say. When clients are too demanding and difficult, I just stop everything. I'm too old, too tired, and too rich to put up with that.

We had a client once, a very short gentleman, and his was the last room to be designed. It seemed that we could never please him. We did a linen fabric patterned with tree forms. Perhaps it was eucalyptus. The scheme was shown to him and he said, "Do you think those draperies are masculine enough for me?" Billy looked him right in the eye and said, "Well, if they're not, I can sew big balls of fringe on them!"

*Once we made the mistake
of missing a client's real message . . .*
We did a house for a couple, and the woman wanted three places to sleep in the bedroom. Fortunately, it was a large room. It took us three years to design it, because we didn't get the message. We just couldn't figure it out. Why three places to sleep in one room? At last, we got it. Her fantasy was that she had been captured and was being held prisoner in a seraglio.

*We used to be able to do a great room
for ten or fifteen thousand dollars. Today . . .*
the average cost of a *quality* room, *not* including art and antiques, is about fifty thousand dollars. It has to be,

"This was a Mediterranean-style house in Holmby Hills, about fifty years old," Mr. Graber explains. "We opened it up—installing the glass wall—to take advantage of living in California." An eighteenth-century English lead garden figure pauses near the living room, where tall potted trees and leafy eighteenth-century Chinese wallpaper reinforce the indoor/outdoor atmosphere. The Regency Carrara marble fireplace and elaborate Chippendale mirror serve as the focus for the carefully balanced traditional arrangement.

when a fabric selling for a hundred dollars a yard today was thirty dollars a yard ten years ago. A fine custom wool carpet might run from six thousand to fourteen thousand dollars.

The tremendous escalation of costs is one reason we discuss budgets in the very beginning. If the clients say they don't know what they want to spend, we lay it out and give them an approximate figure before we go any further. Money has to be talked about immediately. There is the myth of the wealthy client who says, "I don't care what it costs." If anyone says that, you know damn well they don't mean it. Everybody, I don't care who they are, has a bottom to the money barrel.

If someone came to me with very little money to spend on decorating, I would suggest they . . .
go for style. Buy good-quality furniture. There's no difference to me in designing for a young couple's first house than there is in doing an older client's second or third house. It's the same approach. You give them as much for their money as you can. That all-beige look or that all-something look is a fallacy. I don't agree that it's an economical way to decorate.

Stick to simplicity. Balance and scale can fill a room faster than anything else. If the objects in the room are placed properly, open areas will relate to the filled spaces. Then you don't need many things. And if the color's proper, the room looks filled.

Anybody with style and taste can go into our better department stores and do perfectly acceptable rooms for themselves. However, even professional designers make mistakes. I'd never again do some of that early furniture we designed.

For collecting as an investment . . .
paintings have a proven track record. But whatever you buy should be top quality. Only quality holds up as an investment. If you can't buy oils, buy prints. But get the *best*. It's the third-rate work that doesn't hold up, no matter how big the artist's name.

Ted Graber recalls that this guest room in Beverly Hills was "a nasty little room that needed some help. I wanted to give it a richer look and more interest." He had the walls and moldings detailed in pale *faux bois,* and used quilted chintz for the bed, drapery trim and upholstery. Antique Italian botanical prints accent the floral motif. "It's the background and the small chintz pattern that do all the work," he says.

Antiques seem to run in twenty-year cycles. If you buy quality, you can catch the cycle. As long as we live there will be fewer antiques of quality.

When we decorated the American Embassy
in London, I found myself wondering . . .
what it would have been like to have worked with Louis XIV. Everything handed down to us from that period is so magnificent. But I suppose I've worked the same way in the twentieth century, for the merchant princes who are today's royalty.

Decorating likes and dislikes . . .
I dislike wall-to-wall carpeting. I prefer the warmth, the presentation, of wood floors. I can't stand overstuffed furniture. I hate pattern on pattern on pattern on pattern on pattern. Nine times out of ten, they're not at all compatible. It's chaos. Misuse of any material. Fabric on walls so puffed out that it's three inches from the plaster. It belongs in mental institutions so the inmates can't hurt themselves. Gold fittings are dreadful. And a bad reproduction of *anything*. I find it very wrong. If you're going to reproduce a chair, do it properly. Don't take license with it.

The same thing applies with architecture. If you're doing a period house, go to the books and the masters and copy it. Don't improvise. Don't let your ego get in the way of doing it right. That makes it a stage set, not architecture. It's taking somebody's money under false pretenses. That bothers me because I'm involved with architecture and I care.

I like rugs that fit a room. The background and the rug on the floor are the palette a designer has to work with, and the rug should not take over the room so that it is all you see. I like simple rooms, simple rugs.

I dislike big lamps. How many times have you seen a lamp so big that it looks as though the table should be on top of it? Or the lamp is so tall it looks like a column in the corner holding up the ceiling?

And I don't really think the whole center of a room

Ted Graber

Word Association

Color	Anything.
Furniture arrangement	Workable.
Living rooms	Pleasing to the eye and comfortable.
Entrance halls	Knock 'em dead.
Kitchens	Functional and light.
Children's rooms	To fit the child.
Bedrooms	Madame's desire.
Bathrooms	Functional and attractive.
Dining rooms	Pretty.
Studies	The womb.
Floor coverings	Simple.
Window treatments	Appropriate.
Lamps	Light source.
Fabrics	Quality.
Wallpaper	Antique.
Lighting	Muted.
Television sets	Necessary evil.

Chinoiserie table garniture and vase lamps, Chinese wallpaper panels and an English chandelier accessorize the refined elegance of a formal dining room in Beverly Hills. "I like good chandeliers in scale," Mr. Graber says. "There's nothing worse than sitting down for dinner with the chandelier hanging so close to the table you can't see the person sitting across from you." Graceful Chippendale-style chairs surround the highly polished triple-pedestal table. "I like comfortable dining room chairs, regardless of their period, and chairs with attractive back legs, because that's what you basically see—the silhouette of the chair."

should be a mesa of coffee tables. A coffee table has a function, and the most successful is placed in front of a sofa, and both are in scale.

I like good chandeliers in scale. There's nothing worse than sitting down for dinner with the chandelier hanging so close to the table you can't see the person sitting across from you.

Tablecloths are gone. I like comfortable dining room chairs, regardless of their period. And chairs with attractive back legs, because that's what you basically see, the silhouette of the chair. The dining room is used once a day, if then, in most houses. Sometimes once a month.

And I really can't say that I like beds that look like a room within a room. It's constructed and then it's draped. With Henry VIII, there was a reason. It was cold and drafty in those castles.

The tree-trunk furniture numbers are misused. The twig beds, too.

I'm so bored with the misuse of mirror. And mirrored ceilings. If one decorator does it, they all do it.

I love to see a house full of fresh flowers.

I'm one who likes lamps with simple shades, in perfect proportion. And I guess I've lived too long to be caught in a room that's lit from under a sofa.

In the next few years I would long for quality and simplicity to come back. Maybe we'll have an Age of Reason. It depends on the young designers coming up.

If I were given millions to do a house for myself . . .
it would have a huge family kitchen where I could cook and entertain. That's the first requirement, because cooking is my avocation.

I would love to do a proper early-California adobe house in the country. In a meadow. I might cheat just a little and give it more scale than was done originally. It would probably have a great center court, a fountain, and a decorative pool.

Entertaining . . .
Some do and some don't. No matter what your means, when you're entertaining, you can't chintz. It shows. Do the absolute best that you can possibly do. And if you don't have a lot of money, don't be pretentious with it. Keep it simple.

My own home is an apartment in . . .
my own building, which I altered five years ago. It has dark wood floors. The walls are painted white. When I go home after a day's work of coloring, I want to wash my eyes, so to speak. I'm happy in this kind of environment. Not to say that each area isn't dotted with color, but, in the main, it's off-white, beige, and brown. It's furnished with antiques I've collected over the years, and masses of accessories, really too many, but it all happens to be what I like to live with. And pictures of all periods, from Chinese to early Dutch to modern. Lots of books. Dark hardwood floors throughout, with rugs. A fireplace in the living room. As much light as I could manage, and filled, in the main, with plants.

The most exciting interior design in the world is in . . .
southern California. We have been the most innovative. The things that are being done in New York now are only pick-ups of what started here.

Between Europe and the United States I do see a certain similarity today in the modern interiors. I think they all lift from each other. It's slightly incestuous. How could it not be, with communication the way it is? Of course, a thought in the air can light in more than one place.

You must remember this: Style has a twenty-year cycle.

Many people fear decorators, and they're right . . .
They have been taken.

The rich may be able to express themselves more fully but . . .
I think we're all the same.

BRUCE GREGGA

*Chicago-based, Bruce Gregga is regarded throughout the design
community as the best interior decorator in the Midwest. His work
is now unfolding in the Los Angeles area, where he has a second
residence, a "cottage" on the George Cukor estate. Outspoken and
straightforward, Gregga still has the look of a college athlete,
although even sports could not arouse his interest in school, which,
he candidly states, he hated. He educated himself in design, to the
delight of clients including Maria Tallchief Paschen and fashion
photographer Victor Skrebneski.*

*O*ne day when I was five years old,
I began moving furniture . . .
Then I painted the mahogany dining room chairs and my mother was very angry. It all began at that age and it's never stopped. I've tried other things but have always come back to decorating. I worked in advertising for a few years with Victor Skrebneski, the photographer. We set up his studio and I did sets for films and photography. Then back into decorating. Eight years ago I started my own design firm.

I never studied design. I hated school. I had nuns and I hated the nuns. I went to a junior college for two years and hated every minute of it. I'm doing now what I should have been doing since I was five years old. I didn't need school. I really don't think formal training is necessary. The day you're born, whatever you're bent for, it's all together in your body and your head.

Today I have a staff of nine and thirty-three current jobs, residential and commercial.

My home base is Chicago and my second home is in Los Angeles. I've started to work there, too. I like that, but I have to be very patient. It all comes. I can't push it. That's part of being a Capricorn. I just keep going in a straight line. And it's the same way when I'm trying to get a point across to a client. They keep saying, "No, no, no, no." But I know eventually I will have a purple rug if I want a purple rug.

When I began, my first clients were friends . . .
who weren't wealthy at all. I did six rooms on about eight thousand dollars. It looked like gangbusters. And like a lot more money than it was. That's the best way for a designer to get started. You have to do one job for the right group. Then suddenly you're working with the entire group. Then group, to group, to group. I've had national press coverage, but I think most clients come because of friends seeing a house I have done.

I do think to be seen socially is good, but it's not good to be seen in a foolish way. To go everywhere is ridiculous. Often when my clients have parties I do not go. I don't want to be picked apart. People love to get me into a corner at a party and ask about their houses. It's easier to stay at home.

My first step on a new job is to . . .
take field measurements and begin our plans. We might complete plans and bids in six weeks to two months. At the same time, we start our design plans, making selections and choices. I rarely shop with a client. Everything is brought to them, either in my office or in their home. I bring schemes. I bring choices. I might bring four or five fabrics to them. When that's chosen, I pull all the accessory fabrics and pieces together. I sketch custom-upholstered furniture to show the client what it will look like, and I've never had a sofa sent back.

If I walk into a room and it has everything going for it architecturally, I know instantly what the rooms are going to look like on completion. I just know. And when I walk into a turkey and know I need ten hours of thought time to pull it together, it's rough.

Financially, I work on a retail basis, plus . . .
a design fee, draftsman hours and so forth. If people haven't determined a budget, then the best thing to do is put a flat fee on each room. In addition, of course, the client buys everything at the retail price. For a design consultation, my fee is one hundred dollars an hour.

We talk about money in the beginning. We explain our fees, outline what we do, and then try to establish a budget. The client hedges, wanting me to come up with the figure. "What can you do the room for?" I say, "If you leave me alone, I can do the room for a thousand dollars. If you get involved, it'll be fifty thousand dollars." Meaning, I can give somebody a look for not a lot of money—if they don't interfere.

We try to make it all very clear because collecting fees is often a problem. Some people hold back as long as they possibly can. Others pay instantly, even on the costly jobs. And I've spent close to a million dollars for one client in a year.

A proud Senufo carved bird faces the sparing yet sumptuous
living room conversation area of a Chicago apartment in an
updated older building. "I tried for the marriage of some
French things with the softness of contemporary fabrics," says
Bruce Gregga. Paintings by Marcoussis, above the mantel,
and Botero, above the banquette at rear, enhance walls
wrapped in damask; upholstery fabrics are lush satin
and leopard-patterned velvet. "The reason for the big, long
sofa was to expand the space of a not-very-large, irregularly
shaped room—to give it some dimension," he explains.

I will do budget jobs if I like the people . . .
I would still take a ten-thousand-dollar job. Some paint, some color, slipcovers, and pulling it together somewhat. I can do a look for that amount, and a lot of designers would not move out of their chairs for a small budget. The best way would be to work on an hourly rate and let the client follow through. It's good for a designer to establish a room for a client and let the client finish it.

A quality room costs about thirty thousand dollars . . .
And that's without antiques and art. It's a lot of plants. Not even a load of accessories. Actually, there's nothing I hate more than a client who tells me, "I want accessories." They expect the station wagon to pull up and unload. But then it's not their house.

Interior design is just a fancy name . . .
We're decorators. Interior designer is a comparatively new term. Everybody was a decorator until about five years ago. And I'm still a decorator.

Many people use a decorator only because . . .
their friends are using them. It's part of their world. There are a lot of people with very good taste but that's not enough. There is so much more to decorating. Proportion, form, knowledge of construction.

*The most common mistakes
amateur decorators make are . . .*
proportion and scale. But that happens with professional designers, too.

If you're decorating your own house, do it with quality. A wonderful cabinet can set the mood for a room. One thing of quality. And don't use too much color in one room, nor throughout the house. That happens often. You see a rainbow of colors as you walk down the halls. Amateurs don't know how to control color. When I do a house, I do variations of one color.

It's true that good taste is timeless, and anyone with a very keen eye, who will listen, read, and look at pictures, study, and go to museums can acquire taste.

Fabrics instantly establish the taste level of the room. A collector in Chicago has some of the most beautiful antiques I've ever seen. And they couldn't be more wrong, because every piece of fabric was chosen badly.

A home really doesn't reveal much about . . .
the people who live there. Only if it's obvious that they want to show their wealth. Even bedrooms are not revealing, except for bachelors, who always want a fantasy. Even that doesn't mean they are active sexually.

My favorite colors for a sexy bedroom are peach and apricot. And women look marvelous in those colors.

Men are not better designers than women . . .
We've had some fabulous women designers through the years. The late Rosalind Rosier started the whole country mood. She would use wicker with blue and white checked taffeta in a drawing room with velvet upholstered walls. She had fabulous style.

Today women in the field probably relate more to what is happening at the moment. They're all Déco crazy and very showy and glitzy.

The men are much more serious and they are better business people. More controlled. More disciplined. And I don't think women want to work with a woman. They want to work with a man. A woman who's spending money enjoys being with a man. However, there are some very, very successful women decorators making lots of money.

The designer-client relationship can be intimate . . .
some end up in bed. It's not unusual. Women sometimes fall in love with their decorators. At the least, they confide in them a great deal. The decorator has replaced the hairdresser. When the client has a fight with her husband, I'm the first to know.

People on small budgets are more difficult . . .
to work with because they're living in frustration. Wealthy people take the attitude, "We'll have it or we won't." It's that kind of choice. "I don't want to spend that kind of money on that commode. What else is there?" The wealthy are much more practical. Of course, you have to be rich to decorate today.

Clients can drive you crazy . . .
One lady was absolutely out of her tree. We talked about the color scheme and she kept saying, "No peach. No peach." This went on for days. Every time I showed her a fabric: "No peach! No peach!" But I was showing her blues and greens.

There are clients who call every five minutes, instead of making a list and then calling. They'll ask, "Where is such and such?" We tell them, "We'll check." If we don't call back in ten minutes, another call comes in, "Where is it?" This goes on and on. A lot of women don't have anything to do, so they hire decorators and torment them!

My ideal client would be . . .
the duchess of Windsor, because of her incredible taste.

For people on a really limited budget . . .
I would suggest a modern room. You can buy moderately priced furniture that is better looking than reproductions in the same price range, unless you can find in-

In the same Chicago living room, a vibrant contemporary
canvas by David Young contrasts with the aged elegance of a
Chinese lacquered table, and bare bleached-wood flooring
counterpoints the lavishly fringed satin banquette adorned
with Aubusson tapestry-wrapped pillows. "Fabrics instantly
establish the taste level of a room," says designer Gregga, who
is fond of satin: "It's sensuous and reflective."

expensive pine farm furniture in the country. That would give the room quality and softness, mixed with the modern things.

Most of all, keep it simple. Window coverings could be thin slat or bamboo blinds. For today's plain box apartment with a cement floor, I would suggest institutional carpeting. Keep all the colors very neutral. Then a graphic or poster for color wouldn't be objectionable.

However, for anyone, I would suggest acquiring contemporary paintings and sculpture. Young artists are doing good things. It's a joy to live with and a good investment. Quality pieces by old established artists are so expensive, they're almost untouchable for most people.

My own apartment in Chicago is in
a Mies van der Rohe building with a . . .
view of the city and the lake. It was a two-bedroom apartment that I made into one room sixty-nine feet long that L's off for a defined sleeping/dressing area with a fabulous marble bathroom. At that point it's about forty feet wide. The ceilings are only eight feet high. It's an incredible night apartment and very underfurnished. No contemporary furniture. Some antique pieces. The floors are black-stained parquet, walls are creamy. No art. No color.

The house in Los Angeles took one year to redo. It's also very simple. All form and architectural plans. You don't see much furniture when you walk in. There are twelve-foot ceilings and a skylight. Vistas through the floor-to-ceiling windows to the garden. Black granite floors. In the living room, wonderful mirrors that once belonged to Somerset Maugham. I didn't see any reason to have a sofa in the living room. There are six small upholstered chairs, because I couldn't afford fabulous antique chairs. One day I'll have them. The chairs are placed in a circle. Sofas belong in bedrooms or libraries, where people can curl up in them and read. Men are much more comfortable in upright chairs, particularly for conversation and a drink with friends. Lounge furniture is intimate furniture. People in chairs pull themselves closer to the people they want to talk with. You can't move a sofa.

Decorating will be more expensive . . .
in the next few years. We'll be doing more minimal rooms because of escalating costs. Wealthy people will always do a rich house. Good antiques will always be available if you can afford them. We've always had trends in design, whether it's Déco, the minimal room, or a classic contemporary.

If someone gave me carte blanche
to do a home for myself . . .
I'd probably hire a decorator to do it. It would be in

Los Angeles or the south of France, my two favorite places. In France, I would love to have an old stone house. I love to take an old house and redo it. If it were a new house, it would be modern. You can't emulate a period house today. It can be done, but it is costly and difficult. And it still reeks of new. There's no patina. It just doesn't work.

Most people—even the wealthy—
don't know how to entertain . . .
People who do things on a minimum budget can pull a dinner together that is much more exciting, innovative, and tasty, with a much prettier table than those elaborate parties done by a caterer. Few people can keep cooks for any length of time today. Even when you have your own cook, it's just like using a caterer. After a while, everything tastes the same.

A friend who now lives in Santa Barbara creates pure excitement. But dinner is never a big production. She might do an incredibly delicious casserole, the greatest green salad I have ever eaten, and the best dessert ever, but none of it really costs much. It's just pulled together. Little tables for two or three, with guests sitting all over the house. It's always comfortable. Of course, people and conversation make the excitement anywhere.

Mood lighting, candles, or perimeter lighting of some sort help too. Overlighted rooms drive me insane. I want to get out. I feel as though I'm in a cafeteria. And although I love music, I don't like having an orchestra blasting in my ear during conversation at dinner. Six or eight people at a round table is ideal. When you start putting ten or twelve people at an elongated table, it gets very noisy.

Decorating likes and dislikes . . .
I don't like to use ugly objects just because they have belonged to a family. It's very hard to pull things together and make them look decent. The old red Oriental rug that was made in 1920. Things like that drive me crazy. But I work with them if I have to.

Shag rugs are forgettable. And so are kitchens in colors. Country kitchens should be forgotten. I prefer only white in the kitchen.

Bathrooms should be only white or natural. Marble bathtubs can go.

I don't like wallpaper. I do like commercial carpeting. And good Oriental rugs. Durrie rugs are lovely. I love silver and crystal, but I don't have much because I don't want to maintain it.

I really prefer not to have glass-topped dining tables. Marble, beautiful stone or beautiful polished wood is much better.

Also, we've become overplanted, too green. People overdo. Too many small plants and too much maintenance. But I love one sensational specimen plant that is well cared for.

Why does television have to go into an armoire? Or furniture have to be grouped around a television set? It should be accessible. Hiding television under a skirted tablecloth is foolish.

Another thing that drives me mad: people who don't play pool having pool tables. Bars you sit at are a cliché to me. Some men think it's very macho. They think they've arrived when they have six bar stools.

Wasting money on children's bedrooms is foolish. I've done some that have cost thirty thousand dollars and forty thousand dollars. It's outrageous. Six months later, the child doesn't like it anyway.

If I see another deer in a room, I'll go crazy.

My favorite room is the bedroom . . .
I just did a fabulous bedroom with silver and apricot Chinese wallpaper and a wonderful ivory satin bed we designed. Heavy channel-quilted draperies. Instead of drawing them back, you unzip them. Satin is very sexy. Men really relate to a satin bedroom rather than a flowered bedroom. They do not like a really feminine bedroom. The most sensuous floor covering would be carpeting. It's soft. I love doing canopy beds. They are luxurious, but some men go crazy in them and start getting claustrophobic. Most men don't like a tented room either. They don't like to be caged in. Many people are splitting their bedroom today. Women are using the master bedroom, and the man goes off into the sitting room and uses the daybed. I don't know why. Men always want very good light for reading and good-sized tables for keeping their things close to them. Women compromise for the aesthetics, but a man wants comfort.

The best kind of client is . . .
interested in the home. And I like a client who gives me a little intrigue, a little problem to work with. It's wonderful. But it is devastating when very uneducated clients are involved. It just doesn't work. They don't know what they're doing. They don't know what they're saying. They're completely confused. Yet they think they know everything.

I can design a house better than most architects . . .
and I've done it. Being an architect would be wonderful. But I prefer decorating. If I didn't, I'd get the hell out.

The design excitement is no longer . . .
in Italy. That whole thing is sort of silly now. The quality coming from there is not all that great anymore.

Bruce Gregga

Word Association

Color	Natural.
Furniture arrangement	Form.
Living rooms	Comfort.
Entrance halls	Formal.
Bedrooms	Cozy.
Bathrooms	Functional.
Dining rooms	Waste of time.
Studies	Books.
Floor coverings	Depends.
Window treatments	None.
Fabrics	Soft.
Wallpaper	Hope not.
Lighting	Depends.
Television sets	Ugh!

A designer in Europe who is trained and has always been surrounded with fabulous architecture and beautiful antiques can do, better than anyone else, interiors that look as though they've always been lived in.

But the young contemporary American designers are more exciting. Their interiors are easier, more relaxed, not as showy, not as colorful. And not all the crazy forms they do in Italy.

Contemporary is accepted in this country, but what the manufacturers are presenting to the public is bad. Instead of having real designers give them fresh input, they copy and knock off.

Interior design on the West Coast is often very heavy. And if it's contemporary, it's very showy.

Old money is more demanding than new money . . .
Some of the rich are difficult. Some have absolutely no taste. Some have. Some are unkind. Some are kind. Some are showy. Some are not.

A Robert Henri painting titled "Lady in Black Velvet" provides a compelling focal point for the glamorous, theatrical arrangement of a woman's boudoir in a Chicago apartment. Brushed brass flooring and molding contribute a gleaming, hard-surface basis for stylized furnishings—a Regency chair with gilded lion's-paw feet and a chinoiserie lacquered dressing mirror. Smooth satin drapes the table and covers the chair and ottoman. "Satin is very sexy," says Mr. Gregga. "Men relate to a satin bedroom rather than a flowered bedroom; they don't like a really feminine bedroom."

ALBERT HADLEY

Albert Hadley is usually considered to be among the top decorators in the world today. Private, soft-spoken, intensely professional, his work articulates his unswerving taste and sensitivity. He never mentions a client's name. However, there are few secrets in the world of interior design; his clients include Mrs. Vincent Astor, Buffie and Bill Cafritz, William Paley, Mrs. Joshua Logan.

My first job was with a furniture store in Nashville, Tennessee, where I . . .
grew up and went to school. I had always been interested in interior design, decoration, architecture, fashion. I played around with all of it.

I already thought I was a decorator when I got that first job in the late thirties, so I tried to advise people about what to do and what not to do. Even so, I was able to get another job with a man called A. Herbert Rodgers, who was one of the great decorators in the South. In those days, decorators kept a marvelous stock of lovely furniture and objects on hand. Rodgers also had his own upholstery shop, his own paint shop, a furniture refinishing shop and, on the top floor of the house, his drapery workroom, so I had very good training, in that I learned a little bit about all of those things. It was an apprenticeship that was invaluable to me.

After my stint with the Engineer Corps during the war, when I got to New York and the Parsons School I had a very good working background.

I was given a scholarship and finished the three-year course in two years by going to summer school. I'd had any number of jobs to get by, while I was going to school, but my first job after I graduated was with Rosalind Rosier.

I was hired to do everything, but mainly displays for her shop. She was a fantastic woman, with great style and a great, great eye. She was also a demanding person. I almost walked out the first day when she spoke to me in a manner I didn't think appropriate. From that day on, we were friends. Then, after I had worked there only two and a half months, Van Truex, the head of Parsons, called and asked if I would come to the school to teach. I taught for five years. I also had my own business going, which was successful enough, but I didn't like working alone. I was finally able to work for my great friend Eleanor Brown of McMillen. She was one of the first people I had applied to for a job when I came to New York, but because I hadn't been to the Parsons School, I wasn't proper material for her organization.

I was with McMillen for about five years and finally left because I just needed to move on. I had no idea what I was going to do. Through an introduction from Van Truex to Sister Parish, I joined her and we've been working together ever since.

We have an ongoing, rather lengthy roster of people we continue to do things for that are not total decorating jobs. Mrs. Parish and I direct and oversee all the jobs. Our design department works constantly, and each person might be working for from four to ten people, whereas I may be personally responsible for no more than that.

Our staff numbers about twenty, including four junior decorators, each with a secretary; production people; an architectural design staff; a complete accounting department, plus a chauffeur.

When I began designing, I started with my family. And poor friends . . .
My first major client was sent to me by Billy Baldwin, who knew I was just starting. An old client and friend of his wanted some things done in her apartment. At that time, Billy was unable to help them because they wanted it done right away. I was thrilled. I went to see them and we had a perfectly marvelous, sometimes stormy, relationship. They were very dynamic and had very definite tastes. I, recently out of school, *also* had very definite ideas. But we worked well together and they turned out to be very good friends and clients for quite a long time.

Today, clients usually come to us through referrals. We do have a lot of new clients who may not know us personally, but have seen our work in magazines.

I think one has to have formal design training . . .
in a school, or one may have the perseverance to study, to look, to go to museums, to lectures, to do personal investigation. Some people can "get it" without going to a school. But for the most part, I think formal education gives security and discipline.

"It's a strong background that holds this assemblage
together," says Mr. Hadley of a living room in a traditional
Manhattan apartment building. "It was designed for a young
couple who are great collectors of furniture and art objects."
The arrangement of eclectic furnishings, including Regency,
Régence and Near Eastern tables, and Louis XVI chairs, is
surrounded by walls lacquered in jewellike emerald green
and punctuated by a Hans Hofmann abstract canvas and the
commanding focus of a Kenneth Noland target painting.

It's a great mistake to think one must be rich to . . .
employ a professional designer. Decorators have the reputation of doing only the richest things, and people become frightened because they think you won't do a
room. A new client asked me the other day, "Mr.
Hadley, do you have a minimum?" And I didn't know
what she was talking about. She explained, "Somebody
told me you won't do a room if it doesn't cost fifty thousand or one hundred thousand dollars." I told her,
"That depends entirely on the room you want. One
piece of furniture can cost that much. Yet I can design
with authority for the simplest budget. It depends on
the level of quality you want, and your preferences."

We work on a retail basis and list everything on an estimate the client signs before we begin. We don't do any
hourly or daily consultations.

It will be nothing except absolute madness
from beginning to end if you . . .
don't have a happy rapport with the client. There's no
possible way you should even think of going on with it,
no matter what their budget is. This is a very personal
kind of business. It's not a package deal where you simply design something, grind it out, and produce it. Ideas
evolve as you get to know people better and they know
each other better. Then, you play it. Your imagination is
freer and you have more chance to do something that is
really tailor-made.

A decorator is someone
who simply adds to whatever might exist . . .
to make it as attractive as possible, but without total
regard for an overall design concept. And by that, I
mean architecture.

Architectural design is the basis of all good interior
work, and without good architectural design anything
that is added or subtracted or applied is sheer decoration. Whether one calls himself an interior decorator, a
designer, a space planner or whatever it is, he is really
talking about someone who has great respect for architectural expression in interiors.

We need someone to help us
see the design picture clearly and to . . .
work as an editor to bring forth the magic and the
beauty. Also, today it's very difficult for the individual
who is not a professional to orchestrate this great production and get it organized. I'm speaking of labor:
plumbers, electricians, floor finishers, painters, fabric
houses, rug suppliers. It takes an awful lot of manipu-
lation and organization to get all of that together. The
work of the designer goes far beyond what the word
implies, because that person does a hell of a lot of work
to make this dream come true.

Every room speaks. Every house speaks.
You've got to listen to what it's saying before . . .
you know what to do. You've got to see the space in
question and to get some sort of vibration of what it really is all about. You can look at floor plans and photographs, but until you see the light and the actual physi-
cal situation, what message it projects, you don't really
know anything.

We start with the architecture, do whatever is needed
for backgrounds. We work with floor plans. We work
with the owner's possessions. I like to work abstractly on
furniture arrangement and ideas of what can happen in
a space. Once that's more or less established and the
space is working the way it should, then you begin to
pinpoint personal possessions and see where they best fit
into an overall scheme. From that come the more decorative aspects: colors, finishes, materials. That's presented usually as a total, carefully thought out for a harmonious overall personality, an aura that one is trying
to establish. Then we work to refine details and continually improve the design.

One of the greatest pitfalls is to waver on your original
concept of what a space is about. The elements within
that space may change drastically between the time you
begin and the actual completion of the project, but you
must never lose sight of what it is you started out to do.

If a scheme is not working, or if you realize the client is
really not going to be happy with it, then you must say,
"Let's take a new look. If you don't feel comfortable
with this concept, let's scrap it. Let's talk awhile, relax,
put it aside, come back to it later, and take a fresh approach." That's perfectly okay. But don't compromise
along the way, or it just gets to be a mishmash.

It's not only the amateur
decorator who makes mistakes . . .
The most common mistake *anybody* makes is negligence
about studying and being totally aware of the architectural background he's working with.

I can think of one example, a quite vast apartment on
Park Avenue. It was a famous apartment, once owned
by a very prominent family. The first day I walked
through the empty rooms and long galleries with the
new owners, I said, "If you don't mind, the first thing I
would like to do is change the proportion of the doors
and rip out the fake French paneling. This will clarify
the architectural background." Their answer was,
"Well, if it was good enough for so-and-so, it is certainly
good enough for us." I fought for quite a long time,
dropped it, but kept going back to it. Eventually we did
what I wanted, and it made all the difference.

Too often people assume that because it's a perfectly
nice door in a perfectly okay position, it's not worth
moving it six inches one way or the other to make the

The living room of Albert Hadley's Manhattan apartment is
dramatically deep-toned, with lacquered walls that seem to
float between mirrored, recessed cornices and bases, and a
reflective Chinese tea-papered ceiling—a sleek contemporary
background for a tradition-rich interior. Satin-covered
eighteenth-century Italian armchairs in front of a blazing
fire are accented by objects that represent "what is left after
a good deal of stringent editing," the designer says. "These
are the things that I feel comfortable with." He adds: "It's a
room with a wide variety of pleasures, from just gazing alone
at the fire to being comfortable with guests."

For the living room of a country house in New York State, "it's all period furniture and contemporary fabrics," says Mr. Hadley. The fragile eighteenth-century feeling is achieved with Louis XV–style paneling and a grouping of Louis XV furniture, accented by one of a pair of Chinese Chippendale mirrors and a red-lacquered tray holding ormolu-mounted porcelain jars made into candlesticks. Sun-bright silk draperies, hung simply from a gilded rod, and a chintz upholstery fabric specially made for the room, freshen the setting and relate it to the country milieu.

room work better, to establish an architectural balance. If a room is good, it's perfectly fine empty. It doesn't need any decoration.

*I don't think there is such a thing
as highly cultivated taste . . .*
Taste is relative. There is a gypsy taste, a bohemian taste. All kinds, all degrees and all forms of taste. Anything that is good is good whether it happens to fit in with my *personal* taste or not.

We work with Mrs. X, for instance, who has, let us say, a rather debutante kind of taste. That's okay, but if one has debutante taste, it's tougher to make it look grown-up. But you can still achieve a certain look of softness and a certain quality of romanticism that would not suit another person. One is not right and another wrong. They're just two different points of view. A good designer has to discover that personal taste in the person with whom he's working and then develop it along the best possible lines—not allowing the cheap pottery roses and the vulgar display of knickknacks to come into it.

A couple came to me a number of years ago who realized that what they bought when they married was banal. Not only were they moving to an uptown location, they were also evolving into another life style. Not necessarily climbing, but simply growing. One's personal taste changes with time and with knowledge. It's bound to, if one is alive and has any sense at all. We learn to recognize that which is better if we're growing. In this case, they were very relaxed, adorable, attractive people; both very bright, both professional. They knew what they had was not right for the space they were moving to, that they had psychologically and aesthetically outgrown what they owned. We studied the situation together for quite a long time, and through exposure and direction, we were able to give them a background that was very comfortable for them. It was a *giant* step and yet they were ready for it. They accepted and responded to the things they were shown. If they didn't respond, I never pushed. I push for things that I know are right, but one can't be stubborn. Either you like the table or you don't like the table. If the table isn't right for the client, then we have to work a little harder to find the one that is, because I have to make it theirs, not mine.

Tasteless rooms are immediately identifiable . . .
Banal, ugly objects. Or banal, ugly rooms. Vulgar moldings, ill-proportioned openings, badly laid out floor plans, furniture arrangements. Basically the arrangement of furniture in a room must relate in some way to the whole room, to its architectural background.

A home is so revealing . . .
It must be. Otherwise, it's a sham. Every room reveals—

by the way it's put together, the way it looks, the objects, the way it's arranged, the colors, the kinds of materials. There are many, many rooms encountered where one feels immediately that the people who live there have cultivated tastes. It may be a decorator's nightmare, but at least it's personal, and it has the charm of personality whether or not it follows all of the so-called rules. The best rooms are sometimes the rooms that break the rules, but still there is an essence, a magic, a quality that speaks louder than anything else. The way one puts flowers in a pot and what the pot looks like. It may be nothing more than a mustard jar, but if attractive flowers are put in it with care, one recognizes a quality of taste. The books that one sees around, things that are loved and perhaps have sentimental value. You can tell immediately if a house is a sentimental scrapbook.

Bedrooms. If it's sloppy, you can be pretty sure . . .
the lives are sloppy. One's bedroom is *the* most personal room in the house. The average person does wish to have an attractive background for his very private life. As one attempts to put together an attractive bedroom for people, naturally one thinks of the quality that makes one's private life happy. The kinds of colors, materials, arrangement of furniture, the arrangement of objects, if any. The bedroom should speak rather clearly about how that person is in his private moments, but not, of course, blatantly spell out that one likes to be beaten with chains or sprinkled with rose petals.

*The really good, sensitive female decorator
has a quality no man can ever have . . .*
The whole thing of home, of comfort. A woman can put together a woman's bedroom in a far more feminine, seductive way than any man can. Not that it's better design, but there are certain *touches* the woman designer has that the male animal can't, no matter how much he understands the necessities.

And there is a certain rapport of one woman to another that can never be totally interchanged, no matter how much a man might understand the woman. Sister Parish is an absolute genius at putting together *the* most comfortable, luxurious, beautiful rooms for those people with whom she works where the rapport is so complete. There's nothing that compares with that. I might do a beautiful room, but I would never quite have that touch. I'm not saying that some other men might not, but I would find it very difficult.

There are very strong designers and there are designers who are not so strong. They may be men or women.

Some people are very difficult to work with . . .
but others are very easy. And it has nothing to do with money. A lot of people are difficult because they are

spoiled. Obviously some are more spoiled than others. They have perhaps less regard for time on a professional level, not realizing that what one is doing is, in fact, a very demanding business.

If you're really working closely with someone and you're lucky enough to have that marvelous feeling of being on the same wavelength, you naturally become part of that person's scene, part of the family, in a sense.

When one behaves and performs in a professional way, there is mutual respect. A professional person does not become *too* personally involved.

My worst client, and most embarrassing situation . . .
was working with a very nice, most attractive woman who had taken a fabulous apartment. We did a lot of the backgrounds, but when it came to selecting the proper furnishings she had a very difficult time deciding. We had tried some things and looked at a lot of things, but really hadn't gotten very far yet, and the backgrounds were all there. She was going away, so I asked, "May I bring in the things I think would be suitable, so you can get the overall picture when you return?" She was rather hesitant, because she really wanted to be involved in everything, but she agreed. Everything was to be moved in the day before she returned, because I didn't want to keep them out on memo too long.

Two days before everything was to be delivered, I asked Sister Parish to come with me and look at it. Just as I started unlocking the door, it opened, and our rather irate client stood there. She said, "This is not going to work. I intended to come home and find my apartment furnished. Never mind now." And that ended *that*.

Interiors of quality are very costly today . . .
Probably the most expensive I ever did was well over a million. The least expensive was a few thousand dollars, many years ago. It may have been five thousand, but today it would be at least double.

Consider that a good upholstered sofa costs about three thousand dollars and take it from there. How many sofas? How many chairs?

If you want a space done with good quality and good workmanship, it will cost a lot of money. There is no way you can do what I call "budget" decorating if the client wants quality. If you're willing to rely on taste rather than quality, you can do a *very* attractive space for comparatively little money.

Buy a good sofa, cover it in a tough, attractive canvas; put a straw rug on the floor, get a few interesting pieces of furniture, use the simplest kind of surfaces. If you have the eye and the knowledge, you can put those things together with a certain style and a certain flair, and it can be extremely attractive.

Often people on a budget love the idea at first, and then begin to get cold feet because they think, "If we're going to spend that much for the straw rug, maybe we'd better spend a little more and get a better rug." But the better rug really pulls down the whole idea, rather than keeping the concept of simplicity as the keynote. But it can be done, and it can be done with great style, using simple, basic, beautifully designed things.

*I try not to get too much involved
in the financial end of the business . . .*
but I like to know basically what kind of budgets we're talking about, although even without asking, one can usually have some idea.

For instance, if we're asked to remodel a very expensive apartment on Fifth Avenue, we're not talking about peanuts. Yet we also know that unless that person is a collector of really super antiques and important art, we're not necessarily working with a "sky's-the-limit" budget. Quite often we try to come to that kind of discussion very early on: "Are you interested in buying really outstanding antiques?" or "Do you really want the best quality?" If they own anything you're to work with and that's the level they are more or less remaining on, that's your key right there.

*There are two ways to approach
a very limited decorating budget . . .*
Take the entire budget and do a total finished job with the idea of using it for a few years, then throwing it out or moving it to some secondary place later on. That is one way.

The second way is to buy the best you can find. Even if it's just a little straw stool to use as a side table. When your budget allows, if you really wish to have a lacquer drum, that straw stool is going to be perfectly happy in your bathroom, in a child's room, a guest room, or on your porch. You're not throwing it out, because you choose each object for what it is, not as a disposable. The eye must be discerning. You buy the best design. If it is a three-dollar straw basket, you might keep it for years because it will also look very beautiful on a lacquer table later on.

*Don't spend unnecessary money
on things that are half-baked grand . . .*
If a beautiful Louis XV desk is your dream, it's better to live with a kitchen table covered with a cloth until you can buy the real thing, rather than to buy a reproduction. I'm not saying I don't approve of good reproductions, but if your dream is the real thing, stick to the simplest possible table until you can have what you really want. The right scale and the right proportion is far more important than the cost of the object. From an

aesthetic point of view, the only advice to give anybody ever is to remember that scale makes the impact. I'd rather have two soapboxes of the right scale than two good tables of the wrong proportion.

At the last minute, some people came to me who . . .
had a lot of furniture but wanted their apartment updated, revitalized.

It was traditional furniture, lots of French and English stuff. We worked out some very attractive floor plans and it all went quite well. But the dining room was absolutely hopeless because the pantry door was in the center of the long wall. There was no possible way to screen the pantry from the dining room, and there's nothing worse than having the light glare into a room every time a door opens. Anyway, I worked out a screening situation, and the room was painted a marvelous green. We used their own mahogany furniture and their chandelier. The windows were hung with hand-painted fabric in a rather bold blue and green. The entire apartment was done in painted canvas and simple cottons. It was very young, very fresh and very attractive. But the dining room was a disaster.

My mistake was in putting a dark blue rug on the polished dark-wood floor. Since there was no daylight in the room, the dark blue carpet simply sank into the floor and you felt that you were stepping into a big, deep, black pool every time you walked into the room. Perfectly hideous. I hate blue carpets of all description as a result of that.

Often you can sense insecurity in people . . .
In the professional world of selling, which is what we do, one begins to learn certain things about people just on meeting. Often you sense insecurity early on, and you realize you have to work in a way to help them along. One thing people say is, "I know exactly what I like, but I don't know why." Then you find out they really *don't* know what they like. Or they like *everything*. Or they like *nothing*.

A very good friend that I do a lot of work for sometimes looks at something and says, "What am I looking at?" If it says, "I am a chair," then it's a good chair. If it doesn't say, "I am a chair," then it's no good for her. That's very positive, very attractive. I like that quality. All you can do is try to size people up the best you possibly can, and nine times out of ten you're wrong.

Decorating likes and dislikes . . .
I like a clarity of viewpoint in a room. I like to see furniture and objects of character and of directness and of scale and proportion that are meaningful to the overall picture. What I really hate is rooms that lack that direction. That doesn't mean that a room full of all kinds of

things can't make a very definite statement. In such a room, each tiny thing has impact because of what it is in the overall picture. But I hate rooms that lose sight of a definite point of view, and that's very hard to explain.

By and large, I hate anything that's intended for one thing and used for something else. A cobbler's bench as a coffee table to me is just about as bad as you can go. Or a coffee grinder made into a lamp. It's unsuitable. The intention of use must be logical and it must be authentic. Anything else to me is gimmicky and an affectation to be avoided.

There's nothing more beautiful in a room than having marvelous flowers well positioned. We're all slightly guilty at times of expecting plants and flowers to form the decorative impact where perhaps they shouldn't. From time to time, we've all relied on *the* plant or *the* tree in the corner to save the room, or *the* bunch of flowers on the coffee table. The room seems incomplete without them. The room should be beautiful without the flowers, but more beautiful with them. Flowers and plants that are naturally and casually used are more effective than the rigid, studied placement. And one of the things I hate most are flowers so crammed into containers that they look as if they couldn't possibly live. It's a very minor thing, but it's one of the things that can break the room or make a space seem restless. A living thing should not be used in a way that doesn't seem natural. For instance, I hate daisies in glass vases, because they muddy the water. Daisies should be in a pot or a basket, so the slightly murky water doesn't show. That's a very silly thing to say, but it's a pet peeve.

We've been through design minimalism
in the last few years . . .
and it's been an excellent influence, because it has caused people to look differently at the space in which they live. They have at least thought of housecleaning and keeping only those things that are meaningful. Today we live more simply and more within a framework of reality, because service and maintenance are more and more a problem. There is certainly a great indication that there will be a simplification of life style.

My house in the country and apartment in town are
very much the same and yet they're very different . . .
My apartment is very pared down and extremely simple, with a few things that are beautiful to me that make it agreeable and pleasant. It's relatively empty, which I like. I even have the luxury of empty closets.

My house is the total opposite. It's put together to work comfortably for the way I live in the country, but it's a scrapbook of all the things I've collected or been given or found on the street or inherited or whatever. It's much more romantic and easy.

Albert Hadley

Word Association

Color	Subtle.
Furniture arrangement	Comfortable and stylish.
Living rooms	Family.
Entrance halls	Severe.
Bedrooms	Cozy.
Bathrooms	White.
Dining rooms	Cool.
Studies	Warm.
Floor coverings	Simple.
Kitchens	Functional.
Children's rooms	Bright.
Lamps	Minimum.
Window treatments	Simple.
Fabrics	Honest.
Wallpaper	Decoration.
Lighting	Exciting.
Television sets	Honest.

Town is another statement, yet each has a personal point of view about the way I live.

Entertaining . . .
Some people have a wonderful sense of hospitality, warmth, and entertainment, while others are simply cold fish and don't know how to entertain.

Many people get nervous because they're "giving a party," when what they're really doing is seeing their friends under the best possible circumstances. A party is no more than that.

I love decorating entrance halls because . . .
they are the introduction to the house and afford the opportunity to work in a very architectural and sculptural way. The entrance hall should be the most austere part of the house, and yet must be inviting.

European interiors, obviously, have a much stronger . . .
historical background and, therefore, more substance and authority than there can be in this country, which has done nothing but emulate the styles of European architects and designers from the day we landed on these shores, except for purely regional influences.

To me, contemporary is a point of view. And there are many people with the contemporary point of view who still are not going to accept a Parsons table as a table. But they're still very contemporary in thought. I don't think it has to do with what the material is or what the object is. Contemporary is one's own acceptance of life today and arranging one's possessions to fit the pattern of today. Contemporary really has to do with the intelligence and the intellect of the individual.

I suppose many people fear decorators . . .
They hate them. But I also think more and more people are beginning to understand the validity of design and decoration as a legitimate profession.

The rich certainly are . . .
different! They're *much* better off.

"This living room was designed for a music-minded young family moving into a traditional New York apartment building with some period furniture and a collection of modern paintings," Albert Hadley says. "We bleached and stained the floors in a herringbone pattern and stippled and glazed the walls a deep sapphire blue." The rich background enhances an eighteenth-century Italian mirror above the Georgian marble mantel, Regency consoles and a Louis XV fire bench. A painting by Deforest hangs near one of two pianos back-to-back in the room; drawing by Reuben Nakian.

ANTHONY HAIL

*Tony Hail's living room in San Francisco is one of my favorite
places to be. His scholarly knowledge of antiques contributes to his
ability to design interiors that look as though they have been lived
in for generations. When I became editor of* Architectural Digest,
*he was one of the first important decorators who believed in me and
my plan to turn the magazine into an international design force
that might someday influence the way many of us live. He has
certainly influenced the way his clients live: among them are
Mr. and Mrs. Howard Johnson and Mr. and Mrs. James Garner.*

*At Harvard I studied architecture
under Gropius and Bogner . . .*

but I never wanted to be an architect. I was always interested in interior design. Travel was a major influence. I lived in Denmark for ten years—until I was fourteen—and of course I spoke Danish. Then the war came and we went back to America. After the war I had to finish my education. Until I was twenty-four, I was pretty much in America, then I traveled again. I really didn't settle down until I was thirty.

Decorating was not as accepted then as it is now, so I decided to go to architectural school and branch out from there. The *insides* of houses interested me. After World War II, I studied in the architectural school at Harvard, but my degree was a B.A. I never was interested in the engineering side of architecture.

After school I worked for Ed Wormley, with Dunbar, the furniture manufacturer, where I learned about furniture, upholstery, cabinet work, and I met all the leading people in the design world.

My next work was on the White House, during the Truman administration. It was an enormously prestigious job. I worked as an architect and draftsman. Three hundred people worked in the White House on that project. It was very interesting because it got me into eighteenth- and nineteenth-century work again; I had been more interested in modern, before. Then I went to London and worked for *Vogue* and *House & Garden* on special assignments as an interiors photographer and reporter. They sent me all over France, England, Scotland, and Wales.

When I came back to New York, I found there were lots of decorators working there very successfully. A friend suggested there might be a better future for me in San Francisco. The minute I arrived, I felt there was a place for me. That was twenty years ago, and it's been lucky for me ever since.

Classic training is not necessary for a designer . . .
Many things learned have to be unlearned. My best advice for anybody interested in this profession is to get an excellent liberal arts education, travel as much as possible when you're young, then go to work for a decorator or an architect as quickly as you can. Or a showroom. Even a department store. Somewhere you can meet people and start to feel what it is like to sell them curtains and slipcovers. Even though you're selling things you might not approve of, you learn.

Today I handle twenty to thirty jobs per year . . .
Some are large, but the majority are not. Many are for continuing clients. I do commercial work too. Hotels, offices, board rooms, restaurants. But it's only a small percentage of my work.

There are three people on my staff, one of whom is my partner, Charles Posey, who handles all the business. I do all the designing. When clients come to me, they want me. I've never been able to delegate authority.

*There are many rules decorators
should bear in mind. One is . . .*
never tell clients the house they've bought is wrong for them. They'll keep the house and hire another decorator.

When people come to me, I try to find out what they want from their house. Some people want very fancy lives and, therefore, very fancy houses. Others want extremely understated interiors. You try for a rapport with the person because it's a very intimate relationship. I'll never forget what Mrs. James Garner said when we first met. "I'm Hollywood. I'm nouveau riche. I don't want any of that to show and that's why I've hired you." She also told me, "Jimmy's the most important man in my life, and next to him *you're* going to be, because I'm going to see more of you than anybody else." That was twelve years ago.

Financially, the first step is . . .
to set up a budget. Eventually, after selecting fabrics and furniture, we present an estimate, and that estimate is my bill. My fee is the difference between wholesale and retail, unless there's a vast amount of drafting. There is a deposit of either a third or a half of the estimated total, in which my profit is included.

For the drawing room of an imposing Italianate residence
near San Francisco, Anthony Hail arranged an extensive
collection of antique furnishings and objects. "That enormous
room," he says, "the flowers, the soft lights, the exquisite
furniture, someone waiting for you with a silver tray full of
champagne glasses. It's so enormously elaborate—and so
enormously simple." In one corner, a nineteenth-century
Chinese gold-thread tapestry backdrops a suite of Louis XVI
furniture covered in Beauvais tapestry that depicts La
Fontaine's *Fables*. Nearby, family photographs sewn with
bows to a velvet-covered screen personalize the grand scale.

I don't like to work on a consultation-fee basis, because I feel that once I walk into the room, I'm expected to perform my job and that if I stop to straighten my tie, I'm taking up the time they're paying for. And I feel *they* feel that way, too.

I've never understood the difference between
an interior designer and an interior decorator . . .
I've called myself a decorator ever since I can remember. And the old-school people are all called decorators. *Interior designer* implies that you do a lot of drafting, and I don't think many of them do. I'm a *decorator*.

You should use a decorator to save your sanity . . .
How would anyone not in the business professionally know how the springs are supposed to be built in a sofa, or that stereo speakers don't work behind silk walls? A decorator who works every day with these things knows most of the pitfalls and can save you a great deal of money and mistakes, not to mention time. And I haven't even mentioned the decorator's expertise, taste, and talent, which you get in the bargain. With any luck.

When I begin a new job . . .
I bring samples and present definite ideas within the framework of what we talked about initially. If the client doesn't want a certain color, I can change it. I explain that will be plain and this will be pattern. Before I leave, perhaps two hours later, I have a pretty good conception of what it is the client wants and a pretty clear idea of what the interior is going to look like.

The next meeting may make it jell. Or the one after that. And if that doesn't work and I can't really understand what they want, I come back and come back and come back until I do. If they have an architectural plan, so much the better. Otherwise I make a floor plan, but it has to be explained. Some people understand a plan, but most laymen do not. You have to say, that's a sofa over there, there are two tables and they both have lamps, and so forth.

If I have a client who loves shopping, I'll take her along; that teaches me a lot about what she wants.

Frankly, most decorators are not knowledgeable about antiques. I plan in color and texture and weights. Heavy furniture here balancing something there. I think in color, but I'm not exactly famous for vivid color.

The mistake most amateur decorators make is . . .
trying to be up to date. They learn from home magazines that red is *in* this month and orange is *out*. That's absolutely ridiculous. For a while, everything was chrome and glass and those arc lamps *everywhere*. Wildly expensive—and two years later, you're sitting under your arc lamp, wondering what to do with it. You can't move it. It weighs a ton. You're stuck with it.

I hate to hear, "I'm going to do it in English," or "I'm going to do it in French Provincial." What does that mean? It's just silly. You buy a piece of furniture you love and it happens to be English or French.

I always say, begin with four good chairs. Then you can add upholstered pieces and lamps. Tables can be covered with fabric skirts. Later you can replace them with pretty tables. You can get better and better things as you grow, and your budget grows. But if you have five or six pretty things in a room, the room takes on an air that it can never get without them.

Do go easy on color, because you will get so tired of it. Too many people think, "I'll have a green living room, a blue hall and a red dining room. And yellow in the bedroom." Let the house flow. I hate houses that are all cut up with colors. It makes you very nervous.

Make every room in your house count. Particularly if you don't have a big house. If you have three or four rooms you really use, why give one over to a formal dining room with a silver tea service on a sideboard, when you only entertain at home once every two months for ten people? When what you really do at home is read, look at television, listen to music, paddle around, and cook dinner for one or two. If you want to give a dinner for twelve, rent chairs and tables.

Remember who you are and how you *really* live. That's suitability. Suitability is important. In the South, where I was born, they say " 'tain't fittin'." That just means it isn't suitable.

Please don't collect. Those people with collections of rocks! If you didn't find them yourself in Wyoming or the Yucatan, they don't mean anything to your life. I hate those instant collections. Suddenly, there they are. All those marble eggs! Fossils! Minerals! That was a great fad for a while. Recently, a man told me he collected cookie jars in the form of fat people. What do they do with those things? Give them away and start with something else, I suspect. Also the pretentiousness of *name* things today is a scourge. Valentino and Gucci and Pucci, for clothes. But it goes further, even into the realm of fine art. I saw a house recently with Motherwell, Morris Lewis, Warhol, Stella, and other contemporary "name" artists. But they were all second-, third-, or fourth-rate works. Only the "names" were right. There's nothing wrong with not knowing, but one can damn well learn.

Good taste is absolutely timeless . . .
My scrapbooks are filled with things from forty and fifty years ago that I got from my mother's scrapbook. And

In another corner of the same drawing room, designer Hail
created an intimate conversation area with a graceful
grouping of Directoire and Louis XVI upholstered pieces
around a low table inlaid with seventeenth-century marble.
Attention to detail is strictly acknowledged: All small
treasures resting on tables throughout the house correspond to
typewritten slips of paper describing dates and provenance.
The seventeenth-century Dutch painting is by Hondecoeter.

taste can be acquired by exposure. Do you think all those "best dressed" women started out being "best dressed"? If you earnestly try, earnestly look around and develop your inner resources, you will acquire taste.

You can recognize a tasteless room if you see a modern Oriental rug. One that was made today. Made synthetically, by machine, without the hand-tied yarn that made them possible in the first place. That's a real giveaway. Bad lines on pretentious furniture is another.

Lampshades are one of the most dangerous things. Especially the ones with fringe on the bottom, two or three colors of braid here and there, sometimes a bow, and they're all madly out of shape. Either the lamps are too large or the shades are too big.

Scale is such an important thing. You can tell immediately if somebody has an eye for scale and volume. If the arms of a sofa are too small for its scale, that tells you.

Most people don't give a damn about their house . . .
They have no feeling about it at all. They may be brilliant scientists, doctors, actors, lawyers. They simply aren't interested. Some people with superb taste in decoration have no taste with clothes. My grandmother always said, "That woman can't get in out of the rain, but she plays bridge like Culbertson." It has nothing to do with IQ or general intelligence. In the same way, I don't think you can tell much about people by looking at their houses.

Although I do think the bedroom is revealing to a certain extent. I found out early in my career that many men like feminine bedrooms. They like to feel they are going *into* their wife's bedroom. They *love* the idea. I used to try to make bedrooms pleasing for both men and women. But the man would say, "I don't like it." Then I realized men *wanted* lace and blue and fluffy things in the bedroom. He's *in* there. It's *her* bedroom. That reveals a lot about their sex life. Tight bedspreads, tight twin beds and neat little night stands with everything put away reveal another kind of person.

If you want a sensuous bedroom, have padded walls, luxurious carpets, fresh white linen sheets, deep, down pillows—twice as many as you need. Wonderful scents.

Today people think bedspreads are unnecessary, a nuisance. But I still think an unmade bed is like wrinkled underwear. Without a spread, a bed just is not made.

Years ago the great decorators were women. Today . . .
I would find it hard to name four or five women in decorating. That sounds terribly chauvinistic, but I don't mean it to be. It doesn't matter to me. But the women decorators have lost ground.

One of the reasons is that in the old days, the client was

Mr. Frick. Who ever heard of Mrs. Frick? The great clients for decorators were men. They liked working with women. Men were the patrons. Today, women are the decorator's clients. And they seem to prefer working with a man.

This profession has turned into a plaything for the rich woman whose children have left home and whose husband is thinking about his business. There she is. Forty-eight or fifty and nothing to do. So she decorates. That takes her mind off everything. And the husband is delighted that his wife is kept busy.

Designer and client often have
a very close relationship . . .
but it would be extremely stupid of the decorator to assume the role of a lover. However, clients do get personal, do get intimate, do get involved in your life. They tell their decorators things they would never tell a person equally known to them, but since they've already told you how the beds are to be made up, it's very easy to go just a step further. You become a confidant.

There was one woman
who was never to become a confidante . . .
A friend introduced us, and I was told she wanted me to decorate her house. She looked like a lovely matron from Ohio—beautifully dressed, navy blue suit, diamond circle pin, little hat, white gloves, neat as a pin. She said, "I have a big English house, but I want to build a 'motel' for my husband's business associates, so I won't have to have them in the house." Then she added, "We have a house in Palm Springs and we infinitely prefer living there." I asked, "Well, why don't you?" She seemed astonished: "He's in the motion picture business." We chatted on and on until I suggested again that they live in Palm Springs, because she kept mentioning how much they liked it there. "We can't," she told me quite firmly, "he *has* to be in Hollywood around his business." Finally I asked, "What does your husband do?" She said, "Don't you know who Bob Hope is?" I lost the job.

Wealthy clients are difficult to work with because . . .
they're spoiled. They are used to instant obedience from various staff all around—secretaries, their household staff. Money brings service, and service brings obedience.

They resent it terribly if I leave town. There is one client from way back who still talks about how often I'm in Europe. I'm in Europe once a year, just as she is. Clients don't want you to live as they do. It's a great temptation to live like them. And that's the great danger of this profession—to think you're one of them.

You are decorating their houses and they're talking about demitasse cups and how many extra people for dinner, and before you know it, you want to give a little dinner and you want some demitasse cups, too. Slowly, without realizing what's happening, you're building up a miniature Versailles.

Billy Baldwin told me a wonderful story about that kind of thing. He was working for Ruby Ross Wood, a great decorator in her day. She came to Billy and said, "I see that you're going around to all the dinner parties in New York. Let me just tell you something. Those wealthy ladies and gentlemen are going to like you, and they're going to take you up socially. You have good manners, you're amusing, you can dance, and you're nice looking. But I brought you here to be with all these people for one reason only—*to get their money.*"

Socializing does help if that's going to be your clientele. A few years ago, I just decided I wouldn't go out to dinner anymore. I was tired of turning to the left and to the right four nights out of six. My business went way down. Now I go out a lot.

Although most of my clients are wealthy . . .
I did a small apartment not too long ago for fifteen thousand dollars. That was a complete job, kitchen, hall, bedroom, sitting room, bathroom. And the most expensive interior I've done cost about a million dollars.

I used to say a young couple starting married life in an apartment would expect to spend one hundred and twenty-five thousand dollars for everything except silver, china, glass, and linen. Now I've had to double that. That means the living room is probably going to cost eighty-five thousand dollars or one hundred thousand dollars, if it has any quality at all. Some antiques. But no paintings. Good upholstered furniture.

If they were trying to decorate
their own apartment, I would suggest . . .
they buy two or three nice things. A good dining room table, good chairs, and lamps. They should use soft background colors they could live with and put anything against. And I would suggest they buy a Japanese screen, so there would be something pretty for the eye to rest on. The other walls could be bare. Invest in some decent upholstered furniture you can slipcover for the rest of your life. I would tell them *not* to buy inexpensive things just to finish everything right away. If they do that, they will have a whole room of things to be dumped eventually. But it never will be. They'll have that sofa until they're eighty.

For floor covering, I like everything except all those fad things like coco matting and diving-board material. It's been done to death. Unless you're living in Nassau. Nothing is quite as nice as a wool rug, with or without a border. Orientals have gotten a bit prohibitive in price, for most people. The bad ones are terrible. Of course, if you have wood floors, that's all you need.

Anthony Hail

Word Association

Living rooms	Live in them.
Dining rooms	Get rid of them.
Family rooms	Ugh.
Studies	Fine, if you want to go and study.
Libraries	Love 'em.
Kitchens	Don't care.
Bedrooms	Not too many.
Master bedrooms	Dark, extremely comfortable and warm.
Children's rooms	Indestructible, fresh, unpretentious.
Entrance halls	They set the mood for the house. They should be vignettes of the house.
Bathrooms	I live in mine.

Shutters are expensive and tiresome. They take up room when they're open and I don't think they suit most rooms too well. They need painting and dusting continually and they don't control the light. Either they're open or closed. It's light or it's dark.

A lot of style without a lot of money would be . . .
snappy lacquered walls, beautifully tailored, crisp cotton curtains. Extremely comfortable upholstered furniture. For end tables you can get Chinese boxes, and nobody knows whether they cost a thousand or two hundred and fifty or eighty-five dollars. Lighting is one of the least expensive things we have available. Just a beautiful plant with a light on it. Nothing is quite so pleasant as the light given off by lamps. On the other hand, I just loathe those rooms that look like somebody took a shotgun and every five feet, there's a hole in the ceiling. The whole thing looks like a submarine. The light is very unflattering to women, *and* to men.

As an investment for the next years, I would collect . . .
Biedermeier and Charles X. Any furniture in that period we lump under Biedermeier. It was made all over Europe. That furniture has never ever reached the prices that any of the other periods have. It's called *bois claire*—pale wood furniture, clear and light—as opposed to dark wood. It's beautifully made. It has style.

But collectors have caught onto almost everything else. Japanese lacquer is gone. Porcelain is out of sight. Silver of any kind is crazy. You can still go to Scandinavia and, if you know what you're doing, find really beautiful antiques for perfectly acceptable prices. In many other countries they don't know what it is. It's not French and therefore they put the price down. They just look foreign, so the English don't want them and the French don't understand them.

And I don't think people have discovered yet the early-nineteenth-century American artists: Chase, Homer, Bingham. They haven't caught on to Fortuny. Not the man who made the fabrics, but the painter, his father.

Decorating likes and dislikes
I'm tired of all-white rooms. I don't want to see any more of those rooms that have sixteen different patterns. And no more of those fake French rooms we've seen copied so endlessly. They call them French Regency in Hollywood.

I like silk and leather and wool and linen and cotton. I hate rayon and nylon and vinyl kitchen floors. I don't care how soft and cushiony they are for the feet.

I like wood or brick or tile. They've all been perfectly good materials for kitchen floors through the years. There's no reason why we can't continue to use them. Travertine makes a great kitchen floor. It washes well and shows dirt just enough to make you clean it. And travertine tiles are not expensive. They come in twelve-inch squares. I hate cute kitchens with the pots hanging, and the vegetables drying that will never be used.

Banquettes are overrated. They're hard to get in and out of. A woman can't make a dignified movement sliding past other people's feet around a coffee table. If you want to get up, you have to make a big announcement.

I'm sick of indoor/outdoor rooms. I think that's silly. I like the outdoors to be outdoors and the indoors to be indoors. I don't see any reason to have them together.

I love mirrors. I think it makes the room seem larger, and you can see objects that you didn't notice.

I love chairs. I'm nuts on the subject of chairs. Sometimes they say my rooms look like a chair factory. I have twelve chairs in my living room.

If I had unlimited money to spend . . .
I would have a London apartment in Albany, like Pauline de Rothschild. That's my dream of an urban situation. I'd love to live in London, but not if I had to work to earn a living.

I'd buy an old Mediterranean sun-drenched house and then build it inside to suit myself, unless it was already right. Steel doors would come down and close off the

The living/dining room of the same residence is similarly large, but less formally conceived. Framed photographs cluster near the seventeenth-century tapestry that dominates one wall. In the foreground, velvet-covered red-lacquered chairs from Bordeaux attend an English miniature rent table. "I plan in color and texture and weights," Mr. Hail explains. "Heavy furniture here, balancing something there. I think in color, but I'm not exactly famous for vivid color."

house whenever I left. No grounds to keep.

The interior would be whitewashed and clean, with floppy, comfortable furniture. The floors would be wonderful tiles, and the beams would show.

Lacquer-red colors. I love hot colors in hot places. I want to be hot when it's hot. I like cool colors in the mountains with snow and all that. Hot colors in the sun.

Entertaining . . .
I don't think being rich makes you able to entertain, but I don't think being poor helps very much, either. The people I've known in my life who have been the most superb hosts and hostesses have been wealthy.

I like to entertain in my living room with tables brought in and plenty of help. One person helping to serve for every three guests. Fine wine and very simple but good food. A lot of it, but very few courses.

Twelve is an ideal number. Perhaps ten. All kinds of people. It's lovely to have gleaming, clean glasses, beautiful china and nice, big fat napkins. Candles. That makes me feel as though I'm at a party and having a lovely dinner.

I have music going nonstop, and so many flowers you can barely get in the room.

The worst thing about dinner parties, generally speaking, is that after dinner the men and women are separated. I also think there should be something to do after dinner. Games, charades, bridge, dancing. Something to get over the dinner and all the wine. Everyone's a little bit blah and there's an awkward period when a little organized activity comes to mind.

The worst thing is to go to somebody's house and know just who's going to be there. Not a surprise in the bunch. There's nothing better than a duchess and a whore, to make a dinner party go, you know. Sometimes it's one and the same person.

My own apartment . . .
belongs to no country. I was brought up in Europe, but I did not want my apartment to be cloyingly French or typically European. I did want it to reflect all the things that interested me. So it has a lot of Scandinavian things, a great many from my family that I've looked at ever since I can remember.

I have books in every room and magazines at hand. To me, a mantel is the focus of any room, and I have a very pretty French mantel. And I think it's a natural thing to have a mirror above a fireplace. The fire is moving, it's visually active. So I don't want another picture above it competing with the picture below.

I have a collection of very simple but very good furni-

ture. Every piece is authentic. And it's pure. Not necessarily pretentious, although some of it is a little more pretentious than I really like. I love chandeliers, and all three chandeliers are Russian.

There is an entrance hall, and one sitting room, which is about twenty-five feet square with ceilings twelve feet high. The room has very good cornices and paneling, done in the twenties and thirties when the building was constructed. All the walls are padded because it helps to insulate from sound, and I'm right on top of Nob Hill.

My bedroom walls are upholstered in yellow-striped silk that looks like linen. I used to have fur on the bed, but I tired of it. You can't lie on it and you can't lie under it.

I don't have a dining room. We eat in the living room and bring in tables to suit the number of people.

It's just a sensible apartment in the city that has worked very well for me for ten years.

The most exciting interior design is done in . . .
New York. Basically, in the United States we have most of the best of all the European ideas. They're feeding back on most of ours. In spite of their having the most wonderful houses to work with, we've managed to overcome. It's high time we forgot this business of being parvenu, and relied much more upon our own sense of style and innate sense of taste.

I don't think you can name ten great decorators in Europe today without stretching it a bit, but you can name twenty in New York in one ten-block area. As a country, we are much more conscious of decoration than they are in Europe. We're way ahead of them.

People think decorators are . . .
unstable and extravagant. The husband fears for his pocketbook. The wife fears decorators because she's afraid they're going to dictate to her. Decorators are authority figures by the very nature of the game.

*I'll tell you what I've finally figured out
about the rich, after all these years . . .*
Being advantaged and rich and powerful *is* different. Your interests are bound to be different; therefore, you seek other people who have similar interests. How can you sit down and be natural with me, talking about your private jet plane with three bathrooms and four bedrooms, when I don't even have a Piper Cub? The rich have to be continually on guard not to hurt your feelings or sound pretentious.

The problems of the rich are just different from yours and mine. One wealthy woman I know is concerned about having the house permeated with the smell of apples cooking on the stove. We have different priorities.

Original wood paneling, adorned with Italian gilt-framed
mirrors, warms the other end of the same living/dining
room—actually a double room. Offsetting the rectangularity
and deep tones of the paneling and the Chinese screen are
round tables and commodious rounded chairs, all covered in
light-toned brocade. Since the residents prefer the relaxed
comfort of this atmosphere to their formal dining room,
Mr. Hail has arranged one table accordingly.

SALLY SIRKIN LEWIS

When I first joined Architectural Digest, *in 1970, Sally was the first decorator I interviewed for the magazine, and we have been friends ever since. We lecture each other about not working so hard, totally ignoring each other's advice. However, among the celebrity clients who have taken Sally's advice are: Ali MacGraw, Joni Mitchell, Eydie Gormé, and Steve Lawrence.*

My training was in fine arts,
graphic design, and illustration . . .

in New York. Then I married and moved to Florida. I used to sit on the beach and draw. For a couple of months a woman would come by and watch me sketch. Toward the end of the summer she said, "I've been watching you draw and you have great style. Have you ever thought about decorating?" I looked up at her, and said, "What do you mean, decorating?" She said, "My house." I told her, "I wouldn't know the first thing about it. I wouldn't even know where to go." And she said, "I know all the places to go and I can get in. I just don't have the taste to do what I want." And I said, "I guess I could go with you a couple of times and help you." And so I did.

Within five or six weeks, I was making trips to New York with her and buying furniture. I remember coming back on the airplane and thinking, "Oh, my God, I just ordered thirty thousand dollars' worth of furniture for that woman. Suppose it doesn't fit." Then the panic set in. I didn't know about doing scale drawings or measuring. It was just my eye in the beginning. That was 1954 and that's how I started.

About six months later, I received a call from the University of Miami. They said, "We would like you do work in the first Panhellenic building in the United States." I said, "I think you have the wrong number." Half an hour later they called again: "If this is the Sally Sirkin who decorated interiors for so-and-so's house, you've been chosen by a sorority to do their unit at the Panhellenic building." That was the real beginning of my career. And I won an award for that work.

From that point on, I got very involved. I wanted to be a pro. So I worked for some young architects for a couple of years, to learn the basics. I would still like to be an architect, but I can't stand the thought of all those calculus courses.

Then I went to work for Henry End. He's an international designer, originally from London, who was brought to Florida to design a hotel. During the time I was with Henry End, he originated the first design center ever built in the United States, in Miami. He asked me to meet with some of the principals of the big firms in New York to try to induce them to move into his design center. I made some very important contacts and decided to go into business for myself. I moved to New York and started.

Now I've been in the field professionally for twenty-four years. It all started with the woman on the beach.

Formal training is—and is not—necessary
for an interior designer . . .

For basic talent and style, no. Technically, yes. I learned drafting, drawing, and lighting from architects. But I have interviewed many people just out of design school who are twelve to fifteen years behind the times. And they know absolutely nothing about business.

Talent is born within. Talent cannot be taught. And how can anyone teach you style? You've either got it or you haven't.

When I married again and moved to California, I continued designing. Invariably, a few clients wanted something unusual. I would tell them that we ought to shop in New York and they'd say, "Oh, I've never worked with a decorator who wanted to go to New York." It blew my mind. I could not believe it, because at that time, that's where it was all happening. Now, it's very different. But then it was terribly frustrating. I wanted to do things that were very innovative.

So I opened my own showroom. My partner is my husband, Bernie Lewis, a fabulous businessman. We called the showroom J. Robert Scott, named for our sons. At that time, everyone said Los Angeles was not ready for such a sophisticated look. They were wrong. The moment we opened, people loved it.

We've expanded three times. I am personally involved in everything.

I know how I want the showroom to look, how I want it

Describing a first glimpse of the glamorous living room in her
Beverly Hills home, Sally Sirkin Lewis says: "Suddenly this
vista appears, of a room in which all the walls are covered in
gold leaf Chinese tea paper with paintings of cranes soaring
around the walls. A large, white, curving banquette is backed
with lots of soft down pillows in tones of gray. There's a
Déco-inspired black-lacquer fireplace . . . and wonderful
rocklike tables in front of the banquette; a chaise longue and
a pair of French chairs, all covered in white." The stylized
murals, painted by Arthur Fine, were derived from a
Japanese Muromachi screen she had seen in New York.

to run. Therefore, I have had to severely limit my design work for private clients. I really don't care to do more than two or three major design jobs a year.

If I wanted to attract clients, socializing would help. But you have to be that kind of person to begin with. My work is really almost my whole life. In social encounters I'm usually bored to death, unless I'm with people in the arts. But let's face it, status is terribly important. We can all say it has nothing to do with anything, but realistically, it does. People who can afford it want to hire a designer with a reputation, so that when they mention the name, their friends won't say, "Who is that?"

I have to like the clients . . .
and they have to like me, otherwise I can't do the job. I get so terribly involved that I'm always on the job, not just in and out. We must respect each other. I don't play any games, and I say just what I feel has to be said.

During the first meeting, we discuss what they like and, more important, what they don't like. And I ask about their budget in the beginning because I can't afford to waste my time. People will say, "Oh, we haven't thought about the budget." By this time, it has become such a pat comment that I tell them, "If I told you this room was going to cost four hundred thousand dollars, you'd fall off the chair." They agree! So I say, "Then you do have *some* idea. You know you don't want to spend four hundred thousand dollars in this room."

I have to know what the scope of the job is, to start with. If I like the people and they want nice things but can't afford to do the whole house at one time, I'm the first to offer to do one complete room at a time and do it right. I don't mind that, as long as they understand the environment I'm going to do for them.

I would love the day to come when I could work only on flat design fees. But there has to be a major education of the client for that. Generally, the client pays 25 to 50 percent over the net, or wholesale, cost of the items purchased, for the services of the decorator. Let's say the job is three hundred thousand dollars for decorating, and that I'm working on a one-third percentage. I'll be making one hundred thousand dollars on that job. That's a lot of money. If a job is very large, even a one-third fee becomes ridiculous, so I sometimes do things on a sliding scale. I don't want to be underpaid, but I don't want to be overpaid, either.

*Years ago people were terribly insulted
if they were called decorators . . .*
They considered themselves interior designers. True, I do consider myself an interior designer, because I design. Half the items that go into a house, I design, because I don't like to do the same thing. They say that a decorator is one who does draperies, picks a sofa, picks a fabric.

A designer goes in from the beginning with an architect, understands everything drawn on the blueprints, everything about lighting, about structure. A designer may say, "Let's not use anything that's sold in the marketplace." They design the rugs, the fabrics, the furniture, the lighting, everything.

So much good money has been thrown away by the do-it-yourselfers. Anybody who can afford to do so should use an interior designer or a decorator. It saves money in the long run.

When I make a presentation, it's everything . . .
and it's all presented at once. You can't say, "Well, let's go out and buy the carpet today, and next month we'll pick the drapery fabric." You have to do scale, floor plans, lighting, color, furniture, fabrics, carpeting, window coverings, kitchens, bathrooms, tiles, marble, wall covering, chrome, brass, steel, at the same time.

Amateur decorators are frightened of scale . . .
Things are so ditsy. And they usually don't have any sophistication in color. They'll do what is expected, what they've seen in magazines. The "color of the month." Scale, color, and style. You'll find that most people are really a little bit insecure about those three things.

If you are doing your own house, do what's important to make the environment right for you. Don't adhere to any rules. As far as I'm concerned, there are no rules. But avoid "suites" of furniture. Don't use sets. Try to be loose. That will be more interesting than the pat, set thing. Don't look at advertisements. Pick up the good magazines. See what the good designers are doing. Look at the good magazines—which are, of course, *Architectural Digest,* sometimes *House & Garden;* sometimes you see wonderful things in *Vogue.*

*A house is not necessarily revealing.
Sometimes people don't even know who they are . . .*
so how can their house portray them? It may look like what the people *think* they are, but it's not what they *really* are. Lots of houses don't look like the people who live in them. And then there are those that do. If a somewhat weak person is doing it himself, the place is going to be wishy-washy. If he's terribly strong, that shows. If a person is weak, a good designer can make that place a beautiful pastel. The lay person might say it's weak, but it's not. It's simply a beautiful study in pastel—and that can be exquisite.

A macho guy may want a mirrored bedroom so people will think, "He's a very sexy person." It could mean exactly the opposite. He can't get it on at all. And then you can get a woman who is terribly frightened, and not only her bedroom, but her whole house, looks like a fortress. Stiff. Don't touch. That's revealing.

The master bedroom in designer Lewis's home continues the "elegant, bare look that *I* wanted to live with," she says. An enigmatic Japanese bronze Buddha—she has a passion for Japanese art—gazes toward an open-canopy bed covered in contrasting light Indian cotton and dark luxurious silk. "I do not like the typical bedroom with a quilted coverlet, gathered dust ruffle, cane headboard and painted dresser," remarks Sally Sirkin Lewis. "Pretty, pretty, and I don't like it."

A sensuous bedroom has to do with . . .
the furniture, fabrics, lighting, the lines and mood. Not round beds and red velvet walls. I like to design things for a bedroom that are soft and round, with gentle curves. Fabric is soft to the touch. If there is wood, it is silky-smooth. It can be done in beige and white and be the most sensuous, beautiful room because of the form, texture and style. I'm really thinking back to Jean Harlow, who always surrounded herself with white. But you could do a bedroom in brown and it would be sensuous if the designer created the right mood.

The best designers in the field today are men . . .
There's a reason for that, unfortunately. Most women in the field make excuses: home, children, responsibilities, personal care, whatever. I can't say I honestly believe that, because I have had children, a home, a husband, yet I have almost totally dedicated my life to my work. My husband accepted me fourteen years ago as I am. I'm sure there are people who would say the children have to suffer, but I don't believe that, either. I have fabulous relationships with my two grown children. But I do find that most women cannot or will not put in the time nor make sacrifices in their personal lives. They're not willing. It's a lot of really hard work, dedication, involvement. And what is dedication and involvement? Time. It all takes time. The male designers I know are working constantly. They work at night, all day long, and on weekends they're with clients.

Some clients can drive you crazy . . .
Recently, I suggested a client use something I thought would be fabulous in the house, so I sent it out on approval. Later, the client came in, and said, "We're going to return it. It looked too small. And too big."

Once I met with a new client who had seen work I'd done for a friend of hers. We got to the full presentation. She loved it. Budget? Exactly right. All things were beautiful. The next week she called me, "But it all happened so easily. How do I know it's right? How do I know that is the best chair to use? How do I know that is the best fabric? I would like you to take me around to all the fabric houses, the showrooms, lighting places, stone yards, marble yards, all the plumbing fixture places, so that I can be sure what I like is really what I like." I simply sat down and wrote to tell her I could not continue the job, and returned the retainer.

I had other client difficulties when I was in my twenties and early thirties, because male clients would compare their wives to me. "Look what *she* does in a day. See how successful she is. She's a great cook. She arranges flowers. And she has a husband and children, too. All you do all day is shop or play cards and tennis." The women would end up hating me.

Today a quality living room,
excluding fine art and antiques, costs . . .
thirty thousand to forty thousand dollars, including my fee. Some have been a lot more. On every job, there could be anywhere from two thousand dollars to five thousand dollars in lighting. And that's just the electrician's cost. The most expensive interior I've done was between three hundred fifty thousand and four hundred thousand dollars. The least costly was sixty thousand dollars. But that was twenty years ago.

For someone on a limited budget, I would suggest . . .
going to stores like Conran's, in New York, where they have wonderfully styled things that don't cost a lot, but have a great look. In other cities, the import stores. Go to fashion fabric shops. Buy duck fabric at boating stores for two to three dollars a yard. If you have wood floors, just bleach them out. If you have concrete floors, stain them. Work with big mops and color. Paint the walls, use lots of trees and casual furniture. Use lots of baskets. Buy the Oriental plastic-handled flatware that looks like lacquer ware. Do a draped table in the dining room if you can't afford a good table.

For a great look, buy men's suiting fabric in dark green or gray, for about three dollars a yard. Put narrow wood stripping on the walls and staple the fabric on the stripping, then cover it with flat tape and you have upholstered walls. Go to used-furniture stores, junk stores, and find pieces with good lines, and slipcover them with the same suiting fabric. Paint the floors, and perhaps stencil them. Put some big baskets around, filled with big trees. Go to a stoneyard and find an incredible hunk of stone they're about to throw away—or maybe pile two or three pieces of stone on top of one another—and have a great-looking coffee table.

Drape a table for the dining area. Buy dining chairs from a junk shop; spray-paint them for a lacquered look. Go to a glass shop and have them cut a fabulous piece of mirror in a big circle without a frame. Just hang it on the wall. Use inexpensive bamboo roll-up blinds. Stitch strips of the same suiting fabric on the draperies. Just let them hang on the floor with side panels of heavy cotton. Buy some simple surface light cylinders for the ceiling. They cost about ten or twelve dollars. Put a tall, severe cactus on the center of the stone table. Then just throw a few magazines around, some plants and you'll have style without spending a lot of money.

If you want to collect something
that is also a good investment . . .
buy Japanese art. Screens, Japanese lacquer. Buy anything that is authentic eighteenth-century Japanese. I have collected ivory and lacquer for a long time. But if I were able, I would buy every fifteenth-, sixteenth-,

seventeenth-, and eighteenth-century Japanese screen I could put my hands on. The art field today is a very smart place to put your money. Good art, whether it's contemporary or antique Japanese. You see it all over Europe today in all the big auction houses. Collectors are paying incredible prices for good art. All you have to do is look at the art market over the past ten or fifteen years. I'd certainly rather put my money in art than anything else.

We will see more creative design . . .
in the next few years. Things that are not so stereotyped. It's happening already. There will be a greater Far Eastern influence. There's a big swing back to Bauhaus and Déco. It was considered a passing fad a couple of years ago, but it's a very strong thing to come. Egyptian has had it. All of those ridiculous reproductions and tacky fabric designs. That's over.

Creatively, we're coming upon a new age of the designer. I'm seeing it in the showroom. Six years ago, students came in and asked if they could just walk through our showroom. Now they're coming back as customers. They are assistants to designers and they're the ones bringing in their bosses who didn't come into the showroom before. It's the new breed. I think the schools are becoming more aware. Universities have more interesting programs. It's a much more creative time.

My personal fantasy house would be . . .
a small palazzo with limestone floors, possibly concrete walls, and a marvelous terrace overlooking the Mediterranean. Great scale. Ceilings anywhere from twelve to eighteen feet high. Beautiful French doors almost twelve feet high. Great contemporary paintings and Japanese screens. Massive limestone pedestals of great scale. Massive sculpture. A Roman bust. Minimal furnishings. Just very large pieces of contemporary, upholstered furniture. Soft down pillows, which are probably my trademark. Everything plush, comfortable, and overscaled.

Beautiful bedrooms with balconies and four-poster draped beds. Maybe no other furniture in the room, just fabulous paintings on the walls. Almost no color. Ivory, putty, stone colors. A wonderful, almost restaurant type of kitchen, with white ceramic tile floor, black granite counters and stainless-steel cabinets. Lots of apothecary jars. Fireplaces in every room. A great library. That is a great fantasy of mine. I would love to have an old traditional library. Beautiful old boiserie paneling and miles and miles of leather-bound volumes. A beautiful fireplace and a gorgeous old Aubusson rug. Overstuffed mohair furniture intermixed with tubular steel and leather original Corbusier pieces. A stereo music system throughout the house. Beautiful gardens. If there were any plants in the house, they would be life-size trees going up to the sky. I'd feel very comfortable in that.

Sally Sirkin Lewis

Word Association

Color	Personal.
Furniture arrangement	Eclectic.
Living rooms	Entertaining.
Entrance halls	Introduction.
Bedrooms	Reflections.
Bathrooms	The most neglected.
Dining rooms	Stimulating.
Studies	Low key, comfortable.
Children's rooms	Not too serious.
Floor coverings	Backgrounds.
Ceilings	High.
Fabrics	Quality.
Wallpaper	Simple.

"It has a slightly decadent look," says Mrs. Lewis of a small,
narrow living room in Los Angeles that she appointed with
satin-pillowed sofas, a moiré screen, a shimmering gold-leaf
disk against a dark-painted wall. "I used few, but overscaled,
pieces in the room, in order to increase the feeling of space.
I believe in overscale to give a room grandeur and majesty."

People with style know how to entertain . . .
And normally one thinks that people with more money have more style. Sometimes that is the case because they have more exposure, travel more, see how things are done. Yet there are people who don't have that much money, but do have style, and entertain really well.

I like cocktail parties. Cocktail parties with adequate food, not just cold hors d'oeuvre. I find them more interesting than formal dinners. If I do have a sit-down dinner, it's for no more than twelve. I would love to give more parties than I do, but I don't have the time.

The living room is my favorite . . .
to decorate because there's so much more scope. It's usually the largest room of the house and has the most architectural detail. And because I like to use very large-scale things, there's more play in a living room to create marvelous drama.

My own house is . . .
entered through a courtyard. Then you walk into the entrance hall, which is twenty to twenty-five feet of black glass walls, ebony floors, a sisal carpet, and recessed, dramatic lighting. When you walk through, suddenly this vista appears—a room in which all the walls are covered in gold-leaf Chinese tea paper, with paintings of cranes soaring around the walls. A large, white curving banquette is backed with lots of soft down pillows in tones of gray. There's a Déco-inspired black lacquer fireplace. A chaise longue and a pair of French chairs, all covered in white. And I have a lot of lacquer.

The living room faces a view of almost the entire city of Los Angeles. I have just simple roll-up straw blinds on the windows and wonderful rocklike tables in front of the banquette.

The dining room is in the same plane and color. I have a round dining table, draped to the floor with black silk, and really lovely pale beige horn Chippendale dining room chairs and a granite lacquer buffet cabinet.

A lovely little room off the entry hall doubles as my office and a guest room. That room is all black: walls, ceiling, ebony floors—and white furniture. A minimum amount of furniture. White parchment desk, a beautiful eighteenth-century Chinese chair, white quilted draperies and the same straw roll-up blinds.

The bedroom and the study are chocolate brown and off-white. White upholstered walls, Indian cotton rugs, a brown and white geometric carpet, and mirroring on the walls, because the space is really not that large. It's a small house with a big look.

The design excitement now is . . .
in New York. A couple of years ago I would have said

Europe. Not anymore. More and more good things are happening in California. We're catching up quickly. But let's face it, New York is where all the manufacturing is done, where you have the wealth of shops, of galleries. Just by numbers, it's New York.

In Europe, they have great houses to start with. But I do find European interiors less contrived, more natural, soaring, with great scale. So many American homes are decorated-looking. Too many rules adhered to.

America is a more uptight, a pressured, society. Europeans have a more laissez-faire attitude, and it's reflected in their interiors.

People are afraid of decorators because . . .
the word encompasses everyone from the most professional down to the least professional. Unfortunately, our field has more nonprofessionals than professionals.

Decorating likes and dislikes . . .
I like white and ivory and black. And I love Chinese red. I don't like anything weak. I like clarity and strength. I hate rooms that are all lamps. I like a minimum of lamps. I can't stand typical things. For example, a French brocade on a French chair. I hate velvets that have all those markings on them. I love leather. I hate vinyl. I hate anything, really, that's synthetic. I love cotton or wool or silk. Real fabrics.

I hate contrived rooms. And terribly expected things. I love the unexpected. Like the contrast of exquisite antique French chairs on concrete floors. I would love an Aubusson rug hung as a tapestry on a limestone wall. Or a lacquered wall. I love lacquer and almost anything that's Japanese.

I do not like the typical bedroom with a quilted coverlet, gathered dust ruffle, cane headboard, and a painted dresser. Pretty, pretty, and I don't like it. Nor do I like draperies that have a draped valance at the top. For some reason, there is a mentality that feels the bedroom is supposed to look like that.

I don't think anything is supposed to look like anything. I couldn't care less about doing the right thing. I hate it when somebody says, "But is that a bedroom piece?" Or, "Would you leave that in a dining room?" Or, "Would you use that in a living room?" I don't see any geographical connotations for anything.

I find nothing wrong with coffee tables, if one must have them. I don't like them when they're too large. A six-by-seven-foot coffee table is gauche. I love glass tables because they make everything glisten. The china looks beautiful. And I love stone tables. I don't like French provincial dining tables. And I can't stand Spanish refectory tables unless they're in a magnificent

Spanish hacienda. I love square dining tables. They're wonderful for entertaining. But most people are frightened of them. I also like rectangular, round and octagonal tables. It depends on the room.

I love Art Déco furniture. But not the bastardized versions we see so much of today, nor the garish reproductions. Art Déco was such a beautiful form. The Jansen furniture, Jean-Michel Frank, Ruhlmann. They were great designers.

I can love beautiful French country furniture, *used* properly. The problem is that often these things are not used properly nor reproduced faithfully.

Until about two years ago, I didn't want to use a plant in anything I was doing, because I was so sick of rooms that were just overkilled with plants. I use plants instead of furniture. And there are rooms that require no plants at all and they should not be used. Of course, I love plants when used properly. And I love flowers used properly. I hate "arrangements"; I hate artificial flowers and trees.

Wall-to-wall carpeting is wonderful if that's what the room demands. People think they're being so *in* when they say, "I have no wall-to-wall carpeting in my house, only hardwood floors and area rugs." Those people are so *out* they don't know it.

I like a minimum of window covering, if you don't require it for privacy. If you do, use very fine bamboo blinds as opposed to sheers and overdrapes. I do like simple side hangings, panels of fabric tied on to poles. I hate drapery tracks and French-pleated draperies.

I've been in many houses, especially here in California, where people will spend thousands of dollars creating walls of magnificent paneling and carved doors. That's a ridiculous expenditure. I don't see the need for it.

I love mirrors if they're used properly. It always gets back to that. I've just done a job where I entirely mirrored a room: ceiling, walls, mirror on mirror. It was a tiny powder room and I wanted to enlarge it.

Fireplaces are important. And if the room dictates using a furniture grouping around the fireplace, why fight it? Sometimes it is the only answer. I prefer something unusual over the fireplace. A fabulous big Buddha head or a collection of large-scale porcelain.

I love accessories, but I cannot stand clutter. An object can take the place of furniture. Every wall does *not* need a piece of furniture. I love to leave walls just bare or use a wonderful object on a pedestal.

I love quality. I love understatement. I love simplicity. I hate showing off.

It's nicer to work with people
who have money because . . .
it makes the job easier, but if I don't like the people, I don't care how much money they have. I will not work with them.

"When I first saw Joni Mitchell's bedroom," Sally Sirkin
Lewis recalls, "the walls were white and the only furniture in
it was her four-poster bed. The room looked like a bowling
alley. Joni said, 'I want things pure and simple.' And I said,
'Forget pure and simple. Green walls. You have to trust
me.'" The designer created voluptuous, overscale upholstered
pieces and covered them in velvet to match the forest-toned
walls. "I like to design things for a bedroom that are soft
and round with gentle curves," she explains.

LOYD-PAXTON

Loyd Taylor and Paxton Gremillion are the best interior decorators I've seen in Texas so far. And their "trade only" antique shop in Dallas is a knockout. People fly in from Mexico and from almost every part of the United States to see what they have in store. Their clients are celebrities in business and finance; oilmen, cattle barons, industrialists, political figures. When Loyd's and Paxton's Dallas condominium appeared in Architectural Digest, *it stunned decorators in all parts of the world, who, mistakenly, had not associated Dallas with such a high degree of design sophistication.*

We had no exposure to any visual legacy . . .
But we had always been interested in interior design. After college, we moved to Dallas and decided to become antique dealers.

It was one of those hot Dallas summers and we decided to go through the things we had both collected and begin by selling things from our apartment. Then we found a location for our shop and acquired a few good things. The opera singer Mary McCormick had moved back from Italy with some fantastic antiques. She asked us to dispose of her collection. So with our choice bits and pieces and her amazing things, we opened the original Loyd-Paxton shop in 1960.

People would come in, realize that we had style, and a few would ask us to help them decorate. Then our dear friend Martha Hyder discovered us. She was our first important client.

If you don't have formal design training . . .
learn for yourself. Study on your own. We have read and studied more than probably 99 percent of the designers in this country. There are decorators who don't know anything about classic architecture or classic furniture. Even if you're going to do a contemporary room, you must have the background of classics for balance, color, and form. They all work together.

We only take work that excites us . . .
Of course, decorating is so expensive you need lots of money to do something truly exciting. Two really special jobs each year are all we can do thoroughly.

We design everything. When people want your design, they want you. When you delegate, they're not getting your work. We have nine employees and they all help us in one way or another. But not in design.

People tell you they want something,
but that isn't necessarily what they want . . .
A lady came into the shop recently and said she was looking for an English breakfront. She saw a Venetian cabinet, and said, "That's exactly what I want."

You have to use psychology—let people tell you what they want, and then anaylze what they *really* want.

We discuss money right away . . .
with the husband and wife. You cannot allow disagreements over money, although we loathe discussing it.

We work on an hourly fee of fifty dollars. And the client pays the cost of the merchandise plus 30 percent. They see every invoice we pay and all of our canceled checks.

Our clients are offended at the word "contract." All of our agreements are verbal. If, at any point, either party no longer feels comfortable, we can just call it off.

Decorators just furnish rooms . . .
Designers create beyond just putting things in a room. They design backgrounds and furniture. They create an ambience. But we like the word *decorator,* ourselves.

Whatever we're called, we're needed for scale and balance. It takes a trained eye. And most people don't have creative ability or knowledge about decoration. Many don't have the time. They want to go to a professional. A good decorator also saves people money.

We think a great deal
about the people when we begin . . .
an interior. And a great deal about where *our* heads are. Then it just develops. We put it on paper and start thinking what would look fabulous. But showing preliminary floor plans to clients can be very confusing to them. Instead, we generally say, "We want to find special things for you. And we will plan so you will have a livable situation until we find these special things."

Whatever people buy, it should be *real*. Real wood. If it's Lucite, it should have an obvious Lucite shape. Nothing that's fake. If it's antique, fine. If it's new, fine. But it should be what it is.

Today you could spend fifty thousand on one room with good furniture. That would not include antiques.

People decorating their own apartment on a small budget . . .
should plan with the idea of doing something else later with whatever they buy. Stick to very simple lines, simple fabrics. A very simple, basic background. Then go to thrift shops and find a sofa that can be re-covered.

Neutral colors are best. Ivory or gray. An absence of color gives you a great deal of freedom. That's especially true of fabrics. You can change a room very easily by repainting. It's costly to change a room by constantly slipcovering and reupholstering.

A good investment now . . .
would be anything of quality. I'm sure there's something coming out of the forties and fifties period. The creations of the nineteenth century were disdained by people who were able to collect eighteenth century or earlier. The further you move away from a period, the greater your perspective and appreciation becomes.

People are frightened that decorators will . . .
give the wrong image of them. The home is such a personal part of your life, a reflection of you.

If we could choose a client, it would be . . .
Catherine the Great. She was passionate but intelligent and discerning in her taste regarding decoration.

Decorating over the next few years will see . . .
more people of extreme wealth going into condominium living. They will want fewer things. But very, very special things. We have passed through an era in which people found novelty in barrenness, a stark interior, a stark room. And people are bored with it. You will see a sudden upsurge in obtaining things people feel will be increasingly scarce. Consequently, people ask for silk, natural fibers, fine furniture, and beautiful woods.

If we had all the money in the world to spend on a home . . .
it would be right here in Dallas. We would probably do a very extravagant penthouse and buy things that have always been our dream to own. Important eighteenth-century French and great Georgian furniture. Oriental porcelains, sculpture, precious objects. Extraordinary, precious things to be used in everyday living. Fabulous mosaic floors of semiprecious stones.

We live in Dallas in a high-rise apartment with a terrace, a good view and a wonderful library . . .
The furniture is eighteenth- and nineteenth-century French, with two pieces of eighteenth-century English. And one Russian table. The flooring is black marble. There are no curtains. In fact, there is very little fabric in the apartment. The woodwork is black lacquer, and there are mirrors everywhere, to bring light into the apartment and make it look larger than it is. We like the salon idea in a room, where people pull chairs up to a central round table, rather than scattered seating. People in a circle talk and make a unit.

When we put the apartment together, we placed things where they would look best and used them there. We didn't say, "Where are we going to eat?"

When you entertain, you've got to do it small or you've got to do it big . . .
We've always liked fourteen. We use two tables and we each sit at one. A seated dinner party is, without a doubt, the most elegant way you can entertain. But it is also the most extravagant and the most difficult. It is easier for us to give a party for eighty than for fourteen. And it costs just about the same. However, cocktail parties are terrible if everybody is able to sit down.

They have to stand up. So we invite more than the apartment can comfortably accommodate. It forces people to move.

We also invite lots of people who don't know each other. That makes for conversation. We also like to invite out-

The designers' cozy library, slipcovered for summer in cool French checked cotton, contains an array of books pertaining to art, decoration and antiques; interspersed objets d'art include a nineteenth-century Russian silver and gold building-shaped clock. The Sèvres bust of Napoleon is dated 1805, the Jean-Charles Delafosse engravings were published in 1768. "Many duties and responsibilities are assumed when you become the caretaker or keeper of art, be it a great painting, a superb chair, an exquisite box," the designers contend. "It is a burdening task to see that the piece is restored expertly, then preserved and kept safe."

of-town people. We never have just local parties with local people. And we try to have live music, usually a harp and a flute. Music is vital; even if it's records. We start with very quiet music, then build up. When people wear out, the music keeps going.

Decorating likes and dislikes . . .
Pattern, pattern, pattern is very much out. And rooms with tons of plants and trees have become very ordinary. The cluttered look is out. We never want to look at another piece of African art. The craft movement is boring. And nostalgia drives us insane.

Lucite is fabulous, but it's been worked to death. We like to use glove leather whenever possible.

What ruins a great concept or trend is the proliferation of the bad knock-offs. Even a simple thing like malachite, which is a sought-after gemstone. But you see so much that's fake, when you do see the real thing, the impact is gone.

We like permanent surfaces like hardwood floors, marble, slate. Is there anything worse than seeing a gorgeous Louis XV leg disappear into a thick carpet?

Reproduction furniture is dreadful. Buy something for what it is. And it has to be the real thing. If it's new, buy a new design.

We dislike houses where every room has a different color or fabric, or pattern, or feeling. The boredom of sameness is preferable to the exhaustion of passing from one completely different room into another. We are not for shock interiors.

Fabric on walls is an excellent solution to decorating a space that has absolutely no character. But padded walls are just awful. Fabric should be applied directly on the wall surface. We used to be extraordinarily anti-wallpaper. But now we like good handprinted or woven wallpaper. Chinese wallpaper can be very exciting. And, just lately, we've become very interested in glass surfaces—glass that is textured to distort vision intentionally. It's another attachment to fantasy.

We like a round dining table or an extreme oval, because it makes everybody face each other. It should seat a maximum of eight people. We have never cared for coffee tables. But sometimes they're absolutely necessary so you can put down a drink or an ashtray. We prefer tea table height.

We have never cared for a sofa pushed against a wall. Furniture is better out in a room. It brings the people out, too. Rooms are for people. If you have things lined up, the people line up.

There's nothing worse than a fake fireplace. Fireplaces in themselves are a fabulous start for a room. It's very easy for the designer, because a fireplace in a room is obviously one of the most important features—it provides a central point to work from. It is difficult to work in a room where there is no focus to draw your attention.

Interior design in the East is . . .
less important than ever before. Designers are scattered throughout the world now, and communication is so quick. It used to take years for styles or trends to come from New York to Texas; from Paris to New York. It's not like that anymore.

Now good things and bad things are done everywhere. There are some horrible things being done in Paris and London. And there are fabulous things being done in the Southwest, some of the best architecture anywhere. And exciting things are being done in South America and the Orient.

There is a largeness about California decoration. A less restricted feeling on the West Coast than on the East Coast. But in the East, people are retreating into smaller and smaller apartments. You lose the luxury of the large residence. Whereas in Texas and on the West Coast, you can still do big things occasionally.

Someone trying to get started in decorating today . . .
should try to back this up with education. A strong, basic knowledge of architecture would be phenomenally important. Do something on your own to get recognition. Decorate your own apartment or a friend's.

The most exciting part of the house is . . .
the entry. It should make a statement of what the entire house is going to be like. It is an introduction, but never a full disclosure. The entry should have a starkness about it, a somewhat impersonal look, because it is a stopping point as much as a passageway. We like mirrors, consoles, pairs, symmetry. Simplicity, with something very strong, such as a piece of sculpture, a piece of furniture or a fabulous painting. And definitely hard-surface flooring: marble, stone, brick. A carpeted floor in the entry is far too personal, too soft.

We like mood lighting, a change from the outside. And we like the entry hall a little smaller in scale. Then when you walk into the interior, you have a change. We also prefer an entry hall without windows, so that it becomes a total transition area.

There is no great reason for plants in entrance halls, but there must be fresh flowers. And we love a center table, a place for packages and mail.

Sometimes the rich seem to envy other people . . .
And some would prefer a lot more freedom and a lot less responsibility.

A rich harmony of color, pattern, and texture characterizes the carefully organized eclectic mélange that fills the Hyder residence in Fort Worth, Texas. "Our dear friend Martha Hyder discovered us," the designers recall. "She was our first important client." The Hyders, they explain, are avid and confident collectors, who avoid a static environment: "Every two or three months things get moved around." In this view of the living room, an eighteenth-century English chinoiserie leather screen and a Tabriz rug combine with Régence fauteuils, eighteenth-century Hungarian embroidered silk draping the sofa, and an Oskar Kokoschka painting. "We've seen too many homes that looked as though the owners were scared to move an ashtray after the designers left."

BILLY McCARTY

The tall, articulate American from Florida has worked in London for some sixteen years now, commuting to the United States for major design jobs. His manner and appearance have naturally been influenced by his long residence in England. However, the year of association he recently completed with the New York branch of Paris antiquaires Didier Aaron has stimulated the homing instinct; he is delighted that design projects in Palm Beach, New York, Los Angeles, and Houston will keep him in America for a considerable time.

*I live in London, was born
in Miami, Florida, and reared in the Far East . . .*
My father was an architect, among other things, and he was also in the Air Force Reserve. I've been interested in design, my mother says, since I was about two and a half, when I started criticizing her clothes and the arrangement of my room. I'm stuck with decorating. I'm too dumb to do anything else.

I went to the University of Pennsylvania, where I studied architecture and dropped out, way before it was fashionable. It just didn't work for me. I didn't finish architectural school because I ran out of money and sanity. Also, I could not achieve what I wished in an academic situation. One did not have the technical facilities. It was all trying to figure out *how* to build, rather than getting on with designing pretty projects.

Lou Kahn took a certain interest in my work. He stepped in because he had been warned that I was going to jury with an incomplete project, which was all I ever presented. I was not very well liked by the entire faculty, by then. The students understood my problem. Charles Gwathmey was in my class, and Kahn told everyone, in his funny wisdom, that Charlie and I would be the first two to be published. He said, "In every class there is the very good student and the very bad student." I told him, "We know that row of assignments, then." I wasn't much of a student. I was out by the second year.

Next I studied Art History at the Barnes Foundation. After that, I worked with the Philadelphia City Planning Commission on Center City Redevelopment and then came to New York and worked for Harris and Abramovitz on Lincoln Center and the UN Plaza Apartments as a draftsman/designer, even though I had not finished school with a degree in architecture. That was one of my embarrassments. I could draw well and I seemed to know how people should live. I was being paid more than five of my classmates at Harris and Abramovitz who had degrees.

In January of 1963 I met David Hicks, who was looking for an assistant. He offered me a year's contract, so I worked with him in London for about two years, then with another two firms for two years and finally opened up on my own in 1968. I like England, but this past year in New York as decorator-in-residence with Didier Aaron has made me realize that I want to spend more time in the United States.

*There are people who have employed so many
decorators they think they're decorators themselves . . .*
but in the long run, formal education is necessary. The day of the gentleman or lady decorator is over. Costs are too high. I'm working on an interior in New York that will probably cost several million dollars. People like that are not going to go to unqualified designers who will paint it pink and say it's lovely.

Of course, that job is hardly typical. I average about fifteen jobs per year and try to break it down to about one-third commercial, one-third residential, and one-third product—product being carpets, fabrics, wallpaper, furniture. I had a staff of fifteen, but got rid of them all because I discovered I was doing a lot of work I didn't like, just because I had to meet a payroll. If I got rid of the payroll, I could do work I liked. So I slammed the door shut in 1972 and went completely on my own, with a part-time secretary and one assistant who's efficient and purely administrative, thank God.

I met my first major client at a dinner party . . .
at David Hicks's. It was a job he didn't want to do, and I got on very well with the client, who happened to be a Rothschild. Most of my clients are rich, but they want value for their money. I don't socialize to get clients. I've been fortunate enough not to have to, although it probably does help. But I am not a social animal by nature. After my third debutante season in three countries, I decided that it was the same show every time and that was not my future.

The first step with a new client is to . . .
decide whether or not there is a common meeting

"It had to be a house of the times," says Billy McCarty of the London terrace house he transformed for Mr. and Mrs. Stuart Lyons and their three small children. "They wanted a very pretty, relaxed home." A casual yet sophisticated interplay of color and pattern enlivens the drawing room, encouraging an inviting country house look. "I did have almost everything specially made," the designer adds, "such as the rug, the fringes, the pelmets." He used a checked linen to cover sofas and tables. "Because I used a handwoven fabric and had it quilted for extra body, silk brocade would probably have been cheaper," he admits. "But this gingham gave just the right informal look. Nothing else was right."

ground. If the chemistry is not right, there is no point. There are many other decorators who are every bit as good as I am. I usually try to encourage the people who come to me to see one or two other decorators. You have to be sure of each other. It's almost like a marriage. You get involved in things like, do you share a bedroom? Which side of the bed do you sleep on? Who answers the phone? Do you entertain nonstop or occasionally, or do you never wish to see anyone else in your life? Without a rapport that allows this sort of interaction, I can't work for the client.

I try to meet husband and wife together, right from the beginning, and involve both of them in the project. I have a fairly select clientele. It would seem they have to be rich, intelligent, and have taste.

Financially, it's a sliding scale . . .
If I'm paid five hundred dollars a day plus expenses, my commission is going to be much smaller. That may be because the client has access to sources, but wishes me to pull it all together. If I work on an almost retail basis because the client does not wish to be *that* involved in purchasing, then the hourly fee goes down.

The difference between an interior designer and a decorator is almost a seasonal thing . . .
If an awful lot of people who are doing work that I do *not* admire call themselves interior designers, I become a decorator. If people start calling themselves decorators and I don't admire their work, I become a designer.

Whatever the label, the major thing is editing and problem-solving. You must have perspective. And I can also get a finish that most people, not in the business, cannot. And I have access to sources, craftsmen, and people like that.

You always aim for the stars and settle for the earth.

Most people doing their homes don't think enough . . .
Before you do anything, you've got to think out every implication of every decision. Then put it all together.

People who are not professionals usually buy pieces of furniture that don't actually fit into the room. Or find three chairs they think are absolutely marvelous, then discover they'd like to seat eight people.

Think about how you're going to live in the space. What do you already have that you can use? What have you not got? What do you hate? What must you keep because the great-aunt who's going to leave you all the money has given it to you? If that's so, make space for whatever it is. If you like the clients, 90 percent of the time you can develop a rapport with their objects.

Good taste is timeless but . . .
there are always questions of what is fashion, style, and taste. A room that is fashionable will not survive that well. Things that tend to be very fashionable go out very quickly. They look tired.

You can teach a client taste, but I do not think you can teach style. Style is personal. That is what style is about. It is a personal distillation of how you want to live.

The major problem is pretension. Things that are inappropriate for the space, the person, the climate.

Of course, all designers have a certain style, and a client would come to them because they feel comfortable or interested in that. But within that framework, the home should be adapted to the client's own personal needs. I feel very strongly that the place a person lives in should be a part of his being. Bedrooms, especially.

I've had several husbands ring me up and say, "Life was never so great as it has been since we moved into the bedroom. . . ."
It should be a place where you shut the door and feel totally cut off from the hassles of life.

The other big thing is a comfortable bed. I insist that the first thing my clients buy is a good bed. It's one of my early questions, "Are you comfortable in your bed?"

Mr. McCarty describes the library of the same London terrace house: "That's an eighteenth-century pine room that we stuck in." Rich yet muted color—in leather, fabrics, custom carpet, and books—enhances the warmly paneled background. "Color has to be more subtle in England," says the designer. "Sharp, clear color just doesn't work with this light." A Regency mahogany bookcase/secretary, set in an alcove, receives the light passing through a nearby window.

Casual garden bouquets in straw baskets relax the balanced
formality of the family dining room in the Lyons residence.
George III chairs surround a table made from old mahogany.
"I prefer that my clients get a very good reproduction table,
because antique dining tables are terribly expensive and they
get bashed to pieces," explains Mr. McCarty. Fabric in an
early Regency country design covers the walls in bordered
sections that give a feeling of paneling. Swagged and fringed
draperies conceal French doors to the garden. "I do some
of the most elaborate curtains in the world," the designer
contends. "Nine hundred miles of fringe and guimpe."

My fantasy house would be an orangery by the sea . . .
with a large saltwater swimming pool. Also, a pied-à-terre in New York and a flat in London.

The orangery by the sea would be the first place I would build, but I would engage an architect to design it. I would not design it myself. It would be Neo-Classical within contemporary terms.

In decorating, we're going . . .
Neo-Classical.

I went to an opening at the Metropolitan Museum recently, and my suspicion that everything was over by 1927 was well confirmed. Things were so beautiful, and one longs for some designers to actually get out clothes like that again.

*The only mistake people can make
when they entertain is . . .*
to be uncomfortable. You can't receive unless you're comfortable in your own home. I've seen clients go through all sorts of transmutations between being married, then divorced, then remarried, and it's a very different scenario; how they receive as a married couple, then alone, wishing to retain a certain standing, not particularly interested in getting remarried. Then when they do remarry, it again is a unit thing, where there are two personalities receiving. The only mistake is to be uncomfortable in the house you live in.

I like to decorate bedrooms and bathrooms best . . .
because if clients are happy in their bedroom and in their bathroom, they get a feeling of being well sorted, like if all the closets are well organized. That is one of the questions that drive my clients to distraction: "How many pairs of shoes do you have? Do you like your handbags over your shoes?" If you can give people a skeletal system so they can dress, bathe, sleep, or whatever else they wish to do, in comfort, then you can begin to cope with the rest of their lives. After that, the kitchen. Then you can get on with everything else. The major things are the very personal spaces. If those work, you can have orange crates and a bunch of flowers.

My own house in London is . . .
salubriously situated in Fulham between the gasworks and the football ground. It's a four-floor house with a studio in the back and a roof garden over the studio. I absolutely adore the house and will soon start doing it up. It was built in 1850 and renovated by other people. Of course, all my clients are slightly livid because I moved into a house that required nothing done to it. They asked me, "Why should you not suffer what we had to suffer?" And I said, "I don't have the time."

Design excitement is everywhere, but it is limited . . .
Excitement is wherever there is a good designer with a good client. You can't say it is East Coast or West Coast. There are no schools anymore. There are no movements. One thing that certainly has happened, and I think it's happening more and more, is the camaraderie now between designers, which I don't think existed before. That means decorating has actually grown into a real profession. You can't be jealous of somebody whose work is very, very fine. You may see something and say, "Ouch, isn't that marvelous! I wish I'd done it." But it's an "ouch" of respect, rather than of jealousy. If there is any news, it is this.

European interiors for the most part are less fashion-conscious. Certainly in England, people tend to decorate *once* and then it's a fifteen- or twenty-year period until the next generation takes over the space or they move. Most European clients are much more committed to the project as a statement of how they wish to live for a very long period of time. They are not as subject to fashion as in the United States. America decorates too much.

The rich are different because . . .
they have greater choice and less responsibility on an immediate level. Hemingway was right—the rich have more money, but they are still human beings, for the most part. Some more, some less.

MONGIARDINO

Architect and interior decorator Lorenzo Mongiardino
headquarters in Italy, and although he works in the United States
on major jobs, he speaks very little English. My friend and
colleague, Rome-based writer Adrian Cook, conducted the
interview for me in Italian and then translated the voluble interior
designer's words. In any language, it's not the first time
Mongiardino has been interviewed. His work has appeared in
international magazines for many years.

I was born in Genoa and studied at the Technical Institute in Milan . . .

Later, I finished my degree in architecture at the Polytechnic, where I also studied design. I developed an interest in decorating almost immediately after the war. I had already done a few small things when I was at the university, toward the end of the war, but it obviously was not a good time to be starting out. As soon as the war ended, I moved to Milan and began to take an interest in decoration, and to some extent, in construction.

I am not so sure that such schools as there are today are all that useful for a professional decorating career . . .

At the same time, I think it is rather difficult to make a livelihood of decoration without good preparation. I am not, of course, talking only about construction, but decoration. I haven't much faith in decoration without a good structural background. Without structure, you can't have a house. Doors, floors, ceilings, etc., are architecture. I don't believe that you can miraculously save an ugly house with a couple of divans and one or two colors. The house will remain ugly, and whatever you try to do can't change it much.

I accept very few jobs . . .

because according to the way I work, interiors can't be turned out in series. Every job is a different problem to be solved. Generally I do not accept more than two or three jobs a year. Even then they often take longer than the estimated time, and one job will overlap another.

There are only two people on my staff when I am working in Milan. For the jobs I do outside Milan, in London, for instance, I take on free-lance assistants, whom I sign on for that period of time. As a rule, I have two assistants stationed in Milan and two who travel. I don't want to increase my staff, because I don't want to extend my work: I like to follow each job very closely.

I cannot and will not accept too much work. I can't get through it if I have too much. Of course I could with a larger staff but I don't want that. For me, my work is a matter of collaboration. My assistants, artisans, upholsterers and painters are all people who have the same importance on the job as I have myself. The work results from this staff whom I have chosen and can trust. I know that I can trust them to work in *my* way, even if I am not there. I see no point in giving orders for work to be done mechanically by various people who don't even know one another.

My first important client arose from a small job I did at Portofino. A certain person saw the house, liked it and asked me to do a rather important job for him. He was an art collector and owned some very important works.

Today, clients almost always contact me because they have seen some of my work and liked it.

I am very interested in doing houses for people I enjoy being with. It is very hard for me to do a house for someone I do not like.

When I first meet with new clients . . .

it is usually in my office, or I go to see their house. They usually tell me they are desperate, that they have a house they can't live in. Then I say quite frankly, "If you want my advice, you'll start out from scratch again." Or else I say, "You have a house that can be fixed up." Each case is different.

One of the things I don't see eye to eye on with some of my colleagues is that they immediately put things down on paper. I wait for a while before I put anything on paper. I'm not interested in doing a house until I see what kind of a person the client is, the place and its possibilities. I can't just get to work straight off.

No matter where I work in the world, Milan is my base. I like it because it is a place where I can start out from. However, I don't at all prefer Milan to anywhere else in the world. I travel a lot. When I'm in Milan a long time, I get easily fed up and see all its defects. I like London very much, and enjoy being there. But I don't think I'll ever leave Italy, for better or worse, because this is where my friends are.

The free-flowing living room of a romantic villa in Positano
reflects the historical Saracen influence of its location on the
rocky Amalfi coast: the arches and the whiteness reinforce
the traditional North African atmosphere of buildings in this
region. Says Lorenzo Mongiardino: "When I find a piece of
extraordinarily beautiful architecture that has to be brought
back to life, the life of today, then I am deeply involved."
To augment the Mediterranean seaside mood, there are
gilded grotto chairs and shells within huge shells.

A view of an alcove of the same living room focuses on Signor Mongiardino's use of a combination of Italian and Islamic appointments against a background of updated geographical tradition. Globed chandeliers, suspended from wide, banquette-filled arches, have a Neapolitan flavor, while shimmering mother-of-pearl furnishings and gleaming mirrored fabric endow the Near Eastern idiom. Handmade glazed tiles, a regional specialty, reflect the clear Positano light and enforce the glistening whiteness of the design.

Financially, jobs done on an Italian basis are . . .
on the percentage we earn on the work, the normal percentage established by the architects' union. I never go beyond this. I think these basic percentages are much higher in America, so it would be better not to mention it. Usually, we take 14, 15, 16, 18 percent, or even 10 percent when the job is a very big one. However, according to proper Italian usage, we should never take—and I certainly never do—percentages from people we give work to, though I know there are people who take a percentage from the plasterer, the carpenter, the upholsterer. But then probably the fee is very low and the percentage taken from the others very high.

The difference between a designer and decorator is . . .
just a matter of words. Words that have come and gone out of fashion. I am against all that. Ultimately, there is only one person—the person who does the house. I don't think the house or the decoration is achieved by simply knocking down a wall. I don't think you can do things separately. The reason I don't design furniture is that if I made a table lamp, it would have to be for one particular table in one particular house.

People call in an interior decorator because they are not capable of doing the job themselves. If they were, they would probably get better results on their own . . .
I don't want to sound snide, but there are times when I see a decorated house and think how much better it would have been if the father of the family had done the whole thing on his own. This is an example of our civilization. Sometimes, when we call in the decorator, we have to have the house "done" down to the ashtrays. Now these things are not the interior designer's job at all, but unfortunately, a certain type of person has such a tendency to go wrong that we are obligated to supply even the ashtrays. Apart from this, the interior designer should give a room proportion, color, a determining element. Then the client can put up the painting he likes; preferably when the interior decorator has gone.

I always start out with a precise vision of the house . . .
I start with plans, but to my mind there is no such thing as a plan of something I've never seen. For example, I walk into a room and I see what is to be done. I may decide the wall has to come down, or have a niche put in. Or bookshelves. And that triggers the scheme: the design. Then I usually make a sketch, to have an idea of what this house has to offer. Then, out of this, I start on the plans. I don't do the renderings myself. I simply sketch it out and hand it over to a talented group of painters. They usually do the decorative painting work in the house. Then I explain how I want the various elements arranged, and they do the renderings. This gives me a much clearer view of the job beforehand.

One mistake people make when doing their own houses as amateur decorators is . . .
not understanding what a house can give. For instance, somebody sees a house I have done in Paris. He comes to Milan, finds a house with different proportions, different lighting, and tells me to copy it. Ridiculously wrong.

In this case, you have to do another house with another type of decoration and with different things. Also, most people can't foresee how the whole thing will look when it is finished.

If you are decorating your own house, see what you can do with what you already have. Don't ask for too much. You must look at your house with common sense. When you have settled on a certain style or theme, stick to it. Don't do one room one way, and another completely different. Create an overall ambience.

Good taste is a constant factor,
present throughout all periods. Although . . .
there are periods that might have been vulgarly ostentatious, and other periods less so. But even in so-called tasteless periods, there are some very fine things. When a person firmly believes in what he is doing, I think he avoids bad taste. It may be overloaded, or a style that somebody else doesn't like, but I don't believe you can call it bad taste.

A house tells us about the people
who live in it, and it should . . .
tell us more than it does. We decorators are corrupters, in a sense. If there isn't a certain sensibility, the decorator is wrong, because he imposes something that isn't true. You must start with the person, before you do the house, to achieve any sort of integrity.

You can do a beautiful house for a variety artist, and a beautiful house for a chemical engineer. But of course they will be two completely different houses. The architect, the decorator, has to take this into consideration. And if he doesn't, I'm afraid he is a bad decorator.

The greatest thing is the possibility of doing a house that can be more decorative, or more "high society," or more frivolous, or more sporty, or more intellectual. It is absolutely pointless to have acres of bookcases if the person doesn't read. Or a fireplace that nobody ever lights. These, I think, are all big mistakes.

A room the house is centered on becomes the heart of the house. It could be a bedroom or a study. But there is always one room that is more important than the others. Everything is an indication of sexual life, but I don't think a bedroom is revealing in any specific way. A drawing room or any other room can be just as revealing. If a person's sexuality functions, he or she doesn't need a sexy bedroom.

If I really get on with clients, I want to be on the most intimate terms possible . . .
If we don't get on, I find myself in the position of wanting to minimize the clients and impose something of my own. That isn't what I like to do. But if they are crashing bores, I want to see them as little as possible. If they aren't, I want to see lots of them. Of course, by intimacy, I don't mean sexual intimacy. That is the sort of thing that happens to doctors, no?

Contact with my clients is always interesting, and each one is different, which means I can do different houses. There are some who want to spend unbelievable sums on a wall-to-wall carpet and nothing on a chair. There are some who are shockingly cheap about the carpet, and even if it is a fourth-rate one, they feel they have been overcharged for it; then they will spend millions and millions of lira on an armchair.

People should learn to do their own houses . . .
If a house has been built in a determined form by an architect—either by a good architect of an antique period, if the house is old; or a modern architect, who is every bit as good—often there is no reason why a person can't do the house for himself; just as people did in all ages past, without having the architect or the decorator hanging around them like wet nurses. But the person must develop a personal taste, a personal culture. I feel that the personality of the decorator should hold back.

You want a simple approach, without relying too much on established procedures and objects. There are houses that are stylistically acceptable but unpleasant to live in. There are houses with defects, not architecturally sound, but warm perhaps, which can be very pleasant to live in. When you feel the personality of the person who lives there, then the house is warm and "done" by that person, even if there has been a designer at hand. The house lives.

Today there are possibilities of doing something nice with very little money . . .
I would suggest materials from the Far East, which are not expensive. You can do a lot by putting old things together very casually as young people do in their rooms. I much prefer that to a would-be modern décor, which is expensive and is generally pretentious and uncomfortable. Bare bookshelves instead of bookcases, and all that. Anything rational, in the real sense. You need certain things and use them. A table that is two trestles with a board on top. This sort of house, which has been handed down from the thirties, seems to me much more pleasurable than the so-called luxury modern, which I don't like it all.

The one thing I can't stand is "rich modern," because it is a contradiction. People in the past did things much better than we do now. I'd rather buy a beautiful old armchair than a modern armchair. Or a good "frau" armchair, which is much more comfortable than a Mies van der Rohe chair, which is a good design, but particularly uncomfortable.

My own mistakes are more a sum total of many, not just one big one . . .
Attempting to do something in a house that hasn't suited the house. The idea of remaking a thing that came off in house X, in place X, and trying to repeat it in house Y for Mr. Y. This is always a mistake. I often notice this type of error in the work of decorators. Repetition is always a fault. And saying, "I did that in Paris and it was a success. Now I will do it in London." The house that you do in Capri cannot be the same as the one that you do in Milan.

Many people say that because I have done quite a few houses in a mid-nineteenth-century style, it is my period . . .
That isn't quite true. Once a problem arises, I am interested in referring to any period at all to solve it. There are periods I prefer—Italian things, parts of the seventeenth century, and the sixteenth, of course.

I begin by creating an atmosphere in a house; or reconstruct, revitalize an old house, centuries old perhaps. Or else give character to a house that hasn't got any.

Generally, I prefer fine old houses that have been run down or neglected. Some houses in Rome, for example. When I find a piece of extraordinarily beautiful architecture that has to be brought back to life, the life of today, then I am deeply involved. It is the idea of saving the life of things that are beautiful and could easily die.

In the next five or ten years there will be fewer and fewer decorators . . .
With inflation, there will be no need to call in a decorator to do two rooms. I feel that every house I do is going to be my last. Then another appears. But I don't want to make predictions. People say there will be no more important houses. Then, a very important house of an art collector with a magnificent collection turns up.

I love my house, but not to the point of being a "prisoner of love" . . .
My house is something of a free experiment without having a client who butts in. Craftsmanship interests me most in interior design, and in Italy there are still many quite extraordinary craftsmen—painters, men who do decoration in painted marble, upholstery, and so forth. I made my house by experimenting with them all. A few conjuring tricks to transform a certain area. But you must have exceptional workers. These workers are the

people I have been most grateful to in my life. They may be, in a way, lucky to have me to induce such beautiful work; but I am much luckier, because without them I could not possibly do the work I do. Usually, if I accept work outside Italy, I take them along with me. The more I have my own people working with me, the more I like the house, and the more I enjoy doing it.

I am not really a designer . . .
I am a creator of *ambience* in houses; an architect, scenographer, but not a designer. And I'm not up on what is going on in design. I don't have interior designers as friends, and I don't follow it. I do the jobs I have been asked to do. But I spend my free time with literary people and men in other professions. I don't even follow the magazines on reviews of design.

Today, many more people
have accepted modern design than before, but . . .
by now, it has lost its value, just as it has lost its newness. It strikes me that there is a return to many traditional things. I'm not talking about fashions, because all that can be rather frivolous. But I wouldn't call this a time when the modern style arouses great interest. Young people, for example, haven't much time for it. I know quite a few young people who are delighted to live surrounded not only by objects, but also by upholstery, which is not a bit modern. They like going to galleries to see seventeenth- and eighteenth-century painting, and skip the Kandinskys and Mirós. Actually, the generation who love modern art and design are the people today in their sixties, which is as it should be. It was their revolution. I've been amused to see young people stand before some extremely modern architecture, and say, "That is the architecture of Grandma's day."

I have not seen many interesting
things in American decoration . . .
but I don't know it well enough. I haven't seen enough. I have seen things in magazines by designers full of talent and with a great stylistic freedom. Occasionally they seem to lack a tight control. Sometimes they are overinfluenced by cute ideas and I think they should watch out for that. You should create homes based, not on cute ideas, but on sound architectural values from the Parthenon on, passed down through the ages.

I do not consider the rich as a class but as a . . .
varying collection of individuals, as different from each other as people on any other economic level. Luckily, my own relations with the super-rich have almost always been interesting and very happy. Otherwise, the work I've done for them would not have given me, or them, the satisfaction it has.

For the entrance hall of his Milan apartment in a large turn-of-the-century building, Lorenzo Mongiardino set an illusory Renaissance stage: the plaster wall, surfaced to resemble dressed stone, is adorned with classical reliefs and Roman-style busts. Italian Louis XVI chairs and an Empire bench enrich the theatrical setting. "Craftsmanship interests me most in interior design," the designer states, "and in Italy there are still many quite extraordinary craftsmen—men who do decoration in painted marble, upholstery, and so forth. I made my house by experimenting with them all."

FOLLOWING PAGES: "I begin by creating an atmosphere in a house," designer Mongiardino explains, "or reconstructing, revitalizing an old house—centuries old, perhaps." He conceived an exotic Eastern ambience for the living room of an expansive apartment in Rome's seventeenth-century Odescalchi Palace. Colorful Indian raw silk covers the tented ceiling, walls and banquettes; the commodious seating suggests an oasis of relaxed comfort within such palatial scale. The closely coordinated architectural design is enhanced by a large Dutch chandelier, a seventeenth-century Dutch painting, and a collection of blanc-de-chine objects.

MRS. HENRY PARISH II

Mrs. Henry Parish II, the legendary "Sister" Parish, had never been interviewed with a tape recorder. She viewed it with silent alarm, convinced the microphone was a loudspeaker broadcasting her words the length and breadth of Park Avenue. Whether or not she would proceed with the interview was in question. She finally consented, and clutching the arms of a chair, proceeded to answer all the questions with the lucidity and charm characteristic of her.

I was born in Morristown, New Jersey, in 1910 . . .
I went to Miss Chapin's School in New York in the winter, and in the spring I went to day school in the country. But my education was very limited. School then was not strict, but they always said I got in by mistake.

I was brought up in a most beautiful house, and both my mother and my father were interested in decoration. They were among the first to go into eighteenth-century and American furniture. Their home today would still be considered an outstanding example of comfort and love and hospitality. It was filled with flowers, and there were wonderful gardens.

I owe every single thing I have to my upbringing, and the greatest mistake I ever made was the lack of education. I never went to college; it never even occurred to me. I went abroad every year, but got nothing out of it.

I started designing when . . .
I lived in Far Hills, New Jersey, and had been married for a year. We lived in a small white farmhouse, which was unique in its time. Part of the furnishings belonged to my husband's family and part were wedding presents, and things my mother and father gave us to fill in.

The floors were black ebony, the walls were painted white and the curtains were white. This was before the time when anyone ever had white. I remember my father-in-law saying to me, "When do you put the curtains up and take the sheets down?"

The countryside was bewildered by the atmosphere of the house. They had never seen anything like it, and because of that house I was asked to decorate, for pleasure, the Hunt Club. I didn't know wholesale from retail, but I did it, and the countryside was rather astounded, but satisfied. That was the first job I had, although it was unpaid. It was a great learning experience.

The second job was to do over a Howard Johnson's. It was to be perked up. Well, I perked it up too much. It was a dreadful, dismal failure. But people started to be interested in my decorating anyway.

We added more wings to our house, because by that time we had two babies. One wing was unique in that it had an adjoining greenhouse. We really spent most of our time in the greenhouse. It was where we really lived and where the children played.

We painted our bedroom floor in red and white squares, which my husband and a local painter did. They couldn't figure out how the squares were to come out even. My husband would say on the telephone, "It's a nightmare. How did you ever dream up this?" I wanted a fireplace molding made of glass. The craftsmen looked horrified. They hadn't done anything of that kind. The glass was painted red, so it gave an illusion of red crystal. Our bed was a half-canopy made with big ruffles and pale pink roses. The theme was always flowers. People were stunned. I knew some were giggling behind my back and some thought it was charming.

In 1934 I started decorating
professionally for reasons of necessity . . .
With the crash, we knew our whole way of life had to be entirely different. My husband came home Christmas Eve and I knew something had happened. Finally, he said, "My job is changing and we will have to live in a different style, but we'll work it out."

The Monday after Christmas I found, in the village, a room in part of the saddle shop for forty-five dollars a month. I took it for my office and went to New York the same day. I walked into what I was told was a wholesale fabric house. There seems to be a lot of indecision on everybody's part about whether it was Stroheim & Romann or Schumacher, but it was one or the other. I went through the revolving doors, panic-stricken. I'd never even been through revolving doors, but I asked to speak to the president. No one ever knows how I got to see him. I didn't know his name. I simply said, "Our life has changed and I want to make money and help my husband and I want a charge account." He looked completely baffled. I had the definite feeling that he would give me a card right away just to get me out. And he did. I thanked him and then said, "Oh, by the way, may

"It's the most comfortable room," says Sister Parish of a light-warmed Manhattan living room she conceived as a country room in the city. "But it's still very grand, because the furniture is so grand." Furnishings include Louis XVI painted bergères upholstered in a rich, dark, English chintz, and a Louis XV ormolu and black-lacquered desk; the painting on the wall beyond the desk is by Monet. Light filtering through silk draperies flanked by damask overdraperies warms the nineteenth-century Spanish rug.

TOP: A red-lacquered fireplace wall in the library of the same Manhattan apartment provides a rich background for a radiant Cézanne oil above the Louis XVI marble mantel; the Louis XV red tortoiseshell and bronze-doré clock is flanked by ormolu-mounted Chinese porcelain birds. Mrs. Parish comments: "The rest of the room is all books, and there is a Bessarabian rug, from which the deep color tones in the room are derived. This, too, is a country room."

ABOVE: Soft pastel colors create a restful, light mood for the master bedroom sitting area of an apartment in Boston. Bedspreads in embroidered linen coordinate with a fresh floral chintz, geometrically patterned carpeting, and silk pillows. "The top of the coffee table was made from part of an eighteenth-century screen," says Mrs. Parish. Bouquets, both natural and painted, accent the gentle look.

I use the telephone? I want to call my children in the country and see if they're all right." He replied, "Lady, this is not a business for you." But I had the card, and I brought approximately a hundred fabric samples back to my new little office. I set it up right away, brought some furniture in from my own house, put some flowers around, and when Henry came home we went through the village. I asked if he noticed anything different. He didn't, so I showed him the sign, made that day, that said, "Mrs. Henry Parish II, Interiors." That was the beginning of my career.

I opened an office in New York . . .
at the end of World War II and I had quite a big clientele, mostly my friends or friends of my family. When Albert Hadley joined me twelve years ago, we started getting a new look, new clients.

Our staff is now approximately twenty-eight and we do about fifty jobs each year in all different stages.

So many young people have come to our firm over the years, and we've always tried to see them and help them. I find myself saying, "You either have it or you haven't." And I say that as one who had no training at all of any kind. Some people can't help it, it's just in them. And with some, it doesn't matter how many schools they go to, they'll never come to it. Never.

One has to believe men are better designers . . .
than women, because there are so many of them.

You must be involved with your clients . . .
and I get very fond of people I'm working for and have a bad habit of becoming a part of their life, which I feel is not necessary, and actually a mistake.

When new clients contact us, someone in the office speaks to them immediately and asks why they've come, or if we have mutual friends, or if they've seen a house they liked, or whatever the reason is. If it seems tempting, an appointment is made, then we meet and have a small talk to see if we feel we can be of any help and if they are in any way attracted to us.

At first meeting, you have an enormous feeling of personality, of their likes, their way of life, the way they'd like to live, and the way they do live. Of course, they wouldn't be in our office unless they thought that we could better their life or make it more comfortable.

And at that point we say, "Have you a budget?" But the very mention of money puts me in a panic. I have to leave that to other people. I can never discuss money.

A designer is more architectural than a decorator . . .
Both architect and interior decorator are equally impor-

tant, and they should work together. One of the biggest mistakes is that they *don't*. They should combine their efforts and talents.

Some people use a decorator because . . .
they don't really know where to begin. Some people's lives have changed. They have made money and read articles and want to go to the best, if they're going to do it at all. The other reason is the enormous amount of work the decorator does for the client. It is unbelievable, and without that help people suddenly realize there's no way to do it. Plus the fact that they're the gainers because they don't have to move out of their chairs if they don't want to, whereas hours and days and weeks and months are spent by the decorator to satisfy the client.

When we start a new job, the first step is . . .
to ask for the floor plan. That is then discussed in the office and eventually goes to our design studio, where we plot the working arrangement. Then the decisions are made about whether the wall has to come down or up, or if the window is in the right place; if the doors should be tall or thin or wide; and the first presentation is really about how the interior could work.

After remodeling, the job completely depends on what the clients own and what they want to get rid of. If it's a brand-new house, we try to use as many of their things as we can, because it gives the owners a certain satisfaction that it *is* theirs. We are simply helping them with a new look, a better look, a more workable arrangement.

People trying to do their own houses . . .
have limited sources. They have not been exposed to the many outlets, so they can't even visualize what they want. A decorator helps by exposing them to almost everything, and helping them to be selective.

If you have a limited budget, do the most important thing and forget the rest till that's done. And the most important thing to do might be the architectural remodeling. We are always very honest in saying, "Before you do anything, do that."

Don't buy inferior furniture; it has no lasting quality and no value. It's better to have one good upholstered piece that you will have the rest of your life.

This is not typical, but one of our favorite clients was buying a Louis XV chair of great importance, value, and beauty. I heard her saying, "Mother, would you mind trying it? If it's comfortable, we'll keep it."

I do believe good taste is timeless
and that it can be acquired . . .
We have many, many clients who knew nothing, nothing, nothing, but were willing to trust us, believe in us,

Mrs. Henry Parish II

Word Association

Color	Lemon yellow.
Living rooms	The center of the house.
Entrance halls	Dignity.
Bedrooms	Luxury, comfort.
Bathrooms	Cleanliness.
Dining rooms	To use in many ways.
Studies	A room of privacy.
Floor coverings	The options are unbounded.
Kitchens	A working space.
Children's rooms	Color.
Lamps	So far I've yet to find one.
Window treatments	Softness.
Fabrics	Quality.
Wallpaper	Background.
Lighting	Equal spacing.
Television sets	Exposed.

The sitting room of this Manhattan apartment is a
tranquil space of quiet elegance. Used also as a man's study,
the room is appointed with a Regency desk and gilded
Regency armchair, as well as comfortable upholstered pieces,
tailored tweed carpeting and a needlepoint-covered
Chippendale mahogany bench. Sister Parish used an old
English floral chintz that reinforces the luminous outdoor
ambience of the Seurat landscape—a study for *La Grande
Jatte*—above the Directoire marble mantel.

and now they know just as much as we know. Exposure is the most honest way to acquire taste. By following good architectural and decorating books, seeing fine antique shops, galleries, museums, people can acquire an enormous amount of knowledge.

You walk into many a tasteless room and immediately feel a desperate sense of hideousness. You feel in your heart, there's no use, but sometimes the client appeals to you, and you do your best. But in your heart, you know it will never be anything to be very cheerful about.

A home reveals everything . . .
It reveals the life of the people, the children, animals, the servants or the lack of servants. I think a home is one's soul, really.

A bedroom should be more than a bedroom. It should be large enough to make it more of a sitting room, so that one can always have a friend for tea or have the children come in and play. It's a private place, in a sense, and yet it should be a family room.

Times have changed enormously . . .
in that wealthy clients have, for a long period of time, simply done something when needed, and there were no questions asked. Now, wealthy clients have to be as aware of budget as everyone else is, and should be. They are more apt to think twice.

Anyone with a limited budget should start with . . .
a cheerful paint job and the necessary upholstered furniture for the time being. Buy the best you can, and don't do anything more until you can afford it. Even if you have to have a crate as a table, it is more effective than substituting a complete fake or bastard piece.

Someone asked me recently
if I am ever envious of the way my clients live . . .
I said, "Never, except for owning my own airplane."

When I buy for myself, it is not for investment . . .
It's because I can't live without it, and hope perhaps one of the children will want it eventually.

If you're collecting baskets, buy the best. If you're collecting the low-priced antiques, buy what appeals to you. If you're in the high bracket, buy the best quality.

My theory in decorating is that . . .
when things work, they work for every reason, from a household point of view to the last detail of comfort.

If I were to build a house now, it would be entirely planned for the running convenience. Although I have five small farmhouses for sale in Dark Harbor, Maine, I would still build there. But all on one level.

My hope for decorating in the next few years . . .
is that the architect, if there is an architect, and the decorator, and the landscaper, will all work together.

Entertaining . . .
The general opinion of entertaining is very, very low. There are certain people who have a knack that can turn the worst party into a miracle by their personality. It all comes to people's way of life now without well-trained servants. Some people use caterers they've never had before; some people have no idea about seating arrangements or whether they should be seated or not; some people have no sense of what makes it run. Actually, I feel, the less effort the more successful.

The living room is my favorite room
to decorate because . . .
it is the welcoming room, where you see your friends; where your children gather. It's the center of the house.

My own apartment in New York has . . .
a rather grand entrance hall, which we also use as a dining room. The floor is black and white marble. The ceilings are twelve feet high. It includes a dining room table, a sideboard and an old lacquered piece, which is used for stereo inside and a bar tray on top. Not a bar. The living room is gay, full of comfortable chairs, lovely objects, baskets of flowers and antique furniture, both English and French, but mainly comfortable; and the ceiling is gold-tinted tea paper.

In the world today, the best design is done . . .
on the East Coast of the United States. The East has been exposed to a great deal more than the West Coast.

European houses are so different from ours. They're grand and large scale. They've been kept so over generations, and the average rich house in our part of the world will never have the building quality nor the proportions and the scale of living of those in Europe.

Contemporary design in the United States is acceptable today, but not as acceptable as it was ten years ago.

People don't really fear decorators . . .
The word isn't "fear." You want respect on both sides, and that always presents a cautious approach to the client, and the client to you.

Scott Fitzgerald once observed,
"The very rich are different from you and me."
He was, I believe, inaccurate.

LEE RADZIWILL

*We first met for tea, when I went to see her New York apartment
for possible publication in* Architectural Digest. *Lee was gracious
and informal. In the ambience of easeful opulence, the T-shirt and
blue jeans she wore were quite as much at home as a couture dress
would have been. She is at present quite dedicated to her interior
decorating career, and one of her most enthusiastic fans is "the
decorator's decorator," Michael Taylor.*

*I'm very visual and care
very much about my surroundings . . .*

I've only been active in the field, in my own business, for the last three years. But I've been interested in decorating and design since I can remember.

I really don't think formal training is necessary; if you're imaginative and have a good eye, you will immediately recognize something marvelous amid a heap of clutter. If you sense architecture and proportion—the ideal is a square room—you should know what you're doing. If you have the knowledge of history, of decoration and design, you can do a room of any period.

Obviously, there are many people who do go to school and do pass certain requirements, but I know many designers, who haven't had those degrees or courses, who are far better because they have not been taught rules. And I don't think there should ever be any rules.

I can cope with four jobs at a time with the help of an assistant and a secretary, plus free-lance people. The tighter you can keep it, the better.

The thing that holds you up the most—and it's impossible for clients to understand—is how long everything takes to order and to arrive. They think it's entirely your fault, whereas you can do nothing whatsoever about it. You call the upholsterers, the curtain people, the carpenters, every single day, and you just repeat the same thing the next day. Certain clients will blame the designer for it because they don't understand shipments, strikes, and the like.

Little do they know. The repetitive, "Oh, what fun it must be to be an interior decorator!" They think you're just putting up a lot of rose-flowered chintz curtains and strewing the room with lovely pillows. It is incredibly detailed work. I myself have been amazed at the minutiae it takes and how fatiguing it can be, especially when you have a time limit and are under pressure.

What can you do with people who are going to let you down? Workers are going to let you down, usually for very good reasons—illness or family tragedies. So-and-so is on vacation, or so-and-so is ill.

Decorating is very hard work, and I had to learn a lot very quickly. People don't realize the complication of the paper work in ordering things. It takes endless time and concentration. You have to know about economics, financial and bookkeeping things, as well as, obviously, being able to read plans and elevations quickly.

Decorating certainly does not consist of going out and buying some lovely silk and saying to a painter, "Do this room in this shade of yellow." You have to supervise the whole thing. The joy of it all is seeing it get off the ground and then seeing it completed. When you start, it's on your desk for so long, you can't imagine it ever coming together. And it's very difficult to do it if you're three thousand miles away. You cannot make mistakes with plans or elevations.

I simply don't know how clients come to me . . .

I suppose I have had quite a few things published. Mainly they've been my own places, but people remembered them and liked them, because I don't have any trademark and I don't want to have one. I like to be able to do anything a person might want, whether it is very contemporary, Victorian, nineteenth century, even eighteenth century, although that bores me now, because it's so uncomfortable and so stiff. One has seen enough of it lately. But I guess clients come to me by word of mouth. And seeing some good job I did. I know a lot of people want to stick with the same person forever, but a lot of people want to change.

My very first commission was with the Americana Hotel in Miami. They wanted to change its image a bit. I've done a great deal of work at the Huntington Hotel in San Francisco and my point there was to make each suite as livable as a pied-à-terre would be for me. A place where you'd like to have dinner instead of finding it so depressing that you just want to change your clothes and get out as soon as possible. I prefer commercial work by far. Hotels, banks, offices, unless it's an exceptional client with an exceptional place in mind.

When private people call me, I can tell pretty quickly how interested they really are. And I just can't have my

"My beach house at Southampton is incredibly pure, serene, and uncluttered," says Lee Radziwill. "I wanted a house that focused on the natural environment, an unencumbered place that would constantly renew the spirit." She redesigned a long wall of sliding glass that integrates the pared-down space with the ocean; both the David Ligare canvas and the wave-patterned wood floor, painted by Luis Molina, reaffirm the relationship. "I didn't put curtains up anywhere," the designer adds. "The point was to have a view of the sea, and not have curtains you have to brush by, to get out the door."

name on something that upsets me, or if I don't want it said that I did it. I had one job like that and I'll never do it again. It started out so beautifully and it ended up in just a heartbreaking way for me. It was so different from my original conception.

And I can tell if it is merely a bored lady who thinks it would take up her time in the spring, or the autumn, or whenever, to make her dining room chairs. And then I say, "I'm really sorry, but I just can't do this."

I know what my possibilities are very well. For example, I was asked to do a restaurant in the Napa Valley, in California. And I thought that would be very exciting, but then I realized the person who wanted it had a totally different kind of taste than I do and was terribly good with that particular period, which was late-nineteenth century. Western, brass and mirrors, rather the feeling of a pub. So I said, "I would really love to do it, but you have more knowledge about this than I do."

When new clients come to me . . .
they show me their apartment or their house or the office. Then they tell me, though most of them are pretty confused themselves, what they want. Otherwise, they wouldn't call me. Or they don't want to be bothered themselves. You listen to them and look at the potential of the place, and tell them how much you think it's going to cost and vaguely how long it might take. Usually they are stunned, as I am, by the price of the workmanship, craftsmanship, materials, furniture. Then it's up to them to decide. I've turned down more clients than I've accepted, because I felt either they were going to be impossible to work with, or it wasn't going to be interesting. Or that it was going to be a waste of time.

I discuss money with clients in the beginning . . .
I just don't want to get into something and find out in the middle of it that there's been a great misunderstanding, or to give people any unpleasant surprises. However, I have designed several living rooms with dining areas, for about twenty-five thousand to thirty-five thousand dollars. Each room included a few pieces of quality, such as a great desk, or an unusual rug.

Clients pay you to cope with all the dirty work. They don't want to be pounding the pavements and doing these extraordinary detailed things, deciding whether this room should have a molding at the ceiling or not, and calling up the electrician.

I'd love to have somebody do it for me. My apartment has looked the same for thirteen years because I haven't seen anything to inspire me to change it. I keep thinking I must, but all I can do is give it a face-lift, because I haven't seen anything that made me excited enough to start all over. I'd have to do all the rooms, because I want the continuity.

Money doesn't make a great deal of difference . . .
in the way a place turns out. A home can be, if you have the knack, just as attractively done on an inexpensive scale as when the money is no object.

No matter what the budget may be, my fees are the same. I have a consultation fee and a retail fee. Whatever is most comfortable for the client and for me. My consultation fee is five hundred dollars for a day—which is about five working hours. My retail fee is simply the difference between wholesale and the retail price.

I had to learn about all of that. It's so complicated. How to order, how to get 50 percent down before you start to do a thing. Then if you have a client who doesn't pay once the work is completed, you're in real trouble. I've been very fortunate, so far. I've had wonderful clients. But in the beginning, it was difficult for me to understand, and then I realized this situation couldn't go on. You really have to be sure who your clients are and how responsible they are.

Few people realize that decorating is not a lucrative business whatsoever. It's running from one end of town to the other and doing endless paperwork. I'd really prefer commercial work because I'd much rather do that on my own than be with somebody else who has totally different ideas. That takes up an immense amount of time. I've had rather large commercial jobs and, fortunately, been given a free hand. I try to make them look as uncommercial as possible.

The new word is that one is offended to be called . . .
a *decorator* rather than an *interior designer*.
But I think that's because designers have become resentful that people think *decorate* means what you would do for a party. Lovely bowls of flowers, a round table, and something exotic with lighting and trees. I think that's why they prefer to be called *designers*.

Designing does mean a lot more than that. Actually, designing includes architecture, breaking down walls, and having a great sense of proportion. Also, I happen to like surprises. The unexpected. In most cities I like to make it quite different from what one would expect. In my London house, twenty years ago, I did the first comeback of a Turkish room. And then it got so copied that I was disgusted, but still it was so good that I left it.

*The best thing that can happen
to a designer is to have nothing to work with . . .*
to start from scratch. If the clients don't have the mirrors, the desks, the screens their grandmother or great-grandfather gave them, you can start out totally fresh. So far, that's pretty much what has happened to me. I have been very lucky. And that's ideal, but finding something you can build the room or apartment around is often difficult and takes time.

"My apartment in New York is really rather grand," says designer Radziwill, "although the top floor is much more countryish, and the drawing room is much more of the nineteenth century." On the top floor is her airy, light-filled bedroom, an appealing traditional statement of gardenlike charm; the engaging collection of *faux-marbre*–framed nineteenth-century botanical prints contributes naturalistic vitality to the arrangement of antique painted furniture. "I like to imagine I'm in the country when I'm up here."

"I prefer commercial work, by far," Mrs. Radziwill states. "I've done a lot of work at the Huntington Hotel in San Francisco, and my point there was to make each suite as livable as a pied-à-terre would be for me." In the sitting area of one suite, she combined comfortable large-scale seating with sleek lacquered tables, all coordinated by a vibrant color scheme. The shape of the sofa and the decoupage pictures in old walnut frames inject a subtle period quality that serves to contribute warmth to the contemporary setting.

You just cannot go straight to buy the material before you have found the lovely rug or an object that inspires the entire room. I'm not one for changing curtains and slipcovers and sofas frequently. I'm much more for spending the money on objects, a beautiful rug, prints or a painting, rather than curtains and sofas. I don't think they can give enough charm. So, unfortunately, you've just got to tramp the streets until you find your inspiration. I usually start with a rug. Old rugs, actually, or copies, can be marvelous. That's the simplest way to begin. With an extraordinary painting, you take the colors from that.

In a contemporary way of living, I feel the secret is to use only two colors. I also want to create a feeling of purity. Space is a luxury that is often abused. The minute you put a third color in, it ruins all the serenity and gets too busy. But two colors seem to work very well, without just being the boring blue and white we've had down our throats for I don't know how many years. I do love red and coral. Beige and white.

I really dislike dirty colors. They have to be absolutely clean. I've never liked yellow, though I've seen many lovely yellow rooms. But I can't use it. In doing an entire apartment or house, I feel it's important that one room blends into another. No shocks. I also love overscale furniture. I think it is so boring to just have the same old set-up—a sofa with a chair on either side.

People trying to decorate their own homes don't . . .
have enough self-confidence, so they want to be terribly safe. Too safe. And they don't know where to go. Or whom to go to. Where will they find a desk like that or a chair like that? They might go to a department store and get everything there, but it's not going to make much of an impact. It takes awhile to learn how to integrate. It's not personal, not original enough.

Don't keep changing your curtains and your sofas; a room has much more charm when you've lived in it, as the English do. Dogs sleep on every sofa and everything is slipcovered, no matter how grand the people are or how well off. Do have books, plants, and a fireplace, if possible. Do one dramatic thing. Also, make rooms have a continuity. Be sure that a red room doesn't go into an orange room, or something like that.

Although I do like colors that clash. I love to have four or five different reds in a room, because it is so boring if the whole is all the same red. It will look heavy, with no subtlety. By colors that clash, I mean one color in different tones, not in the sense that you'll need to put on dark glasses. I love to use lettuce green and black lacquer with red, because those are usually the colors you find in Bessarabian and Ukrainian rugs, which have always been my favorites. Lettuce green has a freshness that lights up the heaviness of, say, velvet.

Paint moldings and baseboards the same color as the walls, so as not to draw attention to the dimensions of the room. Use plants and bookshelves to redefine the room's space, and use lighting to create atmosphere and focus attention on the room's most interesting features. A dimmer on a light is an extremely inexpensive way to create a maximum effect.

And I find that material on the walls can just perform miracles. It is expensive, but you don't have to get incredibly expensive material. Many people make the great mistake of just gluing the material on the wall, which just gives the effect of wallpaper. There's a wonderful way of practically making it look like a stuffed quilt. I did that in a house I had, and suddenly I realized I had put material on the walls of every room in the house. And it was the most charming house in the world, everybody said. The secret was that each room had something to do with the other. You can't have one room contemporary and the other Victorian.

I really don't think taste can be acquired . . .
Facts and knowledge can be acquired. But I've seen the work of too many designers who have not acquired taste, nor a feeling for color, which is vital. And I do believe good taste is timeless.

The places I've lived in the last fifteen years are . . .
each totally different. My apartment in New York is really rather grand, although the top floor is much more countryish, and the drawing room is much more nineteenth century; whereas the beach house is pure and serene and uncluttered. I don't even have a photograph there, and don't want one. I love the contrast.

I called my house in the English countryside a "house of flowers," because that's the way it was. I painted a lot of silk that we put up. The house in town was very sensuous, with the Turkish living room, and old Cordoba leather gleaming in the dining room.

Bedrooms are all to do with . . .
light. If a bedroom is brightly lit, it turns you off. I'm not saying that you don't need really good lighting to read at night, but if the room is overlit, it can destroy the atmosphere. And color is very important. I never use white except in hot climates, because I think it's such a cold color. It has no warmth. However, in hot climates, it's great. But to me, white offers no background for paintings, and it doesn't show things off as well as other colors would. With a bedroom, you don't want to make a man feel it's too feminine, by filling it with flowered fabric. But there are some marvelous materials. The walls could be in suede. The colors could be anything from beige to coral. It just mustn't look fussy. And it's got to be incredibly comfortable.

LEE RADZIWILL   177

My biggest decorating mistake was . . .
painting my living room in New York white. My wonderful nineteenth-century English paintings looked like nothing against it. You didn't take any notice of them at all. Now, it's red.

And I had another one in London that I made the same mistake with. It was like a bowling alley. No genius could make it come together. But finally, with cut-out patterns of materials, I got the proportions right. I used the fabric architecturally.

It's practically too late to collect anything . . .
unless you're extremely well off. American art, Indian art and primitive art has all gone so high within the last few years. People used to buy it in the sixties for virtually nothing. I don't know the up-and-coming unknown painters very well yet, so I don't know who would be a great investment.

My fantasy client would be . . .
Diana Vreeland. She has such definite tastes of her own, but she would certainly accept great fantasy.

Or somebody who I thought had great taste and would give me carte blanche, and say, "I'm much too busy, but please go to the new house and just do it down to the last ashtray," because they would trust my taste enough, or it would be similar enough to theirs. That would be fantastic. But I would like them to be able to tell me what period they have a preference for.

People are going to simplify their lives . . .
as much as possible. They are going to care more about comfort. Not less about appearance, but rooms will look less cluttered and more serene. We won't have so much taffeta and brocade, those grandmother materials.

Decorating likes and dislikes . . .
I'd like to see more recessed lighting than lamps. And more dimmers for lights. They make an enormous difference in atmosphere. A knowledge of theater helped me with lighting.

I don't want to see any more shag rugs. In a rented house I took for the last few years, there was nothing but those olive-green-mustard-color shag rugs. And in a summer house! I just felt ill the whole time. So I rolled them up and bought some very inexpensive straw rugs.

Less draperies and curtains, unless they're necessary for privacy or light control. At my beach house, I didn't put any curtains up anywhere. The whole point was to have a view of the sea and not have curtains you had to brush by to get out the door.

If I were doing a house for myself today . . .
it wouldn't be in the city. I've always been very much in love with North Africa, so I think I would want it to have a Moorish feeling. I'd want it to be built around a courtyard, to avoid the wind and the rain. It would have a great deal of light and very high ceilings so it would be extremely cool. I'd love to hear water running through it. I love arches. Inside, I'd use exotic, sensuous things. Or perhaps I would make it very cool and modern, rather than carrying you back to the days of incense and nostalgia.

There's not enough money
to afford the period I'd like to work with . . .
It used to be the nineteenth century, because I felt it had such warmth and sensuality. And it was so removed from today, which I want to feel when I walk into my apartment or my house, wherever it may be. But I've gotten interested in contemporary things. I like the serenity. Although I like very few contemporary paintings, unless they are extraordinary Rothkos or Bacons.

Generally, people don't know how to entertain well . . .
The number one criterion is that you have a good guest list. Who's coming? Will they fit? Are they interesting, or fun, or amusing, or exceptionally intelligent? I don't think people realize how important that is. If you have a really good group, the food doesn't matter so much. Whereas, if the food's fantastic but you're sitting between two incredible bores, you wish you were in a restaurant, or home with someone you care about. There are very few people I know who have a wonderful knack for entertaining.

I never like a big dinner party at all. For myself, at home, eight to ten is just absolutely the maximum. I don't feel you can get to know anybody if you have more than that. You're just making polite cocktail conversation, which is a total waste of time. And my dream is to have four people in the living room at a little square bridge table covered with my old silk scarves.

The rich are really scared to go out into the world . . .
And that's why they cling together so much and why their lives are, unfortunately, so narrow. They miss a great deal. I remember a line from a couple who were friends of the Scott Fitzgeralds: "Living well is the best revenge." It is absolutely true. It's an art in itself. And that doesn't have anything to do with money. Take a bottle of wine, some cheese and bread, and go on a picnic, in a boat, or to some charming place, and what could give you more pleasure if you're with someone you like? If it's your sister, your daughter, whomever you're married to, or love, or find amusing. That's living well.

A tailored, brass-trimmed reed four-poster, other simplified
furnishings in rattan and bamboo, a hand-screened print
fabric, and strié-papered walls define a San Francisco hotel
bedroom that projects a clean, light environment. Says Lee
Radziwill: "In a bedroom, you don't want to make a man
feel it's too feminine, by filling it with flowered fabric. But
there are many other marvelous materials, and the colors
could be anything from beige to coral. It just mustn't look
fussy. And it's got to be incredibly comfortable."

VALERIAN RYBAR

Valerian Rybar is the most international of decorators. His work takes him to all parts of the world, and his clients are equally international, with houses and interests in several countries. Valerian worries that people may think him formidable. He insists, accurately, that he is "completely flexible. I don't just say I work with my clients, I really do." A partial list of those clients includes: Mr. and Mrs. Pierre Schlumberger, Mr. and Mrs. Jean Pierre Marcie Rivière, Christina Onassis.

As a young man in Yugoslavia, I studied law . . .
because I was going into the diplomatic service. When the time came to finish my studies, there was no country left to be a diplomat in, which delighted me, because I really didn't relish the idea very much. My prime interest had been, for as long as I can remember, architecture. I looked at architecture, I read about architecture, and I regretted that I studied law instead.

Soon after I arrived in America I got a job with Elizabeth Arden as a package designer. Then Miss Arden asked me to do her salons, and that was my first exposure to interior design. I wish I could say it was a very hard struggle getting there, but it wasn't all that hard.

I quit Arden after three years. By then I had done an apartment for myself, which at that time seemed very "with it," I suppose. People liked it and started asking me to do their apartments.

Formal education doesn't seem at all necessary for an interior designer. A lot of successful designers have not had any formal training. And a lot of designers who have had formal training don't seem to use it very well.

Today my Paris office handles perhaps four residential and three nonresidential jobs a year. The New York office averages about six residential and three nonresidential. The Paris office takes care of Europe, the Middle East, North Africa; and from New York I do America, Mexico, the Caribbean, and Latin America.

Residential jobs take longer and longer. In Europe, if architectural changes are required, it takes at least a year. In America, six to eight months. Of course, I'm talking about quite elaborate installations, new bathrooms and dressing rooms, and changing the walls around. If you build from scratch, you have to add another year. If you go into a residence that is acceptable architecturally, it takes considerably less time.

Although I knew a lot of well-to-do people, I did, especially when I first started, quite a few small apartments. But they always were apartments with a lot of design content, a lot of custom work, and therefore, above-average cost. I rarely worked on a small budget. I don't think it necessarily proves talent to do something inexpensively. With all the things for sale in America, anybody with a modicum of taste should be able to do an interior very well. They don't need an interior designer.

The only reason to use an interior designer . . .
unless there is a lot of conceptual design, custom-made furniture, unusual materials, and so on—is to save the legwork and the coordination of the installation. We do have the know-how the average person lacks. It's easy to pick a pretty chintz; it's another matter to get the curtains properly made. The average person doesn't know where to go to get things done and can't coordinate which comes first: the carpet or the painting. I think that has become, especially in recent years, the main function of the average interior decorator.

I used to think socializing helped . . .
but most clients come to me because of something they've seen; or they're friends of clients. Or they come directly from having seen my work in magazines.

Socializing, when I did a lot of it, was a much more brilliant scene, and you met many more interesting people. What does help is entertaining in one's own home.

I don't start to design for somebody right away . . .
I like to get to know the people at least well enough to know how they really live. Many people kid themselves about that. Some have dreams about how they always entertain, but they really have one dinner party a year. Do the people have an active family life? Are they intellectually inclined? If so, what are their pursuits? Is a library important to them, or isn't it? For an interior to be really successful, all of that must be incorporated into the plan long before you come to the aesthetics.

I don't mind at all, although a lot of designers do, when a client comes with clippings from magazines, saying, "I like this," or, "I like that." They really don't expect me to copy, but I can get a feeling of what they like.

Amid the contemporary milieu of Valerian Rybar's
Manhattan living room is a fine red tortoiseshell Boulle desk
with an intriguing assemblage of exotic objects on it. "I like
to use a few very good and unusual antiques," explains the
designer. "They stand there commanding the room and giving
it quality." Mother-of-pearl articles combine with eighteenth-
century crossed Masonic ritual pieces and an unusual pair of
seventeenth-century Venetian ostrich eggs mounted as
peacocks. Early-eighteenth-century Sicilian candelabra, made
of porphyry, vermeil, moonstones, rock crystal, and other
semiprecious stones, flank the seventeenth-century trompe
l'oeil painting framed in stainless steel.

I don't want anyone to go into a house I've done and say, "Oh, Valerian Rybar did this." That's a negative compliment. A positive compliment is that you've expressed the personality and life style of the clients.

Clients pay the cost of merchandise plus . . .
a percentage. Sometimes I just submit estimates, how much something will be; sometimes I will do something for a fee. It depends on which seems to be most practical. A straight fee usually applies only to nonresidential work. In residential, if there is a lot of architectural work to be done, I usually divide the job into Phase One and Phase Two. Phase One is called *Consultant to the architects and builders,* for which I usually get a fee. I draw up plans and am paid for them.

Phase Two is the *furnishing* of the place, and I submit estimates. We always work at retail on fabrics, that sort of thing. Custom-made things we have to mark up a certain amount. When it comes to antiques—and I don't mean cute old chairs, but serious works of art—we make a separate arrangement, so that I receive a percentage of the value of the piece, if the clients want me to find it for them. Obviously, you can't get 33⅓ percent of something that costs eighty thousand dollars.

I always have signed contracts with clients, no matter if we're close friends. People really like it better that way. In a business that has a reputation for being unbusinesslike, one has to bend over backward to be businesslike. I don't tell them anything about the design before the down payment on the design fee. The design fee is applied to purchases. It's all in a letter of agreement, and I don't start the job unless it is signed.

A designer's overhead can be enormous . . .
There are about ten people on the staff in Paris, and ten in New York. With the exception of my partner in Paris, Jean-François Daigre, who does a lot of design work, I don't have designers on my staff. I like to stay in control of the design aspect. I pride myself very much that our plans are supposedly the best in the business. I have highly qualified draftsmen. That's one of the reasons I can do as much as I do with a relatively small staff.

After I've gotten to know my clients, I ask them . . .
if they have an aversion to certain colors and other very elementary questions. Then I draw a floor plan, showing them the areas, how they work, and at the same time, perhaps, a furniture plan. I go on to show them the elevations of the rooms, with the materials I would like to use, so they can get a complete visual concept.

Then I do everything, room by room, the whole concept, with supportive documents from art books. I show swatches and one scheme. *One,* because that's the one I think is right. Naturally, I can do a library just as effectively in earth tones as I can in red tones. I don't think a room can *only* be done one way. But I'll see it in a certain way, feel it, and present it that way. If it doesn't happen to be what they like, I don't mind at all adapting or modifying the scheme. I used to show two or three alternates and found that it confused people and made them unsure. They are looking to me for an answer, and if I give them a choice, it's almost as if they think I am unsure.

I don't attach as much importance to color as some designers do. It's a secondary consideration. Much more important to me are the materials used, their surface quality, the textures. All of that one can then interpret in a range of colors. I do think it is very important that color flow harmoniously throughout a whole house. That doesn't mean it all has to be done in one color, but you shouldn't jump around from a bright yellow to a bright blue. Color has a lot to do with personality. A lively person can support bright colors. A very wishy-washy, subdued person might feel uneasy and look bad in bright colors. I consider the personality and appearance of the client. Women react strongly to their surroundings. People like one restaurant because it's well lit, but hate another because the wall color is unflattering. That applies much more so to their own homes.

I shop by myself until I spot the right things. It's time-

PRECEDING PAGES: The vibrant living room of Mr. Rybar's apartment offers comfort in a glowing atmosphere of surface contrast. The flooring and chimneybreast are specially fabricated textured steel, while the vertical blinds and all architectural details are shiny stainless steel. Dense linen velvet covers the walls and banquettes, and satin—marbleized by hand embroidery—wraps the oval ottomans. "I try to work in rather expensive materials, so they really cannot be copied," the designer reveals. Antique adornments include andirons that were architectural elements on the façade of a twelfth-century church, and a Renaissance portrait bust of Ferdinand de' Medici in carved rock crystal and vermeil—"The only really good thing that I own."

consuming, but I know my sources well. For certain furnishings, I go to London; for others, to Paris or Milan.

There is an enormous difference
between an interior designer and a decorator . . .
A decorator perhaps makes a floor plan, decides on the furniture, and chooses fabrics, carpeting, wall covering, all from readily available sources.

A designer should be able to give the room an interesting shape, correct an architectural fault, design fabrics and custom-made pieces that will give character to the room. The creative output makes the difference.

A decorator should have a talent for selection; a designer should have a talent for creation.

Great mistakes are made in one area . . .
And that is the sense of proportion. Amateurs often lack that sense completely. You see it all the time. Little itsy-bitsy pieces of furniture in a big room.

In interior design, apart from all the supportive knowledge you must have, such as design, construction, how things have to be installed, and lots of technical things, a sense of proportion seems to me the one great distinguishing talent that a person can have. Amateurs lack that to a great degree.

If you are decorating your own home . . .
do try to visualize what you are doing as a whole. Even if you can't afford to buy everything in one fell swoop, have a master plan tucked away in your mind and go about doing your home according to this plan until it's complete. Very few people do that. They go to a store, fall in love with a sofa, buy it, then buy a lamp out of proportion to the sofa. Don't buy something because you love the way it looks wherever you happen to see it. Be very sure that it fits into your total concept.

Chic is not timeless . . .
Chic is a thing of fashion. A trendy kind of thing that

changes. Fashions, of course, change. But inherent good taste and, above all, a sense of style, are timeless.

A knowledge of quality can be acquired. I don't think that taste, per se, can be acquired. It's one of those subtle things. On the other hand, if you're surrounded by beautiful antiques or very well-designed modern furniture, the danger of being tasteless is minimized. But you must often see people throw all of these things together in the worst possible way, and that's tasteless. It's comparable to women who spend fortunes on clothes and always look terrible. Other women, with relatively little money, look very well.

If you have a limited budget, the great danger is . . .
overextending. There are very many simple, beautiful inexpensive things around, and an accumulation of these will make for a very pleasing interior. Whereas, if somebody tries to overreach for something very expensive, then surrounds this one very expensive thing with a lot of junk, it makes the good thing look cheap and bad. If you keep the whole on more or less the same level, you'll have a much more harmonious result.

I find myself, at this point, not noticing décor . . .
except for the two extremes. If something is really very beautiful, I appreciate it. I look around, take it all in, and admire it. And if something is jarringly awful and it really bothers me, I notice it.

Anything could shock you that's inharmonious and demands your attention without being beautiful. But I have no hates. In a chalet, even a shag rug might be absolutely wonderful, if it's properly used. It's the way things are used that is important. Let's say that you go into a beach house, and the furniture is covered in velvet. That would be a very disturbing element. Appropriateness is a very important element of decoration.

A home should reveal a lot about people
because it's an expression of the way they live . . .
The first time I visited Dallas, I went to a house and

counted something like twenty-five pairs of supposedly antique commodes. That was very revealing. Those people had been taken in by somebody who sold them a bill of goods. Therefore, you have no respect for them. Furthermore, they should know better than to think that people visiting their house will believe that anyone can accumulate twenty-five pairs of matching commodes, because I doubt there are that many in the world. Then, too, the banality of the idea of just one-two, one-two all around is also very boring. And it also reveals that their only interest is trying to show off, to impress. But to impress with fake things also means they think their guests are idiots.

The way a house is kept is very important, too. The little comforts. The table where you need it, the ashtray where you need it, the phone where you want a phone. A certain number of books, plants, and flowers give an agreeable lived-in look. All that kind of thing spells out a cultured, cultivated life. You can come into a very beautiful house and it seems completely sterile because it lacks these personal touches. Obviously the people have no rapport with their own home; it's just there because they can afford to have it. Such people should live in hotels; they shouldn't even have houses.

A bedroom should be sensuous . . .
One very obvious element is lighting. I like a bedroom to be relatively small. It might have a chaise longue, but very little furniture. The surroundings should reflect a little bit of the person's sexual preferences. It might be a very feminine room, almost like Camille, pristine and yet very captivating. Now that would be one way of doing a woman's bedroom. A bachelor's bedroom you would do in much more—let's call it a James Bond type of style— which can be sexy, too.

There are many ways to interpret sensuality. It's not specific colors so much as style, the total concept of the room. Texture is very important. A fur rug is quite sensuous on a man's bed; not so much on a woman's bed. Fantasy has a lot to do with it. A lot of women love canopy beds. It gives them a sense of security and coziness. Of course, psychology comes into play. More so than in other rooms.

There's a theory that American men like to sleep in an ultrafeminine bedroom, that it turns them on. I don't think that's necessarily true. Perhaps in the twenties or thirties it might have been. If a couple uses the same bedroom, who is going to win out in the style of decoration? It's usually the woman. The man is more apt to sleep in his wife's room than the other way around.

Today, people pay much more attention to their own personal comfort than they used to. A young couple furnishing a house or apartment today will usually start out by making their own quarters comfortable, and then work on the living room. Years ago, they'd do the living room first.

In decorating, as in everything else,
Europeans follow American trends . . .
There are many more decorators in Europe now than there used to be. Of course, in Europe, only wealthy people use decorators, which is not true in America. Many middle-income Americans seek the help of decorators. Once a European has established the décor with me, he will leave it to me to implement the design. They don't come and look and worry. Americans are much more apt to be in on all the little details and call up in a panic because the painter has put on a white undercoat and the room's supposed to be green, and how come? You have to explain all that sort of thing. I'm generalizing now, but in Europe they just let you do it. You'd think it would be the other way around.

Perhaps the reason is really quite simple. The kind of people who use designers in Europe have given it more thought. They've chosen the designer because they really expect this person will do just what they want to see done. Here, perhaps, they've chosen the designer for the wrong reason, because of a lot of publicity, or this and that. So they're not completely secure in their choice, and therefore check all the time.

Men are not better designers than women,
but they have more fantasy . . .
Men have a greater facility for disassociating their own likes and dislikes. A woman designer has a tendency to put herself into the picture. But women really excel in office design, which is a paradox.

I don't encourage confidences from clients . . .
Very often the motive for doing a new house might be a failing marriage. A couple will try to have their fights through you, and that is an intolerable situation. A beautiful, finished house has never patched up a marriage, that I know of.

My worst client was also one of my biggest clients . . .
The property in Connecticut had been purchased because their yacht could practically anchor on the lawn. The huge old house was being torn down, and a new huge house built. Everything went along swimmingly. Whatever I suggested was accepted, until it came to the interiors. She made a beeline in the fabric showrooms for anything with a gold thread in it. That's the advantage of the Phases One and Two contractual agreement. It gives both designer and client an ideal cut-off point.

Today, for a room of quality, you have to spend . . .
at least thirty thousand dollars. And that does not, of

For an octagonally shaped conversation/bar area adjacent
to the large living room of a hunting lodge in the Austrian
Tyrol, Mr. Rybar used natural-toned suede for the walls,
ceiling and motorized draperies. Carved walnut moldings
add linear detail to the walls and the tray ceiling; the
lambrequin's similarly edged moldings have carved walnut
tassels as well. "It's all rather luxurious," he says. Banquette
seating is attended by Renaissance-style stools serving as
tables. Mr. Rybar comments: "The strength of Renaissance
furniture seems to live well with contemporary pieces."

course, include art and antiques. Costs have escalated incredibly. You almost have to be a millionaire to do a three-room apartment. The least expensive interior I've done was a studio apartment for thirty thousand dollars. And it was done nicely. The most expensive was about five million dollars.

A trend is set by somebody who is an innovator . . .
who doesn't do his innovation too soon, because then it stands there all by itself and doesn't relate to the life people lead. Timing is terribly important.

Here is an example. The Nicky DuPonts asked me to design their Palm Beach house quite a few years ago. At that time, all Palm Beach houses looked like city houses, stuffed with English furniture or Colonial Spanish. Bunny DuPont was a creative person, so we arrived at a formula that was really trend-setting. We used all-white floors. We had beautiful shutters, beautifully designed millwork. We had gay prints made in sea and sky colors. We did things you see all over the place now, that didn't exist then. We had a whole series of furniture made of carved wood that looked like bamboo. All this was very new then and it was appropriate for the time and place.

People in Palm Beach were tired of big, formal dinner parties. It was the time of palazzo pajamas that went beautifully with the interior. Fashion and interiors are closely related. Interiors have a tendency to follow fashion. Some people have a feeling for what is about to happen. But to set trends, you must have an innate feeling about what people are going to like just before they're going to like it. But not much before.

I'm very much afraid the revival
in style that might happen next . . .
because I don't particularly like it, will be Victorian and Edwardian. I really see that coming. Fabrics are already going toward it. The dull color sense; the little-nothing designs; the Liberty prints that are becoming popular. This again has a lot to do with fashion. It all comes from England. This raggedy, floating, crocheted look. All of that is going to seep into interior design, and I'm not looking forward to it. I never would use it.

A beautiful antique will always be a beautiful antique. But antiques will be used, except by the very rich, as *objets d'art*—one beautiful antique standing, almost like sculpture. And that's the way they should be used. They're all going to wind up in museums sooner or later. In my own work, I like to use a few very good and unusual antiques. They stand there commanding the room and giving it quality.

Everything comes into play with trends . . .
The quickness of transportation. The facility of import-

ing things from one country to another. In J. P. Morgan's day, it was a great feat to get something over from Italy. It cost a colossal fortune. Now, it's just as cheap to buy something in New York as it is to buy in Portugal. You have to be inventive, take advantage of new products, use materials that have been around a long time, in a different way. When that catches on, it will be knocked off. But I try to work in rather expensive materials so they really cannot be copied. It's very unfair to do something for a client and then see it at Bloomingdale's for a fraction of what it cost them. You can protect your client by working with materials that can be imitated, but can't ever be the same.

And, of course, travel has a lot to do with trends. You may see woodcarving in India that costs very little but looks sensational, so you have doors made of that wood for a job. It's unique and looks fantastically expensive when it isn't, really. New inventions might come out of the chemical industry which you can use. You have to be aware, not only of beautiful old things you might adapt, but also new things.

Architects fall down when it comes to houses . . .
They are unfamiliar with a sophisticated way of living. They do not know what a dressing room is. They don't know what a luxurious bathroom is. They don't know that if somebody is very fond of flowers, they need a little place to arrange them. They completely ignore all of that. They might build a beautiful-looking house that is completely unfunctional. They are also very unfair. They resent interior designers a lot and yet they don't do anything about it themselves. I think that's a reason many people ask interior designers to design their houses today, rather than hiring an architect.

For someone with a very limited
budget I would suggest . . .
contemporary furniture. Instead of doing a beautiful lacquered wall, which costs quite a lot of money, use a vinyl, which will look almost as well, like a patent leather. Perhaps apple green. Then put in some nicely designed white furniture. It would be a very definite, smart look.

There's absolutely no excuse for anybody to have a bad-looking home today. The cost of living has gone up, but on the other hand, there are many more home furnishings available at low cost than ever before.

Living like my clients has a lot to do with . . .
understanding them. Some clients are obviously thousands of times richer than I am, but life is very similar. I travel as much as they do, in the same comfort. I entertain, perhaps on a smaller scale, but my tables and flowers are as pretty as my clients', if not prettier.

All the decorating schools teach that you can design for anybody. That's a terrible fallacy. If you are not familiar with the way clients live, if you are not really part of the whole circle, if you do not travel, as a designer, you're at a great disadvantage vis-à-vis the ones who do. And speaking languages. I could never work in all the places I do if I weren't able to speak the languages.

Entertaining . . .
is a very special talent. Some people entertain by calling in expensive caterers, expensive florists, expensive this and that. It will be banal. Attention to detail touches people. For example, guests appreciate little details in place settings. No one today is really impressed if they eat off the most fabulous china; they don't give a damn anymore. They're much more impressed by an amusing napkin, an unusual table arrangement. Instead of using the abalone shells as ashtrays, as most people do, you might use them for individual servings of salads. At the other extreme, wine-tasting parties are corny. One should avoid that sort of thing. A thing we do in Paris for a special occasion is to send napkins to a theatrical embroiderer to have the date sewn on, if it's a birthday, and I often do napkins with all the guests' names embroidered on them, instead of place cards.

Menus are terribly important. Roast beef or lamb are things of the past. People get in a much better mood if they eat something they're not used to eating all the time. And rather than have one very precious service that you use for every dinner party, it's much more amusing to be flexible with several.

When I came to this country,
I asked myself what to collect as an investment . . .
Having grown up and gone to school in Vienna, I was very fond of Klimt. As a child, all my books were illustrated by Klimt. When I came to this country and saw this passion for collecting with a view to future value, I thought, obviously I should collect Klimt. His paintings were going for two thousand dollars. I didn't do it. I suppose two thousand dollars still made a difference in my budget then. Now his work sells for huge sums.

Now it's a very different matter because everything is being collected. But Renaissance is still collectible furniture—those beautiful inlaid cabinets, which are quite hard to place and therefore are not all that sought after. Of course, one can't make a collection of Renaissance cabinets, but I do think Renaissance furniture is very underpriced. I use it a lot on my jobs. The strength of it seems to live well with contemporary pieces. Much more so than a Louis whoever, which looks wrong when mixed with contemporary. A nice, strong Renaissance desk of teak looks wonderful in a modern interior. And it's a good buy now.

Valerian Rybar

Word Association

Color	Red.
Furniture arrangement	Individualistic.
Living rooms	Cozy.
Entrance halls	The cue to the rest of the house.
Bedrooms	Sensuous.
Bathrooms	Luxurious.
Dining rooms	Flexible.
Studies	To study.
Floor coverings	Stone.
Window treatments	As little as possible.
Fabrics	Wonderful textures.
Wallpaper	Out!
Lighting	Subtle.
Television sets	Hidden.

In the Paris residence of Valerian Rybar's partner, Jean-François Daigre, an infinity of reflections fills the salon. The small room is completely mirrored—walls, ceiling, cornices, and baseboards—and curved at the corners for maximum optical effect. The scheme, says the designer, is "all silver and gray, with touches of gilt to give it a glow." Gilded eighteenth-century English dolphin consoles, a Régence mirror, and leather-upholstered fauteuils contribute the golden tones; the modern table, displaying sixteenth-century Persian bone peacocks and a seventeenth-century Japanese round box, is finished in gray Rolls-Royce lacquer.

Interior design will change over the next few years . . .
because we're being forced into smaller spaces. More
things will be built into apartments. Even the space
for the mattress will be poured into the surface of the
building. Eventually, that is how city dwellers will live.

It will be more economical, all hose-downable, work-
saving. Parallel to that, people will turn away from the
hard-surface look that was fashionable in recent years:
the hard lacquers, chromes, Lucites. As things always
move along, others, including myself, will be moving
away from that, toward a softer, more sensuous look.
It's easy and it leaves a lot of room for self-expression.

If I could choose any client I wanted . . .
it would be a historical figure. I've had so many wonderful clients, anyone living would be more of the same.
Thinking of big spenders in the past, I certainly
wouldn't have wanted Marie Antoinette as a client. She
was too self-indulgent.

But I would have liked to work in the Renaissance.
There was good architecture, beautiful *objets,* wonderful space and a great appreciation of natural materials,
which comes close to my own taste. Not that I think I'm
doing the same things they did then; but I like using the
same materials, in the limited way possible today.

I've never had a carte blanche *client . . .*
As far as I'm concerned, they're a myth. I've heard
other designers brag about clients who give them *carte
blanche* but I've never had one. Most of my clients have
spent a great deal of money, but the more they spent,
the wiser their investment. They bought paintings and
very good antique furniture, which have gone up in
value enormously.

*My own home in New York City
was done with a very specific idea . . .*
That was to prove that you can do a very contemporary
apartment using the most modern of modern materials
available, and make it cozy and attractive. Women look
well in it and men are really comfortable. I wanted to
dispel the notion that a modern apartment has to look
sterile. I think I've succeeded in doing that.

It's not a large apartment. Space planning is a great
concern of mine. It had to function for me, for I know
how I want to live. And it does work for me. I don't expect it to work for anybody else.

I don't have a separate dining room. Instead, I set up
tables in the entrance hall. I wouldn't have minded a
little dining room, but the space just wasn't there. A
fifth of all the space is behind panels for storage. There's
a little foyer lined with fake matched bookbindings,
making fun of myself. The "books" are "autobiog-
raphies" divided into segments, each one dealing with
antecedents, childhood, studies, the war years, coming to
America, marriage, loves, career, and so on. All done
tongue-in-cheek.

The living room is in coral linen velvet, which is a very
flattering color. Most of the furniture was designed by
me, with a few antiques added for quality and style.

Status is becoming much less important . . .
This vogue and need for self-expression with people also
applies to their houses and the way they live. People are
quite willing to accept somebody living in a Mongolian
tent, if it's amusing. The status symbol of having French
Impressionist paintings is definitely gone forever.

My fantasy house . . .
I designed a Moorish house in Spain for a client. Green
tile roof, a white tower, six patios, white marble floors,
Moorish fountains, spillways, arcades with carved mar-
ble capitals. Very contemporary furniture and very good
Islamic art.

I really love that house; I'd love to own it. It's been
sold, resold, and is now owned by a wealthy Arab prince
who bought the whole hill, razed all the other houses
around it, extended the gardens and built a few little
guest houses in exactly the same style.

The rich have a sense of everything being possible . . .
They can get on a plane when other people can't. Enter-
tain in a restaurant when other people can't get a table.
They can move around the way they want to move
around, with their own transportation, their own jets.
Of course it makes a difference.

As people, they are not different at all. We always hear
terrible tales about rich people whose money makes
them so unhappy. For every rich unhappy person I
know, there are hundreds of poor unhappy people. The
rich are like you and me, fundamentally. They fall in
love, they have disappointments in love. Rich or poor,
living in more beautiful surroundings should help to
make anybody a lot happier.

JAY SPECTRE

Jay Spectre's clients are all celebrities in various fields of business. Their names are rarely, if ever, mentioned in WWD, and Suzy might not know them at all. However, Jay has become a celebrity himself in the design world, famous for his quality-detailed, bold contemporary interiors. He is generally credited with the first electronic "media" room, created for the Manhattan apartment of Robin Roberts, of the fabric firm Clarence House.

*M*y family is in the retail furniture business
*in Kentucky, so interior design seemed a natural
evolvement for me . . .*

I went on from doing floor displays when I was a kid, to doing windows, to being a star furniture salesman as a teenager. Even today I remain more interested in furniture than anything else, with the exception of art.

My first job was with a decorating firm in Louisville. I always wondered why they hired me, because I really felt I had no talent nor particular ability at the time. Then, after three and a half years, I decided to leave that job and see Europe. That trip was a turning point for me. I learned what I wanted to do with my life. And I developed what I think is essential to this business—a point of view. I also decided that I did not want to work for anyone again.

When I returned, I free-lanced, then opened my own shop. That shop is still there. I could have stayed, and been the biggest decorator in Louisville. But New York presented a challenge, so I moved here about ten years ago.

I have been in the field professionally for almost twenty-five years. I didn't have any formal training and I have never been sorry I didn't. Although if someone asked what they should do, I would tell them some sort of formal training would help later on in their career. It could also help them gain self-confidence. However, if a young person showed exceptional, or perhaps extraordinary, talent, I would say, "Pursue it the best way you know."

This year I am doing about twenty-two jobs. But I have a small office and the work really does vary. It could be five or six jobs in one year if they were all major. Probably ten to fifteen is an average.

There are only three of us on the staff now but it will soon triple because of the work load. My office is next to my apartment. I took two apartments, side by side, for the convenience, and the time saved.

All of my clients have been millionaires . . .
I've never had any other kind. They are people who have achieved a great deal in life. They are risk-takers.

They are presidents, chairmen of boards; they are people who have, mostly by their own means, their own skills, achieved what could be considered great wealth.

Socializing does help, but you must define what you want from both your private life and your professional life. I have never met a client at a cocktail party.

*The first personal encounter
with a client is always an interview . . .*
I try to immediately establish whether there is any basis for going further. I always ask about the scope of the job and the proposed budget. When you ask a client point-blank, "What do you want to spend?," the answer may be, "Well, it really doesn't make any difference." Or, "We haven't decided." Or, "What do you think it will cost?" Or, "I'll have to ask my husband." Or, maybe, "We don't really care how much it will cost." All of those answers are, in my estimation, exactly the same. None of them mean anything. If a client wants a room done for twenty-five thousand dollars, I am not going to waste my time designing a seventy-five-thousand-dollar room. We need some financial basis before we can start.

I charge the retail price for all merchandise, plus hourly fees for office time, drafting time, and any expenses incurred by the office. By drafting time, I mean this: If it takes ten hours at forty dollars an hour to design a cabinet, the client would pay four hundred dollars for the design. The client is not really obligated to order the cabinet at all, but obligated to pay for the design. My consultation fee is sixty-five dollars an hour.

With some clients, collecting the last payment is the problem. They're not ready to say the job is finished. Sometimes it's a personal thing. The client feels he is losing power by paying the last bill.

*A decorator is someone who does
slipcovers, draperies, and wallcoverings . . .*
in the old sense of the word. Somewhere along the way, I think it was in the sixties, we developed the term *interior designer.* That skill is a little more precise.

"My favorite area to decorate is the entrance hall," says Jay
Spectre. "It is the first impression when you walk into
someone's environment." For the entrance hall of a
Manhattan duplex, the designer injected aesthetic intensity
by counterpointing the original, elegant staircase designed
by Stanford White, with a dramatically large second-century
head of Buddha and a vital Jean Dubuffet sculpture. "It
takes much less to do entrance halls, because so little
furniture is required, if any," he adds. Here, only a bench,
stretching beneath an Adolph Gottlieb painting, is necessary.

The interior designer creates an environment and actually designs interior space, an environment inside a structure. An interior designer is competent to design furniture, fabrics, wallcoverings. But I think the confusion still exists. I started out as an interior decorator.

I do not mind being called an interior decorator.

*When you use an interior
designer you are buying style . . .*
You are buying taste. You are buying a point of view. In other instances, you will just be buying help for a job that you may not have the time to do yourself.

The first thing we do on any job is a floor plan . . .
We do the exact measurements, if it is an existing structure. If not, we work from plans. We do a preliminary, then a more precise floor plan. We do a lighting plan. Then we do working drawings of any built-ins, furniture, or closets that require design time. Then we do colors, textures, and fabrics.

Amateur decorators make many mistakes . . .
Not taking accurate measurements. Not being skilled in knowing the scaling that is essential. Suddenly, they order a huge piece of furniture, and it's either a foot too large or a foot too short, or it won't go on the elevator, or it doesn't fit the space, and the scale is wrong. They've spent several thousand dollars on a white elephant. That's probably the most common mistake.

If you are decorating your own home . . .
don't become so emotionally involved that you are immobilized to the point where you cannot complete the job. Do try to put yourself and your environment in the proper perspective and then start the job. Until you do that, don't start. In other words, don't think about design, color, and what you would buy. None of that means anything until you have done the basics. And that is simply knowing your objective. A total concept. Ask yourself, what is right for the next two years or ten years? Where am I in my life at this time? What do I want out of what I am trying to achieve? Once you've defined that, it makes it a lot easier to perceive.

Good taste is not really timeless . . .
Not only is it not timeless; in most cases, it is not even interesting. I don't know what good taste is. It seems like something that somebody who is relatively uninteresting would aspire to. Good taste, by my personal definition, would be a stagnant thing. Something that stopped at a certain time frame. The most interesting people are able to do something that is not in what we might call good taste. It might become good taste some day. Who knows?

Taste can be acquired. It's not something you're born with. It's a question of culture. There are classic things that remain and will always be in so-called good taste. They may be interesting, they may be boring, they may be fascinating, they may be beautiful. But they are classic and we accept them. The simplest way to acquire taste is to make yourself available visually to all the things that are around you. If you want to know what true beauty is, visit the Metropolitan Museum.

*The only thing that would make a room
bad is when it's just too good . . .*
It becomes uninteresting. Too precise.

Any environment is a mirror of the occupant . . .
And it definitely reflects the person who helps them with it. There's a part of me in everything I do. Sometimes that mirror is a little deceptive, sometimes cloudy. And if the people are not reflected in that mirror, it's because they have nothing to bring to that space. My house in the country is a true, accurate and honest reflection of me. That's the reason I didn't allow it to be published for three years after I did it. It was far too personal.

*Decorating is a tough business. Women may not
want to deal with it for that reason . . .*
It's harder work than people realize. It certainly has nothing to do with ability and nothing to do with taste. Some of my design heroes are women—the late Elsie de Wolfe and Syrie Maugham. And I admire Sister Parish a great deal. I don't really think of men as superior in any way in the design world.

Designers become too intimate with their clients . . .
It's very easy for clients to form a dependence on someone they are closely associated with, who is working on something so private and personal to them. I don't really feel that it's necessary, but it has been my experience.

Although I've heard about it, I don't think clients try to seduce their designers. I don't think I'm naïve, but I really don't think that is one of the risks involved in the business. Once someone did try to seduce me, for one reason or another. But I think it was really to intimidate me. That is really a more relevant question. It was a matter of expediency. This person was doing everything possible to get me to do the work, either for nothing or for close to nothing. But I said, "I am interested in clients socially, sexually, or financially. And you just don't fit into any of those categories."

One particular client confided her problems with her husband. I said, "Well, get rid of him." And she did. She's very happily remarried now, and still my client. And a close, personal friend. Most people don't listen to advice. She does.

For the dining room of the same residence, Mr. Spectre
conceived an audacious and theatrical, yet harmonious,
blend of the old and the new. Chevron-patterned glass wall
paneling is edged by restored traditional molding, while
satin-upholstered chairs that echo the Regency attend sleek
glass-and-steel tables. "For conversation, I don't think
anything works as well as a round table," the designer says.
Through the doorway, an imposing Louise Nevelson wood
sculpture adds another dimension to the entrance hall.

"I don't know if there is such a thing as a 'Palm Beach look,'" Mr. Spectre chides. "But if there is, this is not it." His Orient-inspired contemporary approach for the living room of an apartment there is a subtly toned paean to quiet, luxurious comfort. Refined technological solutions—a coved ceiling that provides an even horizon of light, and glass doors, facing the sea, that slide away between double walls—are hallmarks of the designer's ingenuity. A sculptural painting by Charles Hinman graces the far wall, while, in the gallery beyond, an eighteenth-century Japanese screen unfolds.

I will never forget one client.
And she was the worst . . .
It was early on in my New York career and the job was very important for me. I worked very hard at it. The client called continuously. She was overbearing, overpossessive. She wanted to lay all the ground rules. She felt she could run my business better than I could. Finally the job just ended. I took it very hard. Then as time went on, things started looking up, as they always do.

One day I ran into her, and, in her own inhuman way, she asked me how things were going. I said. "You know, you did something very wonderful for me. Sometimes when I get blue, I think of how much worse it could have been if you were my client. That sees me through, and I have to thank you for that."

You can't do a dining room
of quality today for under . . .
twenty-five thousand dollars. I did one recently for a quarter of a million dollars. A few years ago I did an apartment for some very dear friends for thirty thousand dollars, and I show it in my portfolio continuously. I really think it's quite good. The most expensive residence I've done was not as much as people might expect. It was over a million dollars. But not in the millions.

Art is an interesting investment for the very rich . . .
who can afford to gamble. For the person with an average income, there isn't anything. We're living in a time when we cannot buy a piece of Art Déco furniture, or Art Nouveau, or Victorian, or Mission furniture, and expect it to appreciate. If you're thinking of buying great antiques strictly as an investment, you'd be better off buying real estate.

However, I do think pictures by master photographers could become extremely valuable. They can be bought at a good price now and they're not only interesting, but extremely decorative.

In twenty-five years of decorating, I have
never had a client who was not budget-conscious . . .
The super-rich are careful with their money. That's how they got to be super-rich. They don't throw it around.

Entertaining . . .
Part of accumulating wealth is accumulating experience. The rich use their experience. They may have sandwiches sent in and serve it to you with a cup of instant coffee. But that is the way they entertain. And after much experience, I can tell you that if it works for them, then that's entertainment.

I entertain mostly in the country, usually small groups for dinner. Much of the food is from my own garden,

Jay Spectre

Word Association

Color	Black.
Furniture arrangement	Floating.
Living rooms	Comfort.
Entrance halls	Style.
Bedrooms	Practicality and comfort.
Bathrooms	Congenial.
Dining rooms	Elegance. Comfort.
Studies	Comfort and style.
Floor coverings	Slick and polished.
Window treatments	The absence of.
Fabrics	Cotton and leather.
Wallpaper	The absence of.
Lighting	Practical and glamorous.
Television sets	Part of life style.

prepared by me or a friend. The presentation of food is, to me, as important as the food itself. The plate that it's served on, the flatware, the flowers, the lack of music. I never have music in my house when dinner or luncheon is served. Music fills a room, but music is an intrusion during the dinner itself.

Flowers make a dining room work well. You can have a little bud vase next to each person's plate. Have a dozen people for dinner and use a dozen different plates. There are so many ways of taking an extra few minutes to do flowers, pretty napkins, turn down the lights. It does not have to be an extravagant, upholstered, silvered, porcelained, luxurious dining room. And for conversation, I don't think anything works as well as a round table. Six or eight people. That's ideal. Very often, for larger dinner parties, I have two or three or four tables, depending on the size of the room. Three tables of eight works very well, or four tables of six. I like buffet dinners. It gives people a chance to get up, move around and talk to one another.

My favorite area to decorate is . . .
the entrance hall. It is the first impression when you walk into someone's environment. It takes much less to do them, because so little furniture is required, if any. There is something glamorous about entrance halls. Bedrooms tend to be the least interesting, because they're the most personal.

If I could choose any client in the world . . .
it would be a fascinating, beautiful lady. The most glamorous lady of our time. I would like to experience working with Mrs. Onassis.

For the next few years there will be much more . . .
entertainment in the home. I see the media room becoming the most important room in our environment within the next five years. Teaching can be done in the media room. We can hear a concert or an opera at the Metropolitan that was performed and taped five years ago. Or a new film, or the news as it's happening at some remote place in the world, just by dialing it. We'll be able to dial different people in different cities, speak to and see our relatives and friends just by talking to a screen. Our environments will be totally run by the technology that we're developing in this country today. And I think that's where America is ahead of everyone. The Japanese may make it better, but we think of it and develop it. As television sets changed our lives and our rooms in the fifties, the new technology will change our environments in the eighties.

I would like to build a house in the south of France . . .
or on the Italian Riviera. I would look for a large property on the water, as private as possible, with a view. It would be a very classic, very serious house. A lot of glass and a lot of floor space for indoor sculpture, so you could walk around the sculpture and feel that it was not confined. The furniture would probably be minimal, Oriental or my own design. Architecturally, it would be as contemporary as I would know how to do it. It would be today's house. If I built a house, it would be capturing this moment in time. I don't want to capture another century. And I'm not presumptuous enough to think that I can capture the future.

My present apartment was my first in New York . . .
I've been in it for almost ten years and I've never changed it. It's on the seventeenth floor of a large apartment building. There is a living room, two bedrooms, two bathrooms, a small dining room, terrace, a book-lined entrance hall, and a small kitchen with a window. In New York, that's unusual.

When I came here from Kentucky, I did not want to do another beautiful English drawing room or French salon. I knew that people had seen it, and others could do it much better. I had to make my own statement, which I did.

I did my living room and entrance hall in corrugated steel. The vertical blinds are made of galvanized steel. In those days, you could not buy them, and no one did vertical blinds for residential use. All the walls are sheathed in steel. My bedroom is completely done in mirror, black glass, and gray glass. It is Art Déco with Louis XVI furniture, before Déco became something your hairdresser seeks out in used-furniture stores.

I built a house in the country six years ago. That, too, remains essentially the same, except for art I have added or changed. It's comfortable, it's private. It's a miniature of my fantasy house. It has great luxury, and the luxury I refer to is privacy. It does exactly what I want it to do. It says what I had to say at a particular moment. And it works for me. It's all squares. No curves, no angles. Straight up and down. The materials are leather, suede, slate, steel, bronze, wood. The structure is over three-quarters bronze glass. The rest is wood. I have a pool and many, many trees. Hundreds of dogwoods. Large oaks. And a nice garden.

I will tell you about the rich . . .
It will be an unfair generalization, but no matter. The rich are often paranoid. They are scared to death they are going to be ripped off or taken advantage of. They feel that way because in most cases that is how they got their money. The truth is that the rich do not get ripped off. Only the poor get ripped off. There is no way to rip off the super-rich. And if it does happen, they take it off their taxes the following year. The rich *are* different.

An icy Lalique crystal chandelier softly illuminates a
sensuous, Art Déco-influenced master bedroom in Palm
Beach. Framed panels of patterned chintz, overlaid with filmy
theatrical gauze, conceal sliding glass doors and the bright
ocean light, while creating an alternate vista of surreal
mountains. "I understood and bought Art Déco years ago
because I found it interesting," says Jay Spectre, "but I
wouldn't want to be in any sense a 1930s person. We should
strive to be the heroes to the coming generation of designers,
and not encourage them to look back at other periods."

MICHAEL TAYLOR

Even if I had six fingers on one hand, I could not count beyond one hand the interior decorators considered, without qualification, the best in the world by other designers. I doubt there are five who could be agreed upon. However, on any designer's "best" list, Michael Taylor's name ranks high. His home in San Francisco is not, as he said in our interview, "designed." But to be there is an awesome experience. His eye has unerringly led him to collect the most extraordinary objects throughout his years of world travel. Michael Taylor's home is a visual feast. Among his clients are: Jennifer (Jones) and Norton Simon, Nan Kempner, Charles Evans.

*Certain houses were greatly important
to my beginning of awareness . . .*

There was a great house done by Elsie de Wolfe in Santa Rosa, where I lived as a child. It was a fantasy to go there, because it was like no other house. There was an awareness of a way of life that could be described as sophistication. It rubs off immediately. You go home and straighten your room, and get a bunch of flowers to look at, instead of the dead turtle with your name on it.

Part of the American scene is question-and-answer time at a point. "What are you going to do, son?" I had to come up with an answer, and medicine seemed perfectly logical. I liked doctors. I liked what they did. I liked the place they occupied in society. I liked the idea of helping. I couldn't wait to get into it.

So during World War II I joined the Navy at seventeen and was quickly put into the Medical Corps, in the cancer-research unit at Brooklyn Navy Yard. I was exposed to life and death and tragedy. I was too young to accept what I felt was a lack of knowledge in the average doctor. It was disillusioning, a shocker, and it frightened me. I wanted out.

The minute I was discharged from the Navy my father insisted that I enroll at the college he had attended and fall into the routine. But I had things to work out in my mind. I did some traveling and spent a year in New York, just being kind of a rich man's son. My father was bright enough to let me have that year to see what I wanted. And I wanted to go back to California. But I didn't want college. It had to be something creative, either as an artist or in the theater. Decorating was coming into focus, because I could paint, I could draw, I had a good sense of scale and I'd won national awards for design in school. It seemed to be something I couldn't ignore. I quickly took a job in San Francisco so I could be on my own. I was nineteen or twenty, and the first job that came up was as an assistant in a very sophisticated decorator's office.

It was Archibald Taylor, who was the top decorator in San Francisco then.

All I did was run errands. I loved it . . .
because I was seeing beautiful houses. Before long I realized that I could do what this man was doing. I could draw better than he could and I had a lot of ideas about decorating. One day Archibald Taylor walked into the office and said, "I've been noticing your sketches. They're good. Michael, you have a natural talent. I'm only going to hold you back if you stay here. I've talked about you to the owner of the largest furniture chain in this country, and he wants to meet you."

I was accepted and given an important house to do in Carmel. The house had once belonged to writer Henry Miller and it had a lot of charm. We created an interior that was completely designed, every inch of it. The fabrics were woven in special colors to match the tones of seashells, to relate to the ocean. The house was a great success, and because of that I was asked to do other houses. That's how it all started.

Then I was offered a job with an important decorating firm in San Francisco. They had seen pictures of my work. I was about twenty-one, and it was very exciting. I was given a free hand to design my own furniture and develop my own following. During that time I met another designer and we opened our own shop. That was about thirty years ago. It was a great success.

I was probably one of the first to introduce . . .
the use of antiques with contemporary. The richer families were throwing out their antiques and going completely contemporary. I started including wonderful Venetian painted furniture to bring color and line into my rooms. It was very sophisticated, very exciting.

I was the first to bring in big plants and the drama of white walls and white floors. I did it at a time when, if you didn't have a pale celadon-green living room, something was wrong. They were like slumber rooms. I wanted to erase all the concentrated theories on color and start from scratch. And that, to me, meant the white floor, the white wall, the perfect plant, a beautiful flower, a perfect piece of furniture.

For the living room of his cliff-top home/office in San
Francisco, Michael Taylor has effectively blended a
graceful Régence mantelpiece and a low, square Jean-Michel
Frank table; eighteenth-century Swedish candelabra and
antique Chinese vases; a formal terra-cotta bust of Richelieu
and a large opalescent ammonite. "I live with these beautiful
things almost temporarily," he admits. "This is my design
laboratory, a place where I can study forms and effects and
combinations. That's the reason there are so many different
styles and periods represented here—so much that is
man-made, so much that is natural and organic."

The rooms were photographed and talked about and copied. It launched the so-called Michael Taylor look—rooms that could breathe; stripping off fabric coverings and getting rid of wall-to-wall carpeting and matching color schemes. Not taking tones from a painting and having ditsy little pillows and all of that trash. It was freedom. The painting stood on its own and became ten times more exciting. It stopped a lot of decorating theories. Diana Vreeland called me "the Jimmy Dean of the decorating world." I was a rebel. I totally rejected all the accepted theories of decoration: how to treat windows, how to treat floors, how to arrange furniture. And scale. I'm absolutely out of scale in everything I've ever done.

I am an architect. I'm not a licensed architect.
I'm not a licensed decorator. I didn't study decorating
and I didn't study architecture . . .
I can always find an engineer and a draftsman. I want to work with the materials and the scale and the solution. There are people who are geniuses in engineering and drafting; I work beautifully with them because they've seen what I've accomplished. I've worked very well with some of the more important architects in the country and I've done a lot of architecture on my own.

My life is so involved I've never known
the words home *and* office . . .
It's all the same. I live with my own design to find out why it does or doesn't work and how I can improve it. I often have pieces of furniture brought to my bedroom so I can sketch them, study them, and sleep with them. I have wild affairs with furniture.

I have three assistants. The size of my staff varies, but usually it's seven or eight people. I do twenty-five to thirty houses each year, each in various stages.

I have never decorated my own house . . .
I have never put it together. I don't like putting houses together. I don't like putting houses together. I like mixing and creating, but I don't like a format. The excitement is when it happens unexpectedly, on the spur of the moment. Or someone will put something in a place where you wouldn't put it, and it's wonderful.

The number one thing in decorating is comfort . . .
It may be serenity or just because your fanny is more comfortable in a certain chair. I loathe uncomfortable furniture. I can put chairs against walls to look at; but when I sit down, I want comfort. I don't really want to be aware of its line. I want it to be a soft, easy thing that accentuates the beauty of something else. I don't feel decorating should be so much the design of a sofa, as the selection of objects that are exciting for the eye.

A perfect house is never finished. Some jobs take months and some are never finished. It depends on the clients—their need, their involvement. If they want to continually add, and join me in searching for, beautiful things, fine. If they want a package deal delivered, we do it down to the last ashtray, to the fresh flowers and the photographers waiting.

I have clients who have no money at all . . .
And I have some of the richest clients in the world. Peter does not pay for Paul; one price to all. If I have a reputation for being expensive, it's because my eye goes to things that are costly because they are better. But my fabrics don't cost any more, my time doesn't cost any more, the furniture I design doesn't cost any more, than that of any well-known firm. But my eye is different. Perhaps I will tell clients to buy one perfect mantelpiece or one perfect cabinet, then wait, instead of slamming in mediocre furniture just to finish a room. But the client is still the boss. You're spending their money and creating an atmosphere for them.

I have done many interiors that cost in the millions . . .
I understand and respect the obligations I have toward that money. I have saved people financially with investments in furniture. Once, because of a turn of events, a client's source of income was completely wiped out and the property could not be sold quickly enough, so the furniture was sold. It had tripled in value and was easily salable. This has happened many times. That's why we encourage those who are appreciative of fine furniture to buy the best, because the value is there. It's a good investment. I would rather not put money into fancy curtains, fancy carpeting, and all those wallcoverings. I loathe fabric-covered walls. To me, it's embarrassing when I add up the yardage and the price. I feel that fabric on the wall is a tremendous waste of money. Spend on furniture or an art object instead of all that supercilious decoration, like having walls lacquered twenty times to get the perfect glow.

I like working with the husband,
not behind his back . . .
I don't like the wife who says, "Don't worry, I'll handle John." I don't want her to handle John. I want to discuss it all with John and I want it on paper. We don't do one minute of work without a signed estimate. Decorators have a reputation of not being businesslike, but show me a successful decorator, and he's a successful businessman.

The number one thing I have to sell is my time. My average working deal for clients is a straight retail basis. No one has to bother telling me they can buy it wholesale on their own. Anyone can, if they want to. Half of my work is redoing jobs people did on their own.

"I like the bedroom to be sensuous, flattering, comfortable," says Mr. Taylor, whose own bedroom is a case in point. "Colors that flatter flesh. Kind lighting. A generous bed. It may have a fireplace or a view or beautiful things for the eye." His elaborately carved and gilded seventeenth-century Spanish canopy bed, from the Lopez-Willshaw collection in Paris, is complemented by an eighteenth-century English giltwood table with twig-design base.

If people are simply confused and want me to analyze the situation and advise about whether they need to redecorate, reconstruct, or sell the house, then I charge one hundred dollars an hour. And they get their money's worth, because in an hour's time you can discuss a lot of points of view, and work out a lot of solutions.

People have good reason to fear decorators . . .
There are a lot of dishonest people in the field. When I see what's done by people calling themselves decorators, I'm only sorry there isn't a way to protect clients from them. The field of decoration is not easy. You're part psychiatrist, part businessman, and part fly-around-the-room-with-wonderful-ideas. You've got to work with personalities. You've got to create an atmosphere that makes them feel enriched because of this experience.

You can practically destroy a marriage by something that is disturbing to live with. I've been called in to do houses where the marriage was practically on the rocks because of a pretentious attitude by the previous decorator about how the family should live.

Every night is not black tie and candlelight dinners. Sitting in a Marie Antoinette chair is not exactly today. The decorator may have a fantasy and put clients in a place that they're not even aware of. They may not have been to France. They may not even be aware of Louis XVI. Clients may be embarrassed to tell you they love gypsy colors and porch furniture. Or that they want a very sophisticated, formal room. They may feel that you're only interested in doing informal rooms, and they're embarrassed to say they want an Aubusson rug and signed furniture. Nothing against that, as long as they want it.

Decorators can fear clients, too . . .
Once when I was showing something to a client, she turned to me and said, "I love it. Don't I?" Another looked at a chair, and asked, "What does it do?" I said, "It does nothing. It's a perfectly comfortable chair. What is it supposed to do?" And one time, when I was installing a tremendous house, everything had to stop because the cats had decided to nap. They were not to be disturbed. It cost the client thousands of dollars in overtime so the cats could take their nap. Being a cat lover, I almost understood.

I've often wondered why people use designers . . .
It's obvious that we have a talent. I've dedicated my life to my work; obviously I've learned some shortcuts. And I've told as many people not to spend as I have told to spend. That's very important. And an outsider has a clean eye; with experience, he can see the problem.

Times are changing rapidly, and the exciting thing is to be aware. There are so many silly comments in the press by decorators. It's so pretentious for a decorator to say,

"I never use cut flowers," "I never use wall-to-wall carpeting," "I never use curtains at my windows," "I loathe dark walls," "I hate white walls," "I never use indoor plants." All of these statements have been made by some of the more important decorators, and I cringe when I hear them. Wall-to-wall carpeting may be just right for a particular client in a particular situation.

Common sense is the most important rule. If the client calls the decorator and says, "Do whatever you want," it's not good for you, and it's a bore for the decorator. I'm as good as my client. The client doesn't have to have the ideas, but he does have to be honest about his needs and his pocketbook. Trying to have a million-dollar look on a penny bank account is not honest. Some of the best rooms are done on the penny bank account. I've done rooms for five hundred and fifty dollars.

I sometimes meet people
and feel absolutely miserable with them . . .
I may feel they're not being honest with me or that I'm not what they want as a decorator. They may want someone they can brag about, take to lunch, or show off to their girl friends. They may want to say they have hired Michael Taylor. There are a lot of phony personalities in search of decoration. But it's a very serious business with me. I won't take on work unless I feel comfortable with the clients. It's very personal. You're getting involved in their way of life.

I take furniture in vans and try it in rooms . . .
I don't sit in an office and play decorator. I'm on my hands and knees, lifting and shoving and trying things. I get in and work physically in a room, because I feel it that way and I like doing it.

I did a steamship, which I never saw until the day of installation. Everything was made in San Francisco and sent to the shipyard in Bethesda. All the furniture had to correspond to the angle of each floor of the ship. Paintings had to be welded to the walls. It's very technical work, like brain surgery. You have to have marine engineers in your office to do the drafting.

Every day there's a new need and a new solution . . .
I'm creating today something I had never thought of creating yesterday, because of the need and because of the times. Space is the most important thing we have. An awareness and appreciation of space is tomorrow.

Today, taste is the only status symbol. Tasteless things are: pretension, waste, extravagant silliness. I really love simple, functional things. I hate to see rooms that don't wear well. A table filled with obelisks is boring unless it's a collection that means something to you. But to just fill a table because a decorator gave you an instant collection is foolishness.

Michael Taylor

Word Association

Color	All colors.
Furniture arrangement	Comfort. Functional.
Living rooms	Make the room a room that people live in. Not just for entertaining or display or show. People do not live in living rooms as they should.
Entrance halls	Introduction. Very important. First reaction to the entire house is often presented by the entrance hall.
Bedrooms	Sleeping. Comfort. Practical. Functional for reading. Good light.
Bathrooms	Never large enough. Often ignored. Should be more exciting, like using art.
Dining rooms	A room that should be changed from time to time. It should be set like a stage, so the mood can be changed for the guest list or the temperament required.
Study	A room that is congenial for comfort and study. Generally more masculine. I prefer the bedroom to be more feminine and the study to be more masculine, and I like the contrast between the two.
Floor coverings	I love bare floors. I love stone. I love cement. Plank floors, wood floors. I am more interested in the actual material of the floor, than in its covering.
Window treatments	Prefer to work on the problem through architectural means, rather than a superficial covering. Like windows treated architecturally. Love windows undecorated.
Fabrics	Love contrasts. Love velvet with linen; love contrasts of materials. Like simple forms: cottons, wools. Pure fabrics.
Wallpaper	I would rather hang a picture.
Lighting	Extremely important.
Television sets	Very important. Always in my plans because I enjoy television myself; I enjoy it for relaxing. It's not necessary, but I don't like to do a room without a good plan in mind including the television.

There's a place for shag rugs, for wall-to-wall carpeting. Everything has its place, if it's done well. It's just tasteless people misusing things that makes clichés.

My fantasy house for myself would be . . .
a stark room with four perfectly simple walls; or it could be a room filled with fantasy, and collections of wonderful things.

I'd have a suitcase and travel. I like hotel rooms and visiting other people's houses. But I fantasize about all sorts of things. I visualize living in Versailles or living in Greece in a hut. I think of the Indians and their tepees, and the wonder of their design and their way of life.

I might have an absolutely empty room. I doubt if I know of anything I'd share that room with. If there were more energy put into the proportions of architecture to soothe our needs, we'd have less decoration. When architecture is truly beautiful, it's magnificent before the decorator sets foot in the room. Decoration is just that: *decoration*.

*There isn't any difference between
an interior designer and a decorator . . .*
There are creative people and those who aren't creative. I don't understand those terms; I don't even know what I'd call myself. I'm Michael Taylor, the phone rings and I go and we talk about problems and solutions.

But I think the biggest fault of decoration is the decorator. Desecrator. And if the architect were more aware of the interior instead of the exterior, we'd all be ahead. The architect does not solve window problems, the problems of light and ventilation. He is not aware of where and how the client is going to live in the structure, and I find this the number one curse. If there were more good architects and fewer decorators, we'd be ahead.

I begin an interior design with the need . . .
What I actually do first may be a combination of things: an arrangement of seating, sleeping, lighting. Lighting is so important. Color is like breathing. It's vitally important. I probably do far more color work than I do white walls. And the comfort of a place to put a drink, a place to put books near the bed. It starts with a scheme, a scheme of life.

I study the problem with the client and I cannot proceed until I see it. I'm very nervous about starting a project without a full, visual insight on the final look. In other words, I visualize the wall color. I see that final wall. I make sketches. I have the problem stewing in my mind, sometimes for minutes, sometimes for days, and sometimes I have to leave, because it's not possible for me to solve it, because I don't feel that the client is going to be comfortable with it. When I see the room, I go

home that night and may sketch until four in the morning. I do all the color work, place the furniture, fantasize on what pieces I'm looking for and draw them in. Then we all sit down and have fun going over the midnight sketch. Generally, my first reaction is the right one.

Trying to be "with it" is the biggest mistake . . .
Trying to live like something you've seen in a magazine. Not facing who you are and where you are and what you can afford. Not being honest with yourself. Being misled by fantasizing that you're someone else. Or being afraid to do something that might be in bad taste. Some of the most creative rooms on earth are done by people who weren't even aware they had bad taste. They just went out and bought wonderful, mad things. Never thought, "Is that bad taste?"

Be free of all the decorators' spells, all the promises of disaster if you're not with the latest fad. Nothing is new. "Be honest with yourself" is the best advice to anyone, with or without money.

The average room is overdecorated. My primary rule is, "When in doubt, take out."

I know of a famous personality who has not a stick of furniture in her bedroom, but a mattress on the floor and white windowshades. She has a drawing room filled with the most beautiful paintings and furniture on earth. But her bedroom is a sleeping cell. Go copy it. Give that to some unsuspecting little housewife and tell her that's how the movie-star legend sleeps. She's going to do it because that's chic, and the poor thing is going to have a nervous breakdown.

*I've seen rooms done twenty-five or thirty years
ago that are as beautiful today as they were then . . .*
Taste is a very peculiar thing to discuss, because I know people who might be called tasteless, but I absolutely adore their way of life and what they're living with. Who's to put down? I don't think the sterile, perfect object in the room is always the answer either. I may personally fantasize on the perfect empty room, but that doesn't mean that's taste. Who are we to judge who's tasteful and who isn't?

I'm constantly learning. I'm finding new things to see every day. I don't think people should force themselves to develop taste. If there's a natural interest, it will happen. There are a lot of supercilious snobs who are always saying, "Oh, my dear, it's not in good taste." Who the hell are they to say it's not good taste?

*A home reveals so much
that many people are afraid to expose themselves . . .*
That's why the decorator is called in—to create a false impression.

"It's cheerful and it's fun," says designer Taylor of a thirty-year-old suburban Los Angeles home he had stripped of nonessentials and then sparsely appointed with a minimum of large-scale furnishings, backdropped by judiciously placed mirrored walls—all of which work to extend space and reflect light. "Space is the most important thing we have today," he explains. "An awareness and an appreciation of space is tomorrow." In the living room, a Tom Holland work in epoxy and fiberglass stretches across a mirrored wall, and a Michael Steiner bronze rests on the travertine tabletop.

You sense it, feel it,
when a marriage is happy and fulfilled . . .
The bedroom is a very important clue. Some clients don't even have nightstands or proper lighting by the bed, and it always startles me, because I think the bed is a very attractive place to be. I don't like formal decorated bedrooms. I don't like ridiculous things, such as the nightstand that's too small, with a tiny lamp. I don't understand how people can live that way. If you read in bed, why isn't there space for books, to place a tray, or even an art object? I don't like bedspreads. Bedrooms should be airy, fresh and comfortable. Not a display.

The bedroom is basically for the woman. It's her room. I like the bedroom to be sensuous, flattering, comfortable. Colors that flatter flesh. Kind lighting. A generous bed. It may have a fireplace or a view or beautiful things for the eye. I hate the fact that the living room always has the best furniture and the best art. Why can't the best painting be in the bedroom? Each room is equally important. We spend a lot of time in our kitchens and bedrooms and bathrooms, so why not include some art?

A comfortable, welcoming house simply looks as if it's used. There's nothing that bores me more than the term "living room." It's probably the one room that is not lived in. It's for showing off to friends. It should not be a showcase. This ridiculous thing of "Look who we are, and what we found, and how much we paid" is disgusting. The living room is usually the largest room, usually the room with the fireplace, usually the room with the view. For God's sake, why isn't it lived in?

In the English manor houses, people really use their living rooms. I find them comfortable. The French have always created perfectly beautiful rooms, but never know how to live in them. They're never functional, at least in later years. Court rooms may have been more functional. They moved their furniture to fit the need of the occasion, which is about as functional as you can get. Earlier rooms were lit by candlelight, and the candles were movable. Furniture was movable. Today we've got the damn sofa, the coffee table, and the two lamps. It's the kiss of death, because it's static, it's set.

There are just as many women
who are good decorators as men . . .
It's a field many men like to be in. It's glamorous, exciting, and creative. But I don't believe sex has a thing to do with the stature of a talent. Elsie de Wolfe started the whole decorating field.

I'm not a party giver,
but if you really care about your friends . . .
you always entertain beautifully, because you think of what makes them feel wanted. A comfortable place to sit, a place to put a drink. If people want to smoke, let them. Don't make them feel they're outcasts because they want to light a cigarette. Don't put rules and regulations on your guests.

I've always felt the English are the ones who really understand how to entertain. They include children, dogs, art, books, comfort. The French have a false sense of direction. They're proud of their furniture and their history, but when it comes to today, most of them don't understand entertaining. Now lots of them have copied the Americans. They've caught on to the coffee table, to comfortable seating. They've gotten rid of a lot of their restricted fancy little chairs.

The design excitement today is . . .
in the United States. The West Coast is a tremendous influence. It expresses freedom, flexibility.

Europeans don't use decorators as much as Americans do, because they're more secure. They haven't been brainwashed by the magazines. They've never worried about being told they have bad taste. They're not trying to keep up with fads. Also, they don't move around so much. We're constantly picking up and running. Europeans live in their great-great-grandfather's house, and each generation improves it. It's home.

I'm on call like a doctor and I love it . . .
I have three telephones by my bed. If clients care enough to worry about a room at two in the morning, I'm with them. Sometimes I have to hear things I don't want to hear about their personal lives, which I don't feel is really my business, but if I can help, I want to.

My favorite possession is . . .
my life-size Sung bronze deer. I've never seen anything quite like it. I bought the deer when I was nineteen. It took me five or six years to pay for it. But you must never allow possessions to possess you. You have to feel free to walk out that door.

The art market is very interesting today . . .
The old masters are now becoming more valuable than they were ten years ago, and much nineteenth-century art is losing value. But I've never bought a thing in my life for investment. I've only bought what I loved.

I've always thought of myself as rich . . .
I don't think it has anything to do with money. It has something to do with awareness.

Most people who are wealthy have worked awfully hard, and those who inherited their wealth have to work twice as hard to keep it.

The master bedroom of the same suburban Los Angeles
residence basks in similar clarity and transparency, with a
mirrored headboard wall reflecting the warming blaze within
a painted brick fireplace wall, a visual multiplicity of coconut
palms in simple soy tubs, and a large painting by Joe Goode.
Leaning against the mirror, Charles Arnoldi's charcoal
drawing rests on one of two conveniently large bedside tables.
"Your reaction to waking up in the morning has a lot to do
with the success of your day," Mr. Taylor says. "Bedrooms
should be airy, fresh, and comfortable. Not a display."

Photo Credits

Portraits

ARNOLD, VAL	Russell MacMasters
BUATTA, MARIO	Billy Cunningham
CATROUX, FRANÇOIS	Pascal Hinous
CHASE, STEPHEN	Arthur Coleman
CULTRA, HARRISON	Billy Cunningham
DENNIS, LEO	Russell MacMasters
DONGHIA, ANGELO	Billy Cunningham
GRABER, TED	Russell MacMasters
GREGGA, BRUCE	Anthony Soluri
HADLEY, ALBERT	Billy Cunningham
HAIL, ANTHONY	Russell MacMasters
LEWIS, SALLY SIRKIN	Russell MacMasters
LOYD-PAXTON	Robert Hemmi
McCARTY, BILLY	Derry Moore
MONGIARDINO, LORENZO	Robert Emmett Bright
PARISH, MRS. HENRY II	Billy Cunningham
RADZIWILL, LEE	Billy Cunningham
RYBAR, VALERIAN	Billy Cunningham
SPECTRE, JAY	Billy Cunningham
TAYLOR, MICHAEL	Russell MacMasters

Photo Credits

Interiors

ARNOLD, VAL	All interiors: Russell MacMasters
BUATTA, MARIO	Living rooms: Richard Champion Bedrooms: Ernst Beadle
CATROUX, FRANÇOIS	All interiors: Pascal Hinous
CHASE, STEPHEN	All interiors: Fritz Taggart
CULTRA, HARRISON	Pink living room: Constance Smalley Other three shots: Michael Dunne
DENNIS, LEO	All interiors: Russell MacMasters
DONGHIA, ANGELO	All interiors: Angelo Donghia
GRABER, TED	All interiors: Russell MacMasters
GREGGA, BRUCE	All interiors: Victor Skrebneski
HADLEY, ALBERT	Blue living room: Tom Crane Own living room: William P. Steele Green living room: Tom Weir Yellow French living room: Tom Weir
HAIL, ANTHONY	All interiors: Jeremiah Bragstad
LEWIS, SALLY SIRKIN	All interiors: Russell MacMasters
LOYD-PAXTON	All interiors: Max Eckert
McCARTY, BILLY	All interiors: Derry Moore
MONGIARDINO, LORENZO	All interiors: Robert Emmett Bright
PARISH, MRS. HENRY II	Bedroom: Tom Weir All others: Horst
RADZIWILL, LEE	Manhattan bedroom: Richard Champion Huntington Hotel: Russell MacMasters Beach house: Jaime Ardiles-Arce
RYBAR, VALERIAN	Mirrored Paris room: Pascal Hinous New York red living room: Nathaniel Lieberman Hunting lodge: Pascal Hinous
SPECTRE, JAY	All interiors: Jaime Ardiles-Arce
TAYLOR, MICHAEL	All interiors: Russell MacMasters

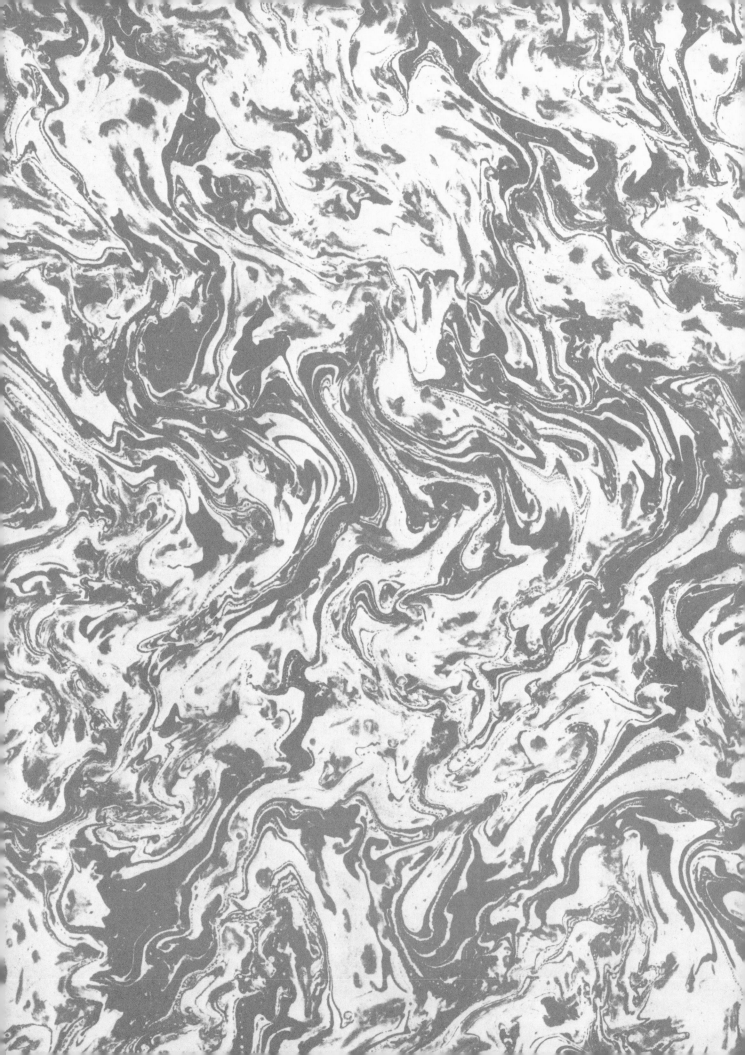